DE GAULLE AND HIS FRANCE

DE
AND

A Psychopolitica

GAULLE
HIS FRANCE

nd Historical Portrait

by Jacques de Launay

Translated by Dorothy Albertyn

HE JULIAN PRESS, Inc.,   *Publishers*

 New York

Published by The Julian Press, Inc.
119 Fifth Avenue, New York 10003
© Copyright 1968 by The Julian Press, Inc.
Library of Congress Catalogue Card Number 68–19017
Manufactured in the United States of America

CONTENTS

PART III ❖ THE WORK

Introduction

On Sunday, June 29, 1965, I was a passenger aboard a Paris–
Barcelona Air France Caravelle. At 12:23, under a cloudless sky,
the plane carried us to a great height above the ancient and famous city of Chartres. At an altitude of 24,000 feet, with the
limitless blue of the summer sky above, we had a panoramic view
of the city and countryside below, the ripening grain of the fields,
while, converging on the city and its center from all corners, a
swarm of people on foot, cars and motorcycles—anything that
could move—was making its way, like so many bees returning to
the hive, to pay homage to their leader.

What had caused this mass of humanity to gather in the city
of a Sunday morning?

General de Gaulle, at the twenty-third provincial tour of his
first term of office, had chosen Chartres for the scene of one of
his famous speeches. Warmed by the adulation of the crowd, the

General ended with the clarion call: "Forward, France! Forward,
France! Forward!" This triple reiteration, applauded by the people, reassured them that their leader would stay at the helm, binding them to union for better or for worse according to the choices
he would make in their behalf.

Charles Péguy, hero and poet of the early days of World War I
(and, like Joan of Arc, closely associated with Chartres), once
declared: "Everything begins with mysticism and ends in politics." With de Gaulle, the progression has perhaps been reversed
—from politics to mysticism.

The best description we have of him was written by himself
when he was a junior officer in 1932; it is an abstract portrait of
the man of character who would be an ideal leader:

> Sure of his opinions and conscious of his strength, he
> makes no concessions to the desire to please. The fact that
> his decisions and firmness are drawn from his own
> strength, and not from a given order, often carries him
> beyond a passive obedience. He considers he has been set
> a task and should be left free to carry it out, an attitude
> many superiors find intolerable, since, unable to grasp the
> whole, they content themselves with details and feed on
> formalities. They fear his boldness, which spares neither
> routine nor the quiet life. "Overbearing, undisciplined,"
> say the mediocre, treating the thoroughbred with the sensi-
> tive mouth like the mule who stubbornly refuses to move,
> not realizing that brusqueness is the reverse of powerful
> natures, that it is possible to lean only on what offers re-
> sistance, and the firm and demanding are worth more than
> the easy-going and the weak.
>
> But should events become serious, the peril grave, should
> the common safety depend on initiative, a willingness to
> gamble, the perspective changes, and justice comes to the

fore. A kind of groundswell carries the man of character to the foreground. His advice is taken, his talents are praised, his qualities trusted. His, naturally, is the difficult task, the principal effort, the deciding mission. Any proposal is duly considered, anything he asks for granted. Moreover, the moment he is summoned, he stays within bounds and shows himself magnanimous. He barely savors revenge, for action occupies his entire being.

The events of his own life were to prove those words strangely prophetic. We have this description of him on his arrival in London in 1940 as a junior officer, during the dark days of the French collapse in World War II:

> For relief I turned to de Gaulle, whose bearing alone among his compatriots matched the calm, healthy phlegm of the British. A strange-looking man, enormously tall even while sitting at the table, he dominated everyone else by his height,[1] as he had done when walking into the room. No chin; a long drooping elephantine nose over a closely cut mustache, a shadow over a small mouth, whose thick lips tended to protrude as if in a pout before speaking; a high receding forehead; a pointed head surmounted by sparse black hair lying flat and neatly parted. His heavily hooded eyes were very shrewd. When about to speak, he oscillated his head slightly, like a pendulum, while searching for words. I at once remembered and understood the nickname of *"Le Connétable"* which . . . had been given him at Saint-Cyr. It was easy to imagine that head on a ruff, that secret face at Catherine de Medici's council chamber.[1]

It was with the author, General Spears, that de Gaulle had

flown to London to embark on what he himself has called "the great adventure of my life," which started on June 18, 1940, with his famous "summons" to the French people to continue the fight.

De Gaulle is a cold man, withdrawn, enigmatic, almost friendless, yet today he is the elected president of the republic, with powers that even the most despotic kings of France have never known.

The story of his "adventure," the events that shaped his destiny, the intense dislike and fervent support he seems able to arouse are not matters for explanation; they can only be presented as facts arising from the life of a most exceptional man.

CHRONOLOGY

NOVEMBER 22, 1890   *C. de Gaulle b. Lille*

1907–1908   *Boarding-school at Antoing (Belgium)*

OCTOBER 1, 1910   *Saint-Cyr*

OCTOBER 1, 1913   *Lieutenant at Arras*

1916–1918   *Prisoner in Germany*

1919–1920   *Polish campaign*

1921   *Professor at Saint-Cyr*

1929   *Headquarters in the Levant*

1932   *Attaché at the Senior Council of National Defense*

1937   *Colonel, commanding the 507th Tank Regiment at Metz*

MAY 17, 1940   *Commanding the Fourth Armored Division*

JUNE 5, 1940   *Under-Secretary of State for War*

JUNE 18, 1940   *The summons*

SEPTEMBER 23, 1941   *Creation of the French National Committee*

MARCH 24, 1943   *De Gaulle-Giraud meeting*

JUNE 3, 1943   *Constitution of the C.F.L.N.*

AUGUST 25, 1944   *Entry into Paris*

DECEMBER 1–10, 1944   *De Gaulle-Stalin meeting*

AUGUST 21–25, 1945   *De Gaulle-Truman meeting*

NOVEMBER 13, 1945   *President of the Provisional Government*

JANUARY 20, 1946   *Resignation*

APRIL 7, 1947   *Creation of the R.P.F.*

JUNE 1, 1958   *Prime minister*

AUGUST, 1958   *Emancipation of Africa*

JUNE–JULY–OCTOBER–DECEMBER, 1958   *Visits to Algeria*

DECEMBER 21, 1958   *Elected First President, Fifth Republic*

JANUARY 3, 1959   *Took office*

AUGUST, 1959; MARCH–DECEMBER, 1960   *Visits to Algeria*

APRIL 22, 1961   *Generals' coup*

MAY 31, 1961   *De Gaulle-Kennedy meeting*

JULY 3, 1962   *Independence of Algeria*

JANUARY 27, 1964   *Recognition of Peoples' Republic of China*

DECEMBER 19, 1965   *President of the Republic by universal suffrage*

PART I ❧ THE MAN

Private View of a Public Monument

❧

From his childhood, Charles de Gaulle was set apart, and seemed to choose this isolation freely. His colleagues at school and college remember that he never took part in any collective games. He was born in a country marked by defeat, in a period of difficulty for France at home and abroad. His family was poor, and his parents, second cousins, were austere in character, an austerity that seems to have become severity; they made no attempt to develop the sensitivity of their second son. Between seven and fourteen, while Charles was still very malleable, he lived with his family through several national crises.

My father, a thoughtful man of culture and tradition, was impregnated with the idea of the dignity of France. It was he who taught me its history. My mother's passion for the country was as great as her piety. My three brothers, my sister and myself had, as second nature, a kind of sensitive pride where our country was concerned. A country boy in Paris, nothing struck me more than the symbols of our glory: night falling over Notre-Dame, the majesty of evening at Versailles, the Arc de Triomphe in the sunlight, captured flags rustling below the ceiling of the Invalides. Nothing affected me more than the manifestations of our national successes; the people's enthusiasm over the visit by the Tsar of Russia, a review at Longchamp, the marvels of the Exposition, the first successful flights of our airmen. Nothing saddened me more than our weaknesses and our mistakes, demonstrated in my childhood by events and sayings: the evacuation of Fashoda, the Dreyfus affair, social conflicts, religious discords. Nothing moved me more than the recital of our past disasters: my father evoking the abortive sorties at Le Bourget and Stains (during the Franco–Prussian war), where he was wounded: my mother recalling her own despair as a small girl when she saw her parents in tears: "Bazaine has surrendered (*Ed. Note: In 1870, to the Germans at Metz, with 140,000 men*)."

From fourteen to twenty-one, the agony increased. France was divided into Dreyfusards and anti-Dreyfusards, and although Charles's father, with fine moral courage, refused to take sides, difficulties multiplied. In 1904, the Jesuits were expelled from France, and Henri de Gaulle lost his teaching job. We have already said that he was poor. From 1907 onward, Charles had to complete his studies abroad, and prepare his entrance examinations for Saint-Cyr.

Among all his professors, the man who made the greatest impression on him was undoubtedly his history master, the Jesuit Father Auguste Butin, an impressive colossus with a lively mind.

⚜

At this period, the Irish were very much in the news with their fight for Home Rule, and Charles de Gaulle was aware of their problems, for his great-grandmother, a MacCartan, came from Ireland, and his grandmother, Joséphine de Gaulle, had published a biography of O'Connell, the great hero in the struggle for Irish independence.

In 1902, the Irish separatists campaigned for the celebration of the Battle of Fontenoy (1745). To wipe out the memory of their defeat at Limerick in 1691, they intended to magnify the part the Irish brigade had played in the victory of Marshall Saxe. An advance guard came to Fontenoy, a tiny Belgian town four miles from Antoing, and set up a plaque:

> *To the memory of the heroic Irish soldiers*
> *Who changed a defeat into victory.*
> *Fontenoy, May 11, 1745.*
> *God save Ireland.*

A grand patriotic subscription was opened in Ireland to pay for a more permanent monument.

Fired with enthusiasm, Father Butin took his pupils, including Charles de Gaulle, to the battlefield to show them the real effect of the marshal's victory. In front of the plaque, he said:

> We can only applaud the idea of perpetuating the memory of the valor shown at Fontenoy by the Irish brigade. It was accustomed to brilliant actions, and while we had the honor of seeing it marching beside our own regiments, in the ranks of the French army, it constantly displayed the qualities of a *corps d'élite*. But this recent inscription cannot be accepted without explanation or correction. The inscription implies: "The French Army was beaten at Fontenoy, and when the day was lost, the Irish brigade,

alone, by its bravery, reversed the battle and turned defeat into victory." That is what it means. Well, we cannot accept this interpretation: we cannot accept it because it is neither complete nor accurate: the highest praise is not minimized if it remains within the limits of truth, and the Irish brigade will lose no jot of its claim to fame when we have re-established its role in the battle.

Father Butin proved that it was "a very French battle" and thus won a second resounding victory for France at Fontenoy. In 1907, the mayor of Dublin unveiled a monument which carries only the legend:

To the memory of the Irish brigade
Who avenged Limerick.

Note the closeness of Father Butin's style to the General's, the emphasis, the periods, the triple repetition noted by students of his official speeches. The nationalistic French spirit of the action and the text is also to be remarked.[2] Moreover, Auguste Butin's political thinking clearly marked the future General. In 1904, he published a small book of great interest whose vigorous thinking can be found again in de Gaulle.[3] It discussed the defense of the northeast frontier of France, where it joins Belgium. After analyzing the geographical situation, the priest affirmed that the defense must be based on its strong points. The only true rampart is the Rhine, but failing that, the greatest efforts must be spent on the organization of an offensive protection based on the fortresses. There must be no question of allowing the enemy to capture Lille–Roubaix–Tourcoing, and the father prophesied: "To spend vast sums on the east and neglect the northern frontier, is a direct invitation to an attack from that side."

⚜

Before World War II, de Gaulle wrote: "One door has been opened to all the misfortunes which have struck France throughout her history: the door through which fled all the lessons of the past."

In another publication, Auguste Butin in 1906[3] praised the father of mobile artillery, Gribeauval: guns protected by camouflage moving toward the enemy. Not so far removed from the armored column.

Charles de Gaulle knew this region well. Whenever he spent his summer holidays at Malo les Bains or in the family villa at Wimereux, where his parents owned a share of the property, he often visited the battlefields. Pierre de Gaulle remembered his brother in 1911 standing on a small rise at Hougoumont while he described the battle of Waterloo.

While Charles was at Saint-Cyr, he spent his weekends at Charleroi with his sister; she married a mining engineer in 1909, the son of a French citizen of Tournai, but of Belgian nationality. It had been arranged that Charles would spend his summer leave in 1914 at his sister's country house at Dinant.

From twenty-one to twenty-eight, Charles de Gaulle's life was dominated by the Great War. Three times wounded: at Dinant in August, 1914; in Champagne in February, 1915; at Douaumont in March, 1916. Prisoner of war for thirty-two months. In the German huts, Captain de Gaulle continued his education, wrote a book, learned German perfectly, gave lectures, directed seminars and kept his fellow prisoners in a permanent state of activity. During this period of exposure to outside influences, de Gaulle, within four walls, found energy in his own will to action.

From twenty-eight to thirty-five: first, the campaign in Poland, where he distinguished himself by his courage, his determination to learn Polish, and his talents as a military instructor. Then followed his marriage to Yvonne Vendroux, which an eyewitness reports as follows:

I knew both families well. My father, *Maître* Ferrand, was a childhood friend of M. de Gaulle *père*. One day in autumn, 1920, I met the Vendroux family in the Paris express. The previous evening, I had seen Charles in the capital. I hadn't met him since 1914, and the lad I knew had grown into a dashing officer. I said to myself, "A fine match for Yvonne," and I sang Charles's praises. "Out of the question," said her mother. "Yvonne is much too young. And besides, she'll never marry a soldier. The garrison life, the constant changes, that wouldn't suit her at all." The truth is that Yvonne had just refused an officer (the son of the governor–general who had decorated her mother). A few days later, I met Madame Vendroux again, coming out of mass. "By the way," she asked, "what's become of your young man?" We decided to arrange a meeting. The Vendroux family was due to return to Paris a fortnight later, so I wrote off at once to my sister. The forthcoming opening of the *Salon d'Automne* would provide an excuse. Charles and my sister duly appeared, and Yvonne and her parents. They both pretended to be surprised, but it was obvious at once that Yvonne hadn't been taken in. The most important item in the *Salon* was a portrait of Maurice Rostand. Yvonne and Charles, who were ahead of us, stayed in front of it for a long time. Next day, I received a letter from my sister: "D'you know that Charles is very taken? We all had tea in a *pâtisserie*, and Charles, probably very worked up, upset his cup over Yvonne's dress." The Vendrouxs went back to Calais. No news of Charles for a whole week. "Maman," asked Yvonne, "don't you think the captain found me rather too small?" The following Saturday, Yvonne was due to return to Paris, to go to a ball at the Polytechnique. I told my sister to pass the news on to

❧

Charles. As soon as she arrived, the tall lanky captain bowed to Madame Vendroux, carried Yvonne off, and danced with nobody else. After the sixth dance, Madame Vendroux saw her daughter returning on Charles' arm. "Maman, the captain has just asked me to be his wife. I have accepted." [4]

Captain de Gaulle returned to France to teach military history at Saint-Cyr and published his first book, *La Discorde chez l'ennemi* (1924).

After a period at the Ecole de Guerre, he joins Marshal Pétain's staff. From thirty-five to forty-two, his devouring ambition attains its peak[5] while he studied the character of his chief and drew the portrait of the man he would like to be:

Faced by events, the man of character must trust to himself alone. His impulse is to put his mark on the action, take it on his own shoulders, make it his concern. And far from sheltering behind his superiors, or hiding behind textbooks, he should take his stand, and face the enemy. Not that he wants to ignore orders or neglect advice, but he is eager for action and wants to make his own decisions. Not that he is ignorant of danger or disregards the consequences, but he assesses them honestly and accepts them frankly. Better still, he welcomes action with a master's pride, for he is part of it, and it is part of him. Rejoicing in victory, if it is due to him, even if he does not benefit from it, and accepting the full weight of defeat, not without bitter satisfaction. In short, a fighter who finds within himself his own ardour and his own support, a gambler who thinks more of success than the profit to be made—and pays his debts with his own money. The man of character ennobles action: without him, it is the drudgery of a slave;

thanks to him, it becomes the divine game of heroes. . . .

The determination to act for himself is inevitably accompanied by a certain severity. The man of character personifies the harshness necessary to the effort. His subordinates feel the effect and sometimes complain, but such a leader is set apart, for their is no authority without prestige and no prestige without a certain aloofness. His subordinates may murmur softly against his haughtiness and his demands, but when the action begins, all criticism is silenced: the crisis reached, he is the magnet they follow, who lifts the burden with his own hands, though his arms should crack, and carries it on his own back, though it break under the strain. Conversely, the trust of lesser men exalts the man of character. He is grateful for this simple justice. His determination grows in answer, but also his benevolence, for he is a born protector. Should the enterprise succeed, he spreads the benefits widely, and should there be defeat, he will not share the shame with others. He wins respect in return for the security he offers.

This appeared in de Gaulle's second book, *Le Fil de l'epée* (1927). After serving at Trèves (Trier), and spending some time in the Levant, de Gaulle returned to Paris (1932) where his driving ambition made him want to play a leading role.

At forty-two, Colonel Charles de Gaulle's character was set. He was a hard man, hard and inflexible. His military career had failed, largely owing to his nonconformist ideas. So from 1932 to 1937, under fourteen ministries, he was attached to the secretariat-general of the Ministry of Defense. During this time, he prepared his thesis on the use of armored columns, drawing on the works of his French predecessor, General Estienne. The idea was very much in the air at the time, for other military writers simultaneously published studies of the same kind, but de Gaulle's own thinking was purely French in origin.[6] This basic work appeared in 1934: *Vers l'armée de métier*.[7]

The time for concessions was past. The death of his father, which took place in 1932, and an estrangement with his protector, Marshal Pétain, left Charles de Gaulle entirely on his own. The publication of the book caused his name for some time to be struck off the list of promotions to the rank of lieutenant-colonel. He needed allies to help get his project adopted, and courted politicians and journalists. The time was propitious, for there was talk of a preventive war against Germany, and Pilsudski sounded out Paul-Boncour in this context.[8]

On December 5, 1937, Jean Auburtin, professor at the School of Social Service, presented de Gaulle to Paul Reynaud, who was "charmed by the boldness of the project."

"For my part," added Auburtin, "I constituted myself its traveling ambassador. I organized meetings with Paul-Boncour, Marcel Déat, Alexandre Millerand, finally with Léon Blum." [9]

Of all these men, de Gaulle particularly remembered Marcel Déat, "on whose gifts he particularly counted," but it was Paul Reynaud who presented the de Gaulle project to parliament on March 15, 1935. In addition, de Gaulle courted newspaper editors.

He made an alliance with André Pironneau, chief editor of *l'Echo de Paris*, subsequently director of *l'Epoque*, who published forty articles in depth on the subject. Other journalists echoed these sentiments, but Paul Reynaud's action had no sequel, and at headquarters, de Gaulle collected nothing but snubs. De Gaulle wrote:

> At the Elysée, at the end of a séance of the *Conseil Superieur de la Défence Nationale* to which I was secretary, General Maurin, the minister for war, called to me sharply: "Good-bye, de Gaulle: where I am, there is no room for you." When visitors mentioned my name, he said: "He has joined up with a fountain pen, Pironneau,

and a gramophone, Paul Reynaud. I am sending him to
Corsica!"

In October, 1936, Léon Blum asked de Gaulle's advice, but
made no changes in the defense plans. Yet de Gaulle was promoted colonel in 1937, and did not go to Corsica, but to Metz,
to command the 507th Tank Regiment. The garrison commander
was General Giraud who, doubtless forwarned, said to him at the
first opportunity: "While I live, my young friend, you won't force
your theories on us here."

In 1938, de Gaulle joined a Catholic leftist club, *Les Amis du
Temps Présent*, and again met the historian Daniel-Rops, who
asked him for a history of the French Army. De Gaulle, who had
time to spare at Metz, redrafted *La France et son armée*, which
appeared the same year.[10] This book had no more success than
its predecessors.

The colonel kept in close touch with Paul Reynaud, flattering
him assiduously, and promising him a great political future which
he felt he could support.[11] But he belonged to no camarilla, and
took no part in political intrigues.

At the outbreak of World War II he was still at Metz; he
contented himself on November 11, 1939, with sending through
the usual channels a note of comment on the lessons to be drawn
from the campaign in Poland: armored divisions must be formed.
This note found its way into the files.

Taking advantage of some leave, he went to Paris in January,
1940, stayed at the Hotel Lutétia and went to see Paul Reynaud
and Léon Blum. Disappointed, on his return to the Fifth Army,
he drew up a weighty memorandum which, on January 26, was
sent to eighty political and military personalities: it demanded the
urgent constitution of an autonomous mechanized force. This
appeal went unheeded. And when Paul Reynaud became *prési-*

✣

dent du Conseil on March 23, 1940, de Gaulle, recalled to Paris, was not named secretary to the war council as he had hoped. Another disappointment. He returned to the front, was given command of the Fourth Armored Division formed on May 15. But as he had said over and over again, it was too late. The division which he organized on the field of battle could not play a decisive role.[12] It fought gloriously, courageously, but without much effect.

On June 6, Paul Reynaud called de Gaulle to the post of under-secretary of state for national defense. At the same time, he was made acting *general de brigade*. But Reynaud had also called on Marshal Pétain to act as minister of state.

The collapse began. The inertia of Pétain and Weygand was set against the dynamism of the General. The armistice was near. De Gaulle traveled to London several times and, after a short interval, stayed there to direct the new battle of France. The destiny of Charles de Gaulle, as political leader, was settled on June 18, 1940.

This rapid survey of the military career of our hero leads us to several clear conclusions. He is a dedicated man, an obsessionist, completely absorbed in the pursuit of his objectives, violent on occasion, but always consistent. Each new element is used by him as a means of activating his driving ideas. Obsessionists are frequently active and emotional. De Gaulle, an exaggerated obsessionist, shows himself to be unemotional; brutally frank, his susceptibilities always on the alert, he has lived completely aloof since childhood.

Finally, the slowness of his progress should be noted. Napoleon ended his career at forty-three (the Russian campaign), Lenin began his great revolution at forty-seven, Richelieu was a minister from thirty-nine to forty-seven, Churchill at thirty-seven, Hitler at forty-four, Mussolini at thirty-nine, to quote only a few examples. De Gaulle came to power at forty-nine by devious ways, and through the back door; his power was only recognized at fifty-four and really admitted at sixty-eight.

"I began my adventure at forty-nine," he himself wrote. Hence a certain fixedness, a marked rigidity of thought.

At forty-two, de Gaulle began to achieve his personal ambitions.

The key lies in *Le Fil de l'epée*, the book he wrote at forty-two: the man of character, the mirror he was seeking in order to find himself. But during his formative years, and his army officer's life, he appeared untouched by the riches of emotion. He will preserve this voluntary, or assumed, moral amputation or suffer an inhumanity which will isolate him more and more till the end of his days.

PRIVATE LIFE

In this epic story, there is little room for private life. Apart from his marriage in 1921, we know very little. His wife went with her husband and shared his garrison life: Mayence, Trèves, Beirut, Paris, Metz. But in 1934, the de Gaulles bought a country place, "La Boisserie," a property of about 5 acres, at Colombey les Deux Eglises, about 200 miles from Paris and roughly the same distance from Metz and Strasbourg. From 1936 onward, when the proprietor died, this house, set in the forest 1,000 feet above sea level, was a home for Madame de Gaulle and her children, while her soldier husband pursued his calling in distant places.

Each time her husband returned, Yvonne de Gaulle reported on her activities, her work, the garden, the rebuilding, and the children's progress at school. Her favorite relaxations were gardening and playing the piano, which she did regularly until the death of their daughter Anne in 1948. Madame de Gaulle played

❧

Liszt, Beethoven, and Chopin, her husband's favorite composers, but she was not above strumming popular songs, and the General sometimes hummed the words of *"Plaisir d'Amour."* Since 1948, Madame de Gaulle has spent most of her time knitting.

Before the war, she joined her husband in Paris during his leaves, and they both went to the theater or cinema frequently. He preferred Sacha Guitry; she had a weakness for Gary Cooper and Clark Gable.

In summer, "La Boisserie" is pleasant because the nearness of the forest tempers the dry heat of the district, but in winter, the cold is intense in this big house with fourteen rooms, whose windows offer entrance to the howling wind. Madame de Gaulle keeps the house temperature at 15 degrees centigrade[13] in the living-room and 18 degrees centigrade[14] in her husband's study, with additional stoves being brought in if necessary. When he lives at "La Boisserie" in winter, the General wears several sweaters and even a cloak, while his wife is happy in a thin dress. A year before the war, the cold was so intense Colonel de Gaulle seriously considered selling the house, but Madame de Gaulle was against it and wrote to Marshal Pétain to ask for his support. The marshal sided with her and extolled the thousand hidden virtues of the property where he would like "to spend a few peaceful weeks," which, of course, he never did.

The difficulties arising from the care of their daughter Anne, and the interest Madame de Gaulle took in mongoloid children, led her in 1945 to support a religious foundation in the valley of the Chevreuse at Vertcoeur which took in these unfortunate children. She became the benefactor of this estalishment, which from 1948 onward was called after Anne de Gaulle. Her husband, at her request, accompanied her several times on her regular visits. But when the institution expanded, in 1946, the financial burden became heavier at the very moment when the General had given up all his governmental duties and retired to "La Boisserie." The nuns who ran the establishment were faced with the closing of the institution in view of their increasing debts. Madame de Gaulle refused to hear of this, and asked her husband to help. The General called in Georges Pompidou, his former chef de cabinet, now a conseiller d'état, who looked after his personal affairs. The conseiller at first considered taking out a mortgage on the house, but a survey of the property showed that the actual value of the building, which was in need of repairs, did not amount to very much.

"Then sell it," said de Gaulle.

Pompidou, who had become treasurer of Anne de Gaulle Foundation, did not carry out this order. He found a way of settling the debts of the institution and restoring "La Boisserie." Later, the General's royalties from the first volume of his Mémoires, 100 million francs,* went to the Foundation, which gave the institution the scope and security it needed. Since then, Madame de Gaulle owes a deep sense of gratitude to Georges Pompidou, who saved the two possessions she holds most dear: "La Boisserie" and the Institut Anne de Gaulle. This particular and personal esteem is not an unimportant factor in the favor the minister enjoys from the General, not always considerate of his wife's wishes, but anxious to have a peaceful home.

On May 19, 1940, at the time of the French collapse, de Gaulle sent his wife and children to Carantec in Brittany. On May 15, on his way to London, he spent a few moments in Carantec and said to his wife: "Things are going badly. If the armistice is signed, take the children and catch the next boat."

On June 17, Madame de Gaulle was doing her daily shopping in Brest when she read in the papers that an armistice had been requested. The same day, as her husband had asked, and through the good offices of Monsieur de Margerie, she received her pass-

---

* Before January 1, 1960, the French franc was valued at 493.7 to one American dollar. The new French franc is valued at 4.937 to one American dollar.

ports. She left at 9 o'clock at night on board one of the last ships to get out of Brest, among the smoke and exploding ammunition dumps. When she reached Falmouth, on June 19, she telephoned her husband. He had had no news from his wife, but merely replied: "Ah, it's you. Come to London. I'll meet you at Paddington." An eyewitness related that he went back to his work without a word, without the slightest trace of emotion.

For the next three years, after various moves, Madame de Gaulle lived in a small house in Berkhamsted, where the General used to come for weekends. His son Philippe, by now seventeen, served in the Free French Navy; his daughter Elizabeth, now fifteen, went to school at Our Lady of Sion in Shropshire, and then on to take a degree at Oxford. Madame de Gaulle spent her time between Marguerite, the faithful old maid who had been with her since Colombey, and her twelve-year-old daughter, Anne.

In 1943, when the General went to Algiers, Madame de Gaulle went with him and set up house at the Villa des Oliviers, and sometimes spent weekends with him in a country house at Kabylie. She returned to Colombey at the end of 1944, and again in February, 1946, as she believed, forever. It was the happiest time of her life. Her son Philippe married Henriette de Montalembert, and on January 3, 1946, Elizabeth's wedding to Commandant de Boissieu, a former officer in General Leclerc's Second Armored Division, was celebrated.

When he left office, Charles de Gaulle at first lived with his wife and daughters in a small house at Marly, then in a country house belonging to his brother-in-law, Jacques Vendroux, at Septfontaine in the Ardennes. It was only in May, 1946, that he finally went back to Colombey.

Pierre de Gaulle and his family were the most frequent visitors at Colombey. Philippe de Gaulle, who was twenty-three in 1946, continued his career in the navy, where he made slow progress. It isn't easy to make a name for oneself, and the General's son had had such a strict upbringing that he had emerged somewhat dazed. Madame de Gaulle never hesitated to use corporal punishment, and the General, finding young Philippe one day in the jam cupboard, said coldly: "You like jam? Very well, stay there," and shut the child up until the following morning. Philippe's promotion, slow under the Fourth Republic, was speeded up under the Fifth: from lieutenant in 1958 to captain in 1967.

As for Alain de Boissieu, who was thirty-two in 1946, he has had a brilliant career, while his wife sometimes acts as confidential secretary to her father. Boissieu was first appointed to Central Africa, then to the general delegation in Algiers, then as commander of the armored forces and the cavalry, and finally director of Saint-Cyr.

The de Gaulles are a large family, nearly fifty of them in all. Xavier, the General's eldest brother, a mining engineer, had to leave his profession during the economic crisis in 1930. He became a tax collector in Mayence and fought the 1940 war as a captain in the artillery, as he had done in 1914. Taken prisoner by the Germans, repatriated for ill health, he managed to reach Switzerland and, after the liberation, became French consul in Geneva. He had one daughter, Geneviève, by his first marriage, and three children, Marie, Louise, and Henri, by a second.

The General's younger brother, Jacques, an engineer at Montceau les Mines, unfortunately contracted encephalitis in 1926 during an epidemic and remained paralyzed until his death in February, 1946. When threatened with arrest in July, 1943, he escaped, and a priest, Abbé Pierre, carried him over the Swiss frontier in his arms. His two eldest sons, François and Bernard, managed to reach North Africa and fought in Italy and Germany. François is now a priest. Jacques' third son, who also escaped to Switzerland with his parents in 1943, joined the Second Armored Division in 1944, and has become a professional soldier.

❧

The youngest of the de Gaulle sons, Pierre, went to work in a bank. He lived in his parents' apartment with his wife and five children: Chantal, Olivier, Véronique, Alain, and René. He was elected president of the Municipal Council of Paris in 1947, then put in charge of the French section of the Brussels *Exposition Universelle* in 1958. He died in 1960.

After her husband's arrest in 1943, Madame Pierre de Gaulle managed to cross the Pyrenees and reach Morocco with her children and the daughter of a Resistance worker who had been shot.

The General's eldest sister, Marie Agnes, had seven children by her husband, Monsieur Caillau, a coffee importer at Le Havre. Of their five sons, one was killed fighting in the Vosges in 1940, and three others fought in the Resistance and in the war.

During the war, two of the eight nephews of the General who were old enough joined him in London; three went to North Africa, and the two others who stayed in Occupied France joined the Resistance. Four members of the family, the Caillaus (husband and wife), Pierre and Geneviève de Gaulle were captured and deported by the Germans according to the law which decreed that a family is responsible for the actions of all its members. Eight de Gaulles escaped to Switzerland and seven remained in France, but they did not use the name of de Gaulle. When there was an opportunity for negotiating the exchange of hostages in favor of his relatives interned in Germany, the General refused to accept. Frequently, heads of state do everything they can to assist the social rise of their close relatives. In the present case, the General would have had every reason to make some move in their favor. He did nothing of the sort. Preoccupied with himself and "his" France, de Gaulle, as a matter of principle, ignored them.

An additional proof of the inhumanity of our subject? Or is it a façade?

The General and his wife are very indulgent to their grand-children. Charles Junior, Philippe's son, who did well in his exams, both baccalaureat and law, has always enjoyed special favor. At Colombey, Madame de Gaulle would intercede for Philippe to spare him punishments, and if she did not succeed, would not hesitate to disturb the General, working in his tower. One day, Charles Junior had been sentenced to translate a long piece of Latin. The General went up to see his grandson and knocked before entering.

"What are you translating?"

"Cicero," says the boy.

"I'd have given you some Livy. His style is magnificent."

And with this pronouncement, the General took the book and reeled off the translation by heart, to the astonishment of the schoolboy.

When the Boissieus came back to France after some time spent in Brazzaville, Madame de Gaulle, seeing that her daughter was still childless, persuaded her son-in-law to adopt a family. Since then they have adopted two children, and Madame de Gaulle looks after them with special care. It is thanks to her that Madame de Boissieu now lives in an apartment on the tenth floor of a new building in the rue de Grenelle in Paris. Journalists of the opposition say that Madame de Gaulle plays a part in politics, but this would seem to be greatly exaggerated. Certainly Yvonne de Gaulle stood by her husband in Paris.

"She saved me from the gulf of uncertainty," said the General, and many times he has introduced his wife as "the leading Gaullist in France."

In 1943, in Algiers, at the Villa des Oliviers, at the peak of his arguments with Giraud and the Americans, it was to her that the General entrusted the task of receiving the most tiresome of his visitors, taking notes of their questions, and answering them according to a schedule he had laid down. She also sorted the secret correspondence that arrived from France and divided it among her husband's trusted collaborators.

Once back in France, she eclipsed herself again, taking no pleasure in meeting politicians. A devout and practicing Catholic, a strict and conservative provincial, she will not receive into her intimate circle those who, if one may believe gossip and the newspapers, have too exciting a love life or, owing to divorce, are in trouble with the Church. The General may pretend that they represent the different spiritual families which make up France, but she refuses to invite this man or that: "He's a Freemason," or "He frightens me," or "Not another boring politician." Members of their entourage maintain that "her strictness has cost various men and women administrative or ministerial posts, although for many years they had given the General striking proof of their devotion." [15]

Madame de Gaulle does not need to support her family. Her brother, Jacques Vendroux, deputy mayor of Calais, has remained at the head of the family biscuit firm, which is related to a Dutch family of tobacco importers, the van der Hoeks. This "burgher of Calais" rallied to the General's side, to the R.P.F., then the U.N.R., and only made a career in politics by accident. During the time of "the years in the wilderness" he gave financial help to the hermit of Colombey.

Forced to give up the joys of "La Boisserie," where she loved looking after her flowerbeds working in a gardening over-all, Madame de Gaulle has had to resign herself to living in the "furnished rooms" of the Palais de l'Elysée, built in 1718 for a friend of the regent, and which sheltered in turn Madame de Pompadour, Murat, and the future Napoleon III. In these "uncomfortable rooms," she lives a sheltered life. Even the few strips of grass are guarded by the security police, and *Madame la Présidente* tries to escape as often as possible. The days are far off when, in 1946, she could go and buy her bread at the local

baker's at Colombey and queue up like everyone else at the
co-operative. Then she could do her important shopping in Troyes
in her 2 h.p. Citroen, but now a "gorilla" has to drive the Ami 6,
which has replaced the small machine.

All the same, in Paris, before lunch, she slips out sometimes
to visit the shops which are still open to her. Police officers follow
her, but she can no longer go to the big stores, as in the old days.
She goes to see her daughter, or an old friend who may be ill, but
she is always back by 1 o'clock, the sacrosanct lunch time, which
lasts for half an hour.

Madame de Gaulle's correspondence, more than 100 letters a
week, is dealt with by a secretary who takes her instructions, and
the afternoons are given up to good works—mostly knitting—
for which she often requisitions the help of ministers' wives, and
to gossip. Farah Diba is her favorite, Jackie Kennedy (who the
General named "a Parisian sparrow") she found "common," and
she thoroughly dislikes Queen Fabiola. None of that matters very
much, except that the General willingly adopts her summary
points of view. Soustelle, Pisani, Malraux are not in her good
books, and this has sometimes done them a disservice.

The evenings are often given up to official receptions, which
bore Madame de Gaulle "to tears," and she can barely hide "a
furious desire to knit." [16] In conversation she uses a series of
stereotyped formulae which the General has taught her, and waits
impatiently for 10 o'clock, when the presidential couple can go
back to their own apartments. De Gaulle insists on seeing the
TV news before dinner, which is followed by family conversation
and reading.

Madame de Gaulle dislikes the presidential life intensely, and
that explains the attempts she made during the last presidential
elections to persuade her husband to give up his crushing task.
Yet Yvonne de Gaulle has always followed where her husband's
destiny demanded. She accompanied him on his propaganda tours

⚜

of France and the French territories during the vital days of the R.P.F. She took part in all the presidential expeditions: South America, Cambodia, and Russia, as well as all the visits to the French provinces. She waited in a small private room in the Hôpital Cochin during her husband's operation: she was in the car that was fired on the day of the Petit Clamart attack, and when the General asked her to travel in a separate car, she refused categorically: "No, Charles, it won't do. I'm a gambler too." Brave and stubborn, Yvonne de Gaulle has chosen, once for all, to follow her husband, and in the final analysis, it was to her that he gave the precious envelopes addressed to the high authorities of the state which contain his will and last instructions.

HEALTH

We know very little about Charles de Gaulle's health. He was brought up in a Spartan atmosphere, discipline was severe, comfort as yet unknown: no central heating, no electricity, no motorcar, no telephone. Charles went on foot every day, including Sunday. At Antoing he slept in a dormitory that the Jesuit fathers could never manage to heat adequately. On Wednesday and Sunday afternoons, he went for long walks with his fellow students, to Fontenoy and Bouvines.

At twenty-six, he experienced thirty-two months of captivity; in 1920, a severe winter in Poland; in 1927, a flu epidemic at Trèves, which caused several deaths in the battalion of *chasseurs à pied* which he commanded. In the Levant in 1929 he contacted malaria, which recurred in London in August, 1942, after a journey to the Middle East, and again in Algeria in 1943. In London, he nearly died, and in Algiers, Madame de Gaulle was very worried, but the fever quickly disappeared.

"The tall asparagus," as his colleagues at Saint-Cyr called

him; "the *Connétable*" to those of the Ecole de Guerre; "the motorized colonel" to the garrison at Metz. He seemed to be impervious to everything: cold, wind, tempest. He is made of stone.

On April 17, 1964, Professor Aboulker operated for the prostate, but by the 30th of the month, convalescence was well advanced. De Gaulle said to his doctor: "I know I'm not an easy patient, Professor, but easy patients are resigned. I'm not." [16]

Summoning his ministers as soon as he returned to the Elysée, he said: "Thank you, gentlemen, for your good wishes. As you see, they have been granted. General de Gaulle is very grateful. Now, let's get down to business." [16]

The ministers endeavored to cut the meeting short. But the General told them: "My mind needs no convalescence, gentlemen." And pointing to his head, he added: "This is not where they operated."

On May 26, de Gaulle, with the grand duchess of Luxembourg and the president of the German Federal Republic, opened the Moselle Canal. In June, he visited Picardy. A doctor was in close attendance. After a speech at Amiens, which was much applauded, he turned to him and, pointing to the cheering crowd, exclaimed: "See there, Doctor, all your pills count for nothing compared to those vitamins." [16]

During a garden party at the Elysée he said to one of his guests: "My doctors have given up being in opposition." [17] And from September 20 to October 17, he undertook a tour of ten republics of South America, which was a real test of endurance. He defied everyone, counsellors and doctors, Americans and local personalities, and exhausted his wife and personal bodyguard. Without any apparent fatigue, he endured changes of climate and altitude, made eight or ten speeches per country, including some in Spanish.

In 1966, after a long and difficult journey through Russia, he

⚜

went round the world via Djibouti and Cambodia. In 1967, the Canadian tour. His physical strength is remarkable, exceptional above all for a septuagenarian. His vitality is prodigious.

Like the majority of those in blood group O, he is predisposed to inflammations and troubles of the circulation, but this never shows. Doctors attend him, but they are nearly always soldiers detached for a certain period from the army health service, and are, obviously, very discreet. The tendencies they have noted on the physical side are: illnesses of the blood, arthritis, cellulitis, stomach ulcers. The uncorrected short-sightedness of his youth has paved the way for the cataract of his old age, which is looked after by Doctor Vallon, a noted ophthalmologist and the wife of Louis Vallon.

A hypertrophia of the hypophysic gland caused the giantism which disturbed his bodily development. On the mental plane, aggravated by this giantism, a hypertrophia of the ego has been noted, a prodigous egocentricity and tendencies to exhibitionism and mythomania, to spitefulness and revenge.[18] Psychasthenia has also been noted, and sometimes a detachment from reality. This doubtless explains the determination of this "man of character" always to remain objective: "to see things as they are." To sum up, a clear orientation toward making demands on, and a struggle against, the outside world.

Jean Lacouture has noted five important stages in this struggle:

1. 1924: At the Ecole de Guerre, Captain de Gaulle resisted the dogma of official teaching, and left with bad marks: "I shall never come back to this filthy hole except as director."

2. 1927: Captain de Gaulle gave three lectures at the Ecole de Guerre in which he showed that a leader sometimes has the right to disobey orders.

3. 1934: Lieutenant-Colonel de Gaulle, in his book, *Vers l'armée de métier*, embarked on a great quarrel with the army leaders,

and in support did not hesitate to call on the press, the deputies of the *Front Populaire*, and the least conformist politicians (Déat, Millerand, Reynaud).

4. 1938: Colonel de Gaulle broke with his former commanding officer, Marshal Pétain, and was not afraid of the scandal.

5. 1940: Colonel de Gaulle, outside official channels, distributes a strange pamphlet which invites dissidence by questioning the actions of the headquarters staff.

"A fine rebellious career, in fact," concludes Lacouture, "and which foreshadows a famous insurgent." [19]

It must not be forgotten that de Gaulle was also persecuted by his chiefs: Pétain, Weygand, Maurin, Giraud. But he invited persecution by judging his adversaries publicly in 1944 and by condemning their successors in 1962. Afterward, he said bitterly: "The army never loved de Gaulle."

Later, he fought Churchill, Roosevelt, every political party, and the Americans, but from 1952 to 1958 he fought himself. From every point of view, he is out of the ordinary, and his destiny, decreed by fate but shaped by himself, could only be exceptional. De Gaulle is a pupil of Nietzsche. Vital energy activates Superman.

A MORPHOPSYCHOLOGICAL APPROACH

De Gaulle before forty looked very different from the man after 1958. The change has taken place in the lower part of the face. The chin, never very marked, has receded. The full lips have thickened, the nose has grown heavier and marks the face more clearly. "His face has changed with the years: two furrows have lengthened his mouth and underlined his chin," said Malraux.

This change, according to the physiognomists, denotes a growing incapacity for adaptation, a certain inaptitude for living in the present; he is thinking of the past and the future, and lives successively ahead of, and behind, his times. He lives with the man of his choice (the man of character) and will not accept other men except insofar as they approach the portrait of the ideal robot.

The internal life of this withdrawn face is very important. Between the ages of twenty and sixty, the forehead has taken on breadth, while the jaw has diminished. The cerebral activity has not ceased to develop, while practical realizations diminish. He uses words less and less to renew himself, and attains a cerebral supermaturity, but contents himself in action with a repetition of the past. A comparison between the portraits of the child and the septuagenarian is very striking. The nose has changed. The nostrils have taken shape little by little; the man has plenty of breath, but decreasing sensibility. The latero-nasal retraction is almost nil at all times, but from the point of view of exterior perception, he has progressively dried up.

The real physical and mental maturity seems to have been reached around 1944, then cerebral growth becomes paralleled by physical decline. The man of action and of thought is only a man of thought from 1952 onward.

His hands are small for his size, square, typical of enthusiasts. With age, they have thickened, the muscles have relaxed and, as flesh takes over, the handshake becomes limp and flaccid.

INSTINCTS

Reading his *Mémoires de guerre* reminds us of Chateaubriand. It is by no means accidental that the latter's *Mémoires d'outre-tombe* have been seen on the General's desk at Colombey.

Little or no imagination, no critical sense, no spontaneity.

Polemics sometimes, directed here and there; hasty compliments that are insincere, and no real self-revelation. Has he no friendships, no feelings other than circumstances dictate?

As André Maurois said somewhat harshly: "De Gaulle says nothing. His *Mémoires* are well written: that is all. For them to be interesting, everything must be revealed." [20]

He has no loves, no secret gardens. It was thus that the Free French saw him in London during the war. Several young women, encouraged by his friends who hoped for a greater kindness from the boss, tried the classic recipes for seduction on Charles de Gaulle. He seems not to have noticed.

After World War II, during his weekly trips to Paris, an unexpected meeting with such and such "pretty lady" seems to have roused in him some slight romantic attachment. But Madame de Gaulle was vigilant, and the General is at heart indifferent to the pleasures of sex. Nevertheless, as a young officer, he was more receptive. In Poland, in 1920, he even behaved like a conqueror.

"I spent a certain time in that forgotten spot," he relates. "When my pay arrived, I lived the life of a boyar. I organized candlelight suppers. Then, cleaned out after five or six days, I had to fall back on my work for amusement." [5]

Polish chroniclers have delved deeper. In the press of the period, they have unearthed the announcement of a duel. Captain Charles de Gaulle was inspired with passion for a lovely Polish lady, the Princess C. As she was being assiduously courted by an officer from the Lithuanian division, the French captain felt himself obliged to fight it out.

This possessive love is in character, and the romanticism of the adventure comes straight out of Chateaubriand. From 1930 up to the start of the war, the colonel remained very attractive and set himself to storming strong points. After 1958, he still paid romantic court to his guests at official receptions—flowery phrases and

⚜

compliments on the material of the dress. But there is no aftermath.

As for the betrothal in the autumn of 1920, it proceeded at top speed. By April 7, 1921, the captain wrote to one of his friends: "I am marrying Mademoiselle Vendroux (Yvonne of the biscuits)." [16]

To the pleasures of the table, Charles de Gaulle is less indifferent. Certainly his appetite is large and equal to his size, and to an outsider, it verges on the greedy.

In London, the leader of the Free French lunched nearly every day at the Royal Automobile Club. To the menu he would add a good Burgundy, a brandy and a cigar. In 1944, the president of the provisional government lunched on *hors d'oeuvres*, meat or fish, vegetable and dessert. At dinner, soup replaced the *hors d'oeuvres*. Among his favorite dishes are *pâté de canard*, or *charcuterie*, and *tripe de chez Pharamond*. He arrives last, sits down after the guests, and is the first to leave.

At Colombey, his guests see him eat enormously and drink more than a liter of wine at a meal, paying particular attention to the vintage of the Burgundy.

After 1958, at the Elysée, the General shows a considerable appetite, and his wife often crosses her fingers on her plate, a signal to stop, which he respects immediately. Before going to table, de Gaulle crosses the anteroom where the little gifts are laid out that he receives from everywhere. He picks out the boxes of chocolates and crystallized fruits sent by those who know his minor weakness. He lays the chosen objects beside his plate and, between two courses, pulls off the string, tears open the packets, and quickly eats several mouthfuls. It is true that this greediness has increased, particularly since he has given up smoking. But his liking for sweets dates from his childhood.

At his grandmother's, rue Princesse, in Lille, in 1907, he ate

Liégeois waffles dipped in syrup. Since 1958, every week he sends for the same waffles from the same *pâtisserie* in the rue Esquermoise in Lille.

In Warsaw, where his rank of assistant to General Niessel allowed him to choose his own billet, he decided to stay with a *pâtissier*, Blikle, who, forty years later, still sends him a birthday cake every year. At the time of his betrothal, he invited his intended to *pâtisseries*. The eyewitnesses of five continents who have seen him eating greedily at well-furnished tables can no longer be counted.

Such a Bismarckian hunger is surprising. It is necessary for his overflowing vitality? Certainly, his huge size must be remembered, but does it not translate itself into an acute instinct of self-preservation? Is the General afraid of death?

It would seem not. In 1914, he faced the enemy fire for the first time:

> The infantry had left the road. Spread out over the fields, in small columns, they moved toward an unknown drama. In silence, with constricted throats, watching their leaders doing their best to smile, the men are anxious, but resolute. . . . Bullets begin to whistle, only a few at first, almost hesitant. . . . Less dangerous than the shells, but frightening because they wound and kill in silence. . . . And running, heart beating, across the fields already harvested at the end of this month of August. . . .

But that is the description of the chronicler. The citations are more eloquent:

> Captain de Gaulle, company commander, well known for his high intellectual and moral courage, whilst his battalion, subjected to a terrible bombardment, was decimated and the enemy surrounded his company on all

sides, brought off his men in a furious assault and a savage hand-to-hand struggle, the only solution he considered compatible with his conception of military honor. Fell in the struggle. An outstanding officer.

This citation is signed: Pétain.

In 1940, on June 2, he was cited again, this time by Weygand, who cannot be suspected of complaisance where he is concerned.[21] As the machine guns open up, de Gaulle is: "under a tree, smoking like a chimney and completely calm. He was dressed like his mechanic, in an old leather coat, with no badges of rank. De Gaulle is a man for hard times." [22]

In 1944, when he returned to Paris, de Gaulle attended a *Te Deum* at Notre-Dame de Paris. Shots were fired from the roofs toward the *Parvis* and rang out inside the cathedral. The General never moved.[23]

At the time of the attack at Petit Clamart, on August 22, 1962, his car was caught in a cross fire. Madame de Gaulle was beside him, his son-in-law, General Boissieu, in front with the chauffeur. "At the first salvo," says Boissieu, "the car skidded to the left, two tires having been hit. I turned round; a shot had broken the rear window, between the heads of the General and Madame de Gaulle. Another had pierced the roof a few inches further on. I cried: 'Get down, for heaven's sake!' but neither of them moved. And to the end they stayed like that, erect and firm." [24]

When they arrived at Villacoublay, the General got out of the car, brushed off the splinters of glass which starred his coat and remarked: "The ones trying to shoot me are just as bloody fools as the ones trying to protect me."

A few days later, he presided over the Council of Ministers at the Elysée: "Be sure, gentlemen, I am very glad to see you again." [16]

He received Mr. Als, the Luxembourg ambassador, at a fare-
well lunch. The diplomat remarked: "What dramatic moments
you have lived through."

"The essential, *Monsieur l'Ambassadeur*, is to live through
them." [16]

No, decidedly, the General isn't afraid of death. He moves
through bullets, shoulders a way through crowds which may be
hiding his murderers, upsets the plans of his police officers and
shows himself coldly courageous. Nevertheless the danger exists,
present, obvious. How sensitive is he? His instincts are completely controlled by his will.

INTELLIGENCE

The General's outstanding intelligence is practical. This avid
reader of philosophers hates abstractions. He was born in Lille,
but he is of mixed blood and his family have been Parisians for
generations. But the northerners have influenced his outlook. He
lived among them at Antoing, where a third of the pupils came
from the cities of the north, then at Arras while he was serving
in the regiment of Colonel Pétain. P. M. de la Gorce has described
it very well:

> The soldiers of the Thirty-third Regiment of Infantry
> are miners from the Pas-de-Calais, peasants from the
> Tarde, the Thiérache, from Valenciennes. They are peo-
> ple formed in the image of a land and a climate, tough and
> hard-working. The quality they cultivate most is the care
> of their dignity. Work is their daily obsession, imposed by
> the rigors of a treacherous climate and the uncertainties
> of a labor market subject to the vicissitudes of industry
> or the mines. Toughness and austerity prevail, but some-

times give way to explosions of noisy enjoyment or of
rage. Such are the men de Gaulle learned to know at Arras,
then during the first two years of the war; he was all the
more prepared for the experience, since, being a northerner
himself, he had an intense fellow-feeling for the men who
would be his comrades or under his command. His image
of the French people was fixed forever. All his life, when
he evokes them, it is the population of the north of France
he will conjure up. When he speaks to the French people,
he is thinking of the Frenchmen of the north. When he
chooses words, he uses terms most likely to arouse a certain northern sensibility. His language nearly always includes terms most likely to appeal to their psychology;
thus we endlessly come across the adjective "tough," an
ideal of fieriness, pride, and even resistance, which comes
to mind when endeavoring to describe a certain northern
attitude.[25]

Charles de Gaulle's understanding is astonishing: immediate
perception, just observation, rapid comprehension. Yet there are
two distinct periods in his life: before and after 1940.

Even before 1932, he showed a very open mind, and was
interested in many subjects. His writings dealt with psychology,
the military arts, politics, history. Then the sphere of his intellectual interest narrowed. *"Vers l'armée de métier"* is only a thesis,
a summary of the ideas of Gribeauval, Father Butin, General
Estienne, and the editors of the *Militär Wochenblatt*. The
speeches of 1940 to 1944 justify "legitimate" rebellion. After
1958, the identification with France is complete. There is no
question of anything except France's place in the world. De
Gaulle may speak of the gold standard, agriculture, or labor-
capital relations, but these are mere speeches learned by heart
and well delivered. The General's opinion on these subjects is

summary or simplified, as were those of Marshal Pétain. At the
Council of Ministers, discussions on the agricultural aspect of the
Common Market are sometimes lively.

"Let us hear from *Monsieur le Ministre de l'Agriculture*,"
says de Gaulle. "He has a will of iron, the tenacity of lead, and
a beard made of steel wool."

Then, after listening to M. Pisani reporting on the difficulties
encountered in Brussels, he continues, solemnly: "These people
mustn't imagine that de Gaulle can't tell eggs from billiard
balls." [16]

To the General, France is an ideal, a purely cerebral creation,
which rests less and less on concrete realities. While the ministers
are occupied with them, he cherishes his ideal making grandiose
and megalomaniacal plans.

At the beginning of his first seven-year term, the General still
drew up long-range views, characteristic of the dedicated man.
In December, 1945, he announced to Robert Prigent the immi-
nence of an East–West conflict, with the heart of the Sahara
occupying the geographic role previously held by the Massif
Central.[26]

In 1928, he wrote to his friend Nachin: "The army of the
Rhine cannot last much longer. The force of events is beating
down the last conventional and precious barriers. We must realize
that the *anschluss* is near, then the seizure by Germany, by force
or by consent, of what was taken from her for Poland's benefit.
Then, we shall be asked to give up Alsace. I'd say this was written
in the skies."

In 1933, he had foreseen the victory of armored divisions.

On June 18, 1940, he announced to the French that they had
not lost the war, an announcement of profound significance.

On June 30, 1940 he said to Maurice Schumann: "If Hitler had
meant to reach London, he would have been there already. I

believe Russia will come into the war before America, but they will both come in. Hitler is dreaming of the Ukraine. He will not be able to resist the urge to settle the fate of Russia, and it will be the beginning of his downfall. In short, the war is a terrible problem, but the outcome is already settled. We only have to bring the whole of France round to the right side."

On December 7, 1941, when he heard of the disaster of Pearl Harbor, he said to Colonel Passy: "Now the war is definitely won! The future will develop in two phases: the first will be the saving of Germany by the Allies: as to the second, I'm afraid it may be a great war between the Russians and the Americans . . . and the Americans will lose. . . ."

In April, 1944, he said to André Philip, who spoke of internal autonomy for Algeria: "Autonomy? You know quite well it can only end in total independence."

Certainly, his appreciation of matters in hand is not always correct. In 1933, he overlooked the tank-airplane combination. In 1941, he perhaps weighed the scales too quickly on the Russian side. In 1945, he was wrong. Nevertheless, his prescience is very fine, and often very close to reality.

Since 1958, the thinking has been more cerebral and the vision too far withdrawn from realities: the tripartite nuclear directory and the confederation of Europe are good ideas, but are not implemented.

After his withdrawal in 1946, he examined himself objectively: he speaks of de Gaulle, referring to himself in the third person to get an outside view. During the generals' coup in Algiers, he said to R. Buron: "What can you expect? There is one factor they can't make up their minds to take into account, an essential factor which upsets all their calculations; that factor is de Gaulle." [27]

To a friend who dared to ask him what, according to him, is his principal quality, the General replied: "Modesty," and after a pause, to measure his interlocutor's surprise: "When you contain the destiny of France, you can never be great enough, strong enough or fine enough!" [16]

Despite this inordinate, pathological pride, de Gaulle knows how to keep calm. On the problem of minorities, he said to Pompidou: "In two years' time, we shall see the independence of the Flemish provinces: in three years, it will be the turn of French Canada: in five years, the Swiss Jura will be demanding its independence. We live in a contradictory epoch: that of the big combines and the revolt of minorities. The paradox is that the big combines are only made up of minorities." [16]

To the United States ambassador, he spoke of his plans for co-operation with the noncommitted countries: "If we do not act immediately, in ten years' time the world will consist of 20 per cent of men who are too rich and 80 per cent who are too poor. That means that the affluent countries, North America, Eastern and Western Europe, will find themselves faced with a frightening reality: either to let themselves be invaded by maddened or famished hordes, or else to strike back by using the atom bomb. By acting immediately, we can still prevent this happening, but we must understand each other and admit that it is more important to safeguard the future than to preserve temporarily various vague interests of private citizens in countries where nearly the whole population lives in the most utter poverty. I'm telling you this, *Monsieur l'Ambassadeur*, for it is time that the United States understands that the world is not made up only of hypothetical supplies of Indians." [16]

In making these forecasts, de Gaulle is helped by a prodigious memory. He trained it under the Jesuits, developed it during his teaching periods, and has always cultivated it systematically. In the old days, he learned the long speeches from *Cyrano de Bergerac* by heart and spoke Latin; nowadays he learns long passages for his press conferences, virtuoso performances which carry a dramatic progression, including literary flourishes, and with colleagues planted in the audience to keep the monologue going. The "performance" at the press conference resembles, step by step, his lessons at the Ecole de Guerre thirty years earlier. His son Philippe remembers being called to his father's study: "For the next hour, we're going to speak Latin," [16] and his closest collaborators have witnessed astonishing feats of memory which are not so surprising on the part of one who, half a century ago, persuaded his brothers to speak Javanese.

Equipped with such gifts, de Gaulle takes pride in finding the *mot juste*. He condemns incorrect terms: integration, supranationality, and resists *"franglais"* and *"volapük."*

To a minister in council who had spoken of the *"force de frappe,"* he replied, banging his fist on the table: "What is this *force de frappe?* A phrase coined by a scruffy journalist. You, sir, would probably talk of the force of dissuasion, or the force of persuasion? When you don't know the right words, you should keep quiet!" [16]

Superficial remarks by journalists annoy him: "Paper, nothing but paper, never a single idea! You'd say de Gaulle was the only one who can think. I can't spend my time talking, merely to provide the journalists with copy." [16]

And again: "I could probably have been a decent journalist at a time when journalists had to know how to write." [16]

Listening to or reading de Gaulle, one sometimes has the impression of being in the presence of the leader of a great crusade. But the depth of his religious feelings can be questioned. In 1944, he replied to one of his colleagues who had complained of the attitude adopted by certain priests: "I don't give a damn! I'm a Gallican." [16]

In point of fact, de Gaulle knows that "the Church considers itself obliged to accept the established order," and that order is dictated by him within the framework of the state. France is

⚜

Catholic and he is France. As for his personal religion, it is a little like Chateaubriand, buried with his face to the wall: "Look at that mound," he said to one of his faithful who had been invited to Colombey. "When I die, I shall sleep there under a granite cross of Lorraine."

His whole intelligence is at the service of his single-mindedness.

WILL POWER

The General's stubborness has caused a good deal of ink to be spilled, particularly between Roosevelt and Churchill. It arises from a certain internal violence which he does not always manage to suppress. On the surface, this violence is expressed by certain biting remarks, and in private he often uses barrack-room language. When Madame de Gaulle one day insisted that he should restrain himself, at least in front of his grandchildren; he said: "They aren't such twerps, Yvonne, that they'd put such words into their school essays, nor am I that I'd use them in my speeches." [16]

The General's "enormous power of irreverence" has been mentioned. This is true, but not necessarily unkind. He said to J. B. Tournoux: "When I have hammered out a good literary formula, I can't resist bringing it out, even if it doesn't correspond exactly to every shade of my thought."

And yet he has known crises of rage and bitterness. The first Council of Ministers in January, 1963 saw the outbreak of a fine fury. George Ball, President Kennedy's special envoy, and Charles Bohlen, American ambassador in Paris, had just brought him the Kennedy–Macmillan proposals which had been worked out in the Bahamas.

"The American proposals," said de Gaulle, "are a lot of words.

⚜

They're talking of a 'screen' which, in the minds of the United States, will give them an opportunity of laying their hands on the atomic force of France, in order to prevent our country from owning its own means of independent dissuasion."

He repeated: "No, no and no!" during his press conference on January 14. But like Arthur M. Schlesinger, Kennedy's adviser, one can wonder if his public rages are not put on, calculated and exploited as a means of gaining authority. The answer will probably be in the affirmative.

De Gaulle is a marvelous actor who can assume a violent rage, but his first, secret and intimate reaction was violent, and he controled himself before preparing a public reply. This self-control requires the exercise of exceptional will power.

The General is a man of impulse. He makes his decisions quickly. On June 14, 1940, at 9:20, he was in Bordeaux at the Hotel Splendide and registered with rage that the atmosphere was full of defeat. "I saluted Marshal Pétain, who was dining in the same room, in silence. He shook my hand, without a word. I never saw him again, never."

He hurried off to Brest, stopping for a few minutes at Carantec where his wife and children had taken shelter. "It's all going very badly. I'm off to London. We may be able to carry on in Africa, but I'm afraid we're in for a total collapse. I'm warning you so that you can be ready to leave at a moment's notice." [28]

He reached England on board the destroyer *Miland*. On the 16th at dawn he was in London. He consulted with Churchill, and telephoned the proposals for a Franco–British union to Reynaud.[29] Then he flew back to Bordeaux, where he arrived at 9:30 at night. "Colonel Humbert, and Auburtin, from my office, were waiting for me at the airport. They told me that the *président du conseil* had resigned, and President Lebrun had asked Marshal Pétain to form a government. This meant certain surrender. My decision was taken immediately. I would leave the following morning." [30]

On the 17th, he left for London. In the afternoon, he called on Churchill, who offered to arrange for him to speak on the radio, as soon as Pétain asked for an armistice.

"The same evening, we learned that this had been done. Next day, at 6 o'clock, I read the appeal you all know. This was on June 18, 1940, 125 years to the day after the battle of Waterloo."

On the evening of the 17th, de Gaulle telegraphed to Bordeaux, offering to continue the negotiations begun the previous day. The answer was a telegram ordering his immediate return. But the General would not be deterred from the decision he had already taken on the evening of June 16. This was based on two assumptions: 1) Churchill would not surrender; 2) the economic arsenal of the United States was at the disposal of Great Britain. He does not seem to have evaluated the chances of Russia and the United States joining in until later. "I have seen treason with my own eyes, and in my heart refused to accept its victory," he said to Maurice Schumann.[31]

He did not know that Churchill, convinced by Spears, saw in him the advance guard of a Reynaud-Mandel government, and had sent Lord Lloyd, one of his ministers, to parley with Pétain on July 19. De Gaulle learned this only after his momentous broadcast on the 18th, after the crossing of the Rubicon and the beginning of his own rebellion.

During the following days, de Gaulle had his doubts. He invited Weygand, then Noguès, to head the overseas Resistance. In vain. On June 23, Weygand, minister of defense in the Pétain government, canceled de Gaulle's nomination as acting general, and put him on the retired list. De Gaulle was unmoved and continued his calls to rebellion. His speech on the 23d took on an aggressive tone against Marshal Pétain, whom he had last seen in Bordeaux nine days earlier.

Churchill still clung to the hope of seeing Mandel and a few

❧

former French ministers constitute a valid French government and only came down on de Gaulle's side on August 7, 1940.[32]

To resume: de Gaulle's decision was purely emotional. His assumptions—Churchill's will to resist (and he could die at any moment) and the economic support of America (in no way guaranteed) were more than precarious. The elements of objective appreciation, information, the probability of American and Soviet intervention on the side of the British were nonexistent. Therefore, only subjective elements could be considered: foresight, flair, historical understanding and, above all, de Gaulle's character, whose impulsiveness verges on genius or disaster.

He thrives on opposition and believes, whether good or bad, a decision to take sides is better in any circumstances than compromise. Other hypotheses can be put forward:

1. De Gaulle knew that he could no longer serve in Pétain's cabinet. His political career was compromised owing to his personal relations with the marshal. London was his only hope.

2. De Gaulle was watchful of an opportunity to seize power. His expectation of a place in the Reynaud cabinet had finally ended in disappointment. He seized the opportunity offered in London. This explains the presence at his side of several officers of the extreme right.[33] This operation is the pendant to the marshal's seizure of power at Vichy.[34]

We do not hold with either of these theories. The decision was exclusively military; de Gaulle was neither interested, nor a plotter; he has said so himself, and everything leads us to believe him. He makes basic decisions alone, under the pressure of his own impulsiveness.

One further example: on August 24, 1962, two days after the abortive attack at Petit Clamart, he summoned Georges Pompidou to Colombey: "I intend," he said, "to modify the Constitution immediately, and make the election of the president of the republic subject to universal suffrage, by referendum. A vote of censure will certainly be tabled in the Assembly. If you are defeated, do you agree to immediate dissolution and a new general election?" [35]

Pompidou was surprised. His eyebrows arched as he confronted the giant kangaroo laying down the law so loftily.

The idea was not new. De Gaulle had put it into words as long ago as April 11, 1961: "Our Constitution is both parliamentary and presidential. . . . I consider it right that men who are concerned with the public good and national continuity should give some thought to what may happen when I am no longer here. . . . It is possible that (the president of the republic) may be chosen by universal suffrage. The idea can certainly be considered. . . ." [32]

The "constitutional successor" to the head of state, Monsieur Monnerville, president of the senate, was against this new development. Nevertheless, on December 30, 1961, de Gaulle said: "I'm still thinking about it. . . . I am thinking particularly of my successor." [36]

On May 15, 1962, he added: "This isn't the moment." [36]

From May 17 to 20, during a tour in the provinces of the center, he recalls the necessity, "of assuring the continuity of government." [36]

In July, he received Paul Reynaud, former president of the Constitutional Council, who advised him against the proposed reform. On the 17th, Reynaud declared: "There has been much talk lately of revising the Constitution which, in fact, needs it badly. Some people have accused the head of state of planning to revise it without taking a preliminary vote in both chambers and having recourse to a referendum. This violation will not take place." [36]

By August 24, the General had made his decision. We can put forward three theories:

❧

1. He made his decision as early as April, 1961, and waited for conditions to be ripe before imposing it.

2. He sounded out parliament and public opinion, was rebuffed by parliament and noted the absence of any reaction from the people. His decision was taken after the attack at Petit Clamart.

3. He was encouraged by his judicial advisers: the Constitution was ambiguous (parliamentarian and presidential), though he had not yet come to a decision. The obstacles raised by MM. Monnerville and Reynaud forced him to act. He took advantage of the opportunity presented by the Petit Clamart attack.

The choice lies between these three interpretations of the General's thinking. We choose the third, which seems more suited to his temperament.

Thought is a slow, decision sudden and impulsive, action immediate.

On September 12, at the Council of Ministers, he moved a few pawns. Christian Fouchet was recalled from Algeria and appointed *ministre-délégué* to the prime minister, in charge of information. Certain ministers demurred. There was a pause.

"Do I hear someone raise an objection?"

No one said a word.

"Very well. The prime minister agrees with me; the affair is settled. The Council is unanimously in agreement." [16]

De Gaulle announced his "intention to suggest to the country by means of a referendum that the president of the republic will henceforth be elected by universal suffrage."

He also declared that he would announce this decision to the country on September 20 and that the ministers could give him their opinions on the 19th. He listened to each in turn, then concluded: "I note, gentlemen, that you are all in agreement." [37]

On the 20th, the official announcement. On October 5, a

violent debate took place in the Assembly. A vote of censure was passed by 280 votes out of 480.

On the 6th, Monsieur Pompidou placed his resignation in the hands of the president of the republic. Then, in accordance with the Constitution, de Gaulle saw Monsieur Monnerville. The scene is described by André Passeron:

> The president of the republic was particularly shocked and angered by the aggressive remarks made by the president of the senate at a recent congress of the Radical party. . . . Although their interview did not give rise to any outbreak, it was unusually brief and icily cold. When Monsieur Monnerville was announced, the General was standing behind his desk, unmoving, impassive. Waving his visitor to a chair, he said:
>
> *"Monsieur le Président,* the Constitution forces me to consult you regarding the dissolution of the National Assembly."
>
> *"Monsieur le Président,"* replies Monsieur Monnerville, "I am in agreement with the dissolution following on the vote taken on the motion of censure. The dissolution will clarify the general situation. On the other hand, the present government does not seem qualified to vote the next budget, unless you will nominate a new prime minister. But I think it would be simpler if a new Assembly could vote the 1963 budget."
>
> "Thank you, *Monsieur le Président,"* replies de Gaulle. He rises, walks round his desk and goes as far as the door with the president of the senate. As they go, Monsieur Monnerville repeats:
>
> *"Monsieur le Président,* allow me to insist on the necessity of having the budget of France voted by a new Assembly."

❦

Both men bow stiffly, and the General, speaking to the *aide de camp* holding the door open, said:

"See *Monsieur le Président* to his car."

The National Assembly was dissolved. On October 28, a referendum was submitted to the French people asking them to vote for the election of the president of the republic. De Gaulle received 61.75 percent of the votes.

This process of constitutional revision shows a fine courage, clear will power, impulsiveness controled and placed at the service of the objective, pursued with single-minded devotion.

As for the General's emotions, we remain perplexed.

Churchill, who knew him well, and saw him through many grave crises, said:

"Under an impassive, imperturbable demeanor he seemed to me to have a remarkable capacity for feeling pain." [38]

This is only an impression. In reality, there is an undercurrent of hardness in de Gaulle. He protects his family, his few friends and collaborators on condition that they serve the cause he has chosen. His invalid daughter, Anne, who died at twenty, was the center of all his attention. He was totally indulgent toward her, and in spite of all his cares, always found time to play with the poor little mongoloid. When she died, he went to the cemetery of Colombey with his wife, then said:

"Let's go home. Now she is like all the others." [16]

His London companions remember the Dakar defeat and the General's despair.

"I went through a terrible time. I even thought of blowing my brains out." [15]

And Passy, who tells this story, says that he saw de Gaulle weep.

The General also tells how during his exhausting struggle to win recognition for France as an ally, the news of the success at Bir Hakim shattered him:

"I thanked the messenger, sent him away, closed the door. I was alone. Oh, what heartbeats of emotion, sobs of pride, tears of joy!"

Later, April 23, 1961, at the time of the generals' coup, everyone in France will remember General de Gaulle's pathetic appeal:

"Women of France, men of France, help me!" [39]

He was overcome, more isolated than ever, but his reaction was that of an actor. The coup had been under way for forty-two hours, and the General was obviously fully informed of its development. He wanted to "strike a firm blow and be sure of success." [40] But his emotion was such that it was communicated to all his viewers.

During moments of crisis, he bends, then reacts violently to the obstacle. But real internal dramas are expressed in melancholy and meditation. After his resignation in 1946, he waited to be recalled. Nothing happened.

He went off to Antibes to meditate for a few days. He prefers the sea, like the majority of the French, while Madame de Gaulle prefers the country. He is drawn to the ocean and wide horizons, while his wife likes to be in the shelter of the forest. Soft hat, formal black overcoat, the tall, solitary man paced up and down the coast, chain smoking.

"Meditating beside the sea, I drew up the way in which I was going to retire, leaving the helm in silence, without blaming anyone, publicly or privately, without accepting any kind of appointment, award, or pension."

His exile lasted for a dozen years. The man of the sea submitted to retirement to his estate at Colombey, among the forests dear to his wife. He lived mostly in the tower he had had added to the building, which dominated the wide countryside and was framed by the age-old forests of France. He left it only during the long struggle for the return to power. In the intervals of writing the thousand pages of his *Mémoires*, he went for long walks in his little park.

"I must have been round it fifteen thousand times," he says. "When I walk in any of the neighboring forests . . . their somber depths drown me in nostalgia."

In all this there is a touch of sado-masochism: the persecutor persecuting himself. Above all, de Gaulle gave up smoking. Before the war, he smoked immoderately: forty cigarettes a day to kill time. He gave it up around 1938:

"I will start again only if there is a war." [16]

In 1939 he resumed his passion: two packets a day, this time English cigarettes. In 1946, on his return to Colombey, he informed his family and friends:

"I don't smoke any more." [16]

He takes cachous (breath sweeteners) instead, and the General's guests remember being greeted by a great booming voice:

"Cachous? You know I've given up smoking." [16]

Deprived of his dose of nicotine, he becomes soured, then counteracts his acidity by eating sweets, which make him put on weight.

He put his surplus energy into his writing, his permanent need for activity increased by this enforced idleness. E. Jouve had counted 1,543 writings and declarations by Charles de Gaulle between 1906 and July, 1965. Among them, seven books, seventeen studies, seven prefaces and innumerable speeches, a total of more than eight thousand pages, of which six thousand were written between 1940 and 1965, that is to say, more than the equivalent of a book a year spread over a quarter of a century. Besides all his occupations, de Gaulle exercises the profession of a man of letters. He says he writes "slowly and with difficulty," which was true for the *Mémoires*, a book of deep thought and action, a perpetual search for synthesis and the *mot juste*. But the rough notes of the speeches show that he writes quickly and with an initial spurt which is seldom restrained.

This abundant and tiresome literature is a need, a substitute for talk, and a discipline imposed on his emotions. He wants to remain in control of himself and not be drawn into a conversation which could reduce the strength of his dedicated action and the force of his ceaseless activity. Like Michelangelo, the works—we are speaking of the written and not the spoken works—translate an irreversible excess of mind over action.[41] There emerges from the reading of this Song of Roland, written by Roland himself, an expressible sadness with which the author fills the reader more and more with every page. It is the struggle to reach an unattainable goal, or the end of a tunnel which perhaps has no exit.

Charles de Gaulle's behavior toward his close collaborators is very instructive. Even the most faithful are periodically changed. Courcel, Debré, Guichard, Guy, Burin des Roziers, Palewski, and many others come and go sometimes, not always. Some, hurt by the master's cold-bloodedness, say how much they have been attracted, fascinated, hypnotized; and then one day, have recoiled, floored, revolted by the bad temper, the bitterness or cynicism of their prince. No one will ever know if he is defying his own emotions or if he has the heart of stone which his detractors say he has.

His vindictiveness is immense, extravagant. Toward Pétain, toward Roosevelt, toward each and every one. When Paul Reynaud, the first of his supporters, the faithful partisan of 1958, decided to oppose his election as president of the republic by universal suffrage, his die was cast.

During the following elections, de Gaulle created difficulties for him in his constituency; a pawn placed in the way of the faithless. In front of his ministers, the General became pitiful, falsely wheedling:

❧

"An old man who has missed all the great moments of his life, what a pity if he has to lose his last election." [16]

This self-control, this restrained aggression, this will power which sometimes stifles intelligence, can only be understood in a real systematic spirit.

The de Gaulle system is France personified in de Gaulle, directed by a Louis XIV-type state and exercising a world policy. Men like leaders who stretch them beyond their limits, and this explains why the French have chosen de Gaulle.

He believes in his star, and always has done so, ever since his childhood.

A PSYCHOLOGICAL PROFILE

To synthesize the personality of de Gaulle we have called in handwriting experts and psychiatrists. Our examination is based on four samples of de Gaulle's handwriting at different ages: a letter to Colonel Nachin, dated June 20, 1929,[42] the inscription in a book given to Marshal Pétain, dated 1933;[43] the appeal of June 18, 1940 and a note to General Leclerc on August 23, 1944.[44] There is a great consistency in the style. First characteristic: speed and dynamism. It is clear he writes a good deal, often and quickly. He writes straight off, except for the appeal of June 18, which needed multiple corrections. When Malraux returned the text of his *Mémoires* and pointed out that the struggles with his conscience on that historic day were not included, de Gaulle replied:

"Malraux, it was terrible! . . ."

From 1929 to 1944 the writing is more and more centrifugal: the writer is less and less concerned with being brilliant; he is sure of addressing a wide audience. He becomes less aggressive from 1944 onward.

The texts of the diplomatic notes or the speeches corrected by hand, after World War II, are softened or made more conciliatory, particularly after 1958.[45] Yet the speed of the writing does not diminish.

Second marked characteristic: the slope to the right. The writing is stretched toward the end, drawn out, very thin and extraordinarily linked. No fantasies, no room for the emotions. All the texts have an exact aim, no room for feeling, everything logical, everything cerebral.

Third marked characteristic: the sameness of the writing. The signature does not alter. Yet the desire to please at first sight in 1929 is simplified in 1933 and has almost disappeared in 1944.

Let us study these facts more in detail and place them according to the graphologists. The reflexes are intellectualized, the impulses very violent, the rhythm driving, and the reaction extremely rapid. Restraint is slight, and often missing altogether. The attitude is rigid, tight and cold in appearance, but with the years, the tension diminishes.

Sensibility is almost entirely cerebral. He forms subtle though sometimes elementary impressions, though these can remain for a long time. The temperament very optimistic, and shyness very slight. Vitality is powerful and permits a strong resistance to emotion: apparently under tension, this resistance is weak, and he finds it difficult to control himself, for his self-control is restricted: the writer is vulnerable.

The instincts are sharp: the tastes eclectic and imitative, settled, more or less in the hierarchy. Possessive instincts are strong and interior, excessively imperious and individualistic, but mastered by habit. Combativity is very marked and the need for expansion very great. Caution is very weak. Preservation instinct is excessive and the defensive apparently very firm: nevertheless the avoidance of danger is bad, and the writer is not assured of his rear guard.

꧁

The intelligence can be applied equally well to the concrete and to the abstract. Synthesis is immediate, proceeding by analogous memorization. Judgment is extremely rapid and sharp, intuition very great and understanding markedly developed. Reflexes are weak, but the imagination powerful. The writer is not creative and shows little ingenuity.

Will power is exercised to a systematic program. Decision is extremely prompt, action dynamic and well oriented. Patience is virtually nonexistent in appearance and in depth. Energy very strong, but the writer makes less effort than he appears to make. He has little discipline, very little self-confidence, and recovers slowly and painfully.

His morale is traditional as is his education. The writer is more or less careful to observe the proprieties. His ideal remains very close to the actual, whatever it may seem. Yet he is very much a moralizer, a mystic with a basis of universal humanism. His circumspection is only a façade, but not calculated. Pride is extremely developed. Courage apparently very great; the writer is stoical, but uneasy. On the whole he is fairly unreflecting.

These are the graphologists' conclusions, knowing neither the writing nor the writer. Starting from these given facts, and other more technical approaches, the psychoanalysts think that the subject is equipped with the qualities necessary for the practice of the following professions, chosen from among eighty-five: actor, preacher, professor, engineer, critic.

The faults which restrict the range of professions open to the subject are above all lack of adaptibility, lack of discipline, and insufficient reaction. It will be noted that the military profession is not included in the list of suggestions.

By way of comparison, it seems that de Gaulle's writing has not the meticulousness of Colbert's, the reformer in love with detail, nor the exuberance of Balzac's, the classicism of Racine's, the majesty of Louis XIV's, the discipline and affectation of

Foch's, the fire and breath of Napoleon's, but is nearer that of Richelieu for its vitality and impatience.

In fact, it would seem that the psychological profile of General de Gaulle emphasizes two essential features which mark his personality: his extraordinary vitality and his passion for action.

His fellow students in Paris, at Antoing, at Saint-Cyr, and the Ecole de Guerre, saw him like that. In spite of examination results which were not always satisfactory, his teachers noted this in the same degree:

> SCIENCES—a good pupil, very intelligent, works hard and very conscientiously.
>
> HISTORY—a very good pupil.
>
> PHILOSOPHY—top of his class.
>
> NATURAL HISTORY—very good pupil, has worked very conscientiously.
>
> MODERN LANGUAGES—has made a serious effort and good progress, distinction.
>
> SPOKEN FRENCH—first prize.

Four years later he graduated from Saint-Cyr 13th out of 211, showed himself from the start as an officer of real value who raised the brightest hopes for his future. Signed: Pétain, 1913.

Very intelligent, loves his profession devotedly. Led his section on maneuvers impeccably. Deserves the highest praise. Signed: Pétain, 1913.

An officer of remarkable courage, very plucky and very brave. . . . Very sound judgment and highly developed tactical sense. A complete officer. Signed: Mercier, 1920.

An officer of high quality, who knows his own worth. Solid and extended understanding, a great aptitude for assimilating a question and presenting it brilliantly. Very much listened to and much appreciated as a lecturer by his pupils, over whom he has a great influence. Preparing for the Ecole de Guerre, will cer-

❧

tainly be admitted and will be successful. Signed: Gombeaud, 1921.[46]

But when he leaves the Ecole de Guerre Supérieure: "Intelligent officer, cultivated and serious, some brilliance and much facility, very gifted: great qualities. Unfortunately spoils undoubted qualities by his excessive assurance, his intolerance of the opinion of others, and his attitude of a king in exile. Seems to have more aptitude for general studies and the synthesis of a problem than for the deep examination and practicalities of its execution." Signed: Moyrand, 1924.

The vitality bursts out all the time: as a child, when he was brought up the hard way; as a prisoner at Ingolstadt; at Trèves, when he organized forced marches; at Paris, as the glutton for work at headquarters; in 1940, at the head of the Fourth Armored Division; after 1958, in his continual journeys, a septuagenarian defying fatigue.

The dedication is imperious: it involves France. De Gaulle feels the need to express his personality in long-term actions.

"He thinks of nothing but his place in history," says Jacques Soustelle.

His actions are placed in a wide perspective: he has been called a man of the day before yesterday and the day after tomorrow. The General does not hide his intentions. To his colleagues who are worried at seeing him mixing imprudently with the crowd and running unnecessary risks, he replies: "De Gaulle interests me only as a historical personality."

And to a historian: "Nothing can be done without great men. And you become a great man only by wanting to be one."

This passion is such that it nearly always stifles the emotions: during the war, surrounded by the mob, and even during attempts on his life. It means that the General neglects subtleties and considers as secondary everything which is not in line with the objects of his aim. He divides business into *"domaine reservé"* and *"intendance"* and uses the others as levers or means of action at the service of his objective in a perpetual acceleration. This is what can be called "the Gaullist system," a means of government and not a political doctrine.

When the tension is relaxed, in times of fatigue or of retreat, such as during the period in the "wilderness" (1946–1958), melancholy appears. The wounded man retires into a haughty solitude and justifies his battles and his defeats. As soon as the struggle is resumed, his dedication controls him, master of the system he has created, and of which he considers himself the center.

Yet it seems that the lack of emotion which prevents de Gaulle from appreciating the aspirations of the common people whom he would like to assemble around him, and leads him to be the slave of an abnormally developed passion, must contribute to his defeat on the personal as well as on the political level. When he goes he promises to leave a great gap.

A PSYCHOANALYTICAL APPROACH

Few men have had the luck to have had, like de Gaulle, an excellent father admired for his qualities as much as for his faults. This "reluctant monarchist," as he described himself, showed himself unshakable on matters of principle and firm in his methods of education. The five de Gaulle children—four sons and a daughter—were brought up strictly, and in order to remain faithful to his convictions, their father had to renounce many amenities. No electricity, no central heating, no extra holidays. In the evening, after dinner, they amused themselves with Latin exercises. On Sundays, visits to the chateau and park of Versailles, on Thursday afternoons, visits to Napoleon's tomb.

⚜

Henri de Gaulle gave lyrical descriptions of his share in the 1870 war, his wound on the battlefield of Stains, and recalled the principles which guided his life: no compromise of any kind. Sometimes he described his future as he saw it, with a touch of bitterness: his unfulfilled vocation, the officer's career which he had to renounce.

The most intelligent son of the family certainly felt his father's frustration more acutely than his brothers. He determined to be an officer. After preliminary successes, he would have the career his father had dreamed of, and then outstripping his father's ambition, he would look for a model to whom he could transfer his need for imitation and competition. This model would be Pétain, colonel commanding the Thirty-third Regiment of Infantry at Arras. There was a gap of thirty-four years between Pétain and de Gaulle. The young officer could have been his colonel's son. The former's career had made very slow progress: he was only a colonel at fifty-six, thanks to his spirit of independence. But de Gaulle knew how to appreciate his leader's qualities as a teacher, the qualities of his own father. In 1914, the war separated the two men for a time, but de Gaulle was not surprised at seeing Pétain become the great war leader at Verdun:

> The day the choice lay between ruin and reason, Pétain found himself promoted. Brilliant at seizing the essential and the practical in everything, he dominated his task by his mind. In addition, he gave it his own imprint. Between this clear mind and the vital actions which henceforth are required by the struggle and the adversaries, the harmony is so complete that it seems to be a decree of nature. Besides, confidence can be given to a master who is known to have disdained the fortune of underlings. A powerful critical faculty safeguards him from banal favors. A great independence which accepts order, listens to advice, but

refuses to be influenced. Glamor of the reticent, enhanced by a deliberate coldness, irony ever watchful, and a pride which surrounds this solitude.[47]

Pétain's theory triumphed: the wearing down of the adversary by weight of artillery. After the war, de Gaulle became a close friend of Marshal Pétain in his apartment in the Square de la Tour Maubourg. On December 28, 1921, he named his son Philippe in honor of the marshal he admired. Pétain supported Captain de Gaulle, who was in difficulties at the Ecole de Guerre Supérieure (1927) for his noncomformist views.

In his lectures at the Ecole de Guerre, lectures organized by Pétain, he sang the praises of true discipline, but some of his statements can be said to have been a little disturbing. Those who have accomplished great things must often go beyond the appearances of a false discipline: like Pélissier at Sevastopol, pocketing the emperor's threatening telegrams and reading them only when the battle was over. Like Lanrezac, saving his army after Charleroi by breaking off the battle in spite of express orders. Like Lyautey, preserving the whole of Morocco in 1941 in spite of orders from his superiors. After the battle of Jutland and the opportunity missed by the English of destroying the German fleet, First Lord of the Admiralty Fisher, on receiving Admiral Jellicoe's report, cried bitterly: "He has all the Nelson qualities except one: he doesn't know how to disobey."

De Gaulle, preoccupied by these questions, repeated his lectures at the Sorbonne at the end of 1927.[48] Then, while serving in the garrison at Trèves, and at Beirut (1929), he polished the text, completed it, and brought it out in a book *Le Fil de l'epée*, published by Berger-Levrault, his fellow prisoner and friend at Ingolstadt. This work is dedicated to Marshal Pétain, and the publication date is 1932.

It was a crucial year in de Gaulle's life. He was forty-two, his father had died at eighty-three, the national government elected in 1928 was defeated in the spring elections and replaced by a union of the left. Above all, he quarreled with Pétain, the idol to whom he had transfered a good share of his filial devotion.

From 1932 onward, de Gaulle became withdrawn and decided to make his way alone. In order to succeed, he meant to excel the marshal and did not hesitate to oppose him on all points. Small incidents took place, then a serious misunderstanding over a book which de Gaulle had written following Pétain's directives, and which he finally published under his own name in 1938.[49]

De Gaulle now loved nothing but France, France alone, and had no other responsibilities. Not having succeeded within the army framework, he scrambled, with the help of Paul Reynaud, onto the stool of undersecretary of state in the ministry for war from June 5 to 7, 1940, but when the marshal took power on June 17, he left for London, where he fulminated against anti-France.

The rest of the adventure is well known: the struggle for the recognition of Free France, the victory and the premature retirement, then after the days in the "wilderness," the return to power. De Gaulle has fought his battle tirelessly with a fine aggressiveness that has never softened, except perhaps during the days in the "wilderness," when he experienced a severe attack of melancholia. Opposition increases the passion of the captain who commanded during the storm, but when the elements are calm, after the end of the war in Algeria, he can think again of his destiny.

In volume 3 of his *Mémoires*, speaking of his meeting with Stalin (December 10, 1944), the General writes:

> Stalin showed himself a good player. In a soft voice he complimented me: "You stood firm. Congratulations. I like dealing with a man who knows what he wants, even if he doesn't share my opinions." He spoke of everything

in a detached manner, as if he surveyed other people, the war, history, and even himself, from the summit of a peak of serenity. "After all," he said, "death is the only winner."

These remarks impressed the General, since he remembered them more than ten years later. It was the first time any disturbance appeared on this one-track mind. After coming to power in 1944, a power so long hoped for and perhaps not very expected, he had outstripped his masters, his natural and his adoptive fathers. In winter, 1944, the desire to excel disappeared, the fear of failure showed again amid the success. The greater the hopes, the greater the fall.

From that time onward, the General withdraws into himself and is isolated with his destiny. He did not reply to Roosevelt's invitation, sent from Algiers (February 13, 1945). Certainly, de Gaulle's reasons were valid. Roosevelt had no right to issue invitations from French territory, particularly after having opposed the presence of France at Yalta. The president of the United States openly expressed his dislike of de Gaulle and the caprices of the so-called "prima donna." But might it not be that at this period the General was examining himself and no longer believed so implicitly in his star?

In his *Mémoires,* de Gaulle described these weeks of anxiety. The purge was at its height:

> 2,071 condemnations to death were pronounced by the courts, apart from those *in absentia.* Afterward the dossiers were submitted to me; after their examination and on the advice of the commission for pardon at the Ministry of Justice . . . I studied them all carefully, with the assistance of councilor Parin, director of criminal affairs and pardons at the Chancellery, and received the lawyers every

time they asked for an interview. Nothing in the world
seemed to me sadder than this array of murders, tortures,
betrayals, calls to treason which passed before my eyes.
In conscience I declare that apart from about a hundred
cases, all the condemned deserved to be executed. Nonetheless, I pardoned 1,303 of them, commuting in particular
the death penalty for all the women, almost all minors, and
among the men, the greater number of those who had
acted after receiving a direct order and had risked their
lives. I had to reject 768 appeals, whenever the condemned
by personal or spontaneous action had caused the death
of other Frenchmen or directly served the enemy.[50]

It is easy to imagine what those hundreds of audiences must
have been like, granted to lawyers who were once more pleading
in defense of their clients. It meant several dossiers a day for
several months. Even if he was advised and helped, he alone had
to make decisions which were often appallingly difficult. The
whole force of this justice hinged on a decision made from the
outset: no compromise. Everyone waited for the new Solomon
to pronounce what was right and what was justice. This daily
confrontation with death would drive any man to reflection and
to doubt. After a year of harassing arguments with members of
parliament, enlivened by victory celebrations and quarrels with
the Allies, de Gaulle resigned on January 19, 1946. Retiring to
his estate, he recovered the fighting spirit which sustained him
until the defeat of the R.P.F. "How many hours slipped by," he
said, "where reading, writing or dreaming, no illusion could
soften my bitter serenity. . . . An old man, apprentice to trials,
divorced from all action, feeling the approach of the eternal
cold, but never tired of watching through the darkness for a
glimmer of hope."
A bitter struggle still awaited him: the decolonization, begun

during the war, in an atmosphere which many times included mob violence and attempted murder. But victory was once more won over the opposition. He returned to bitterness, uncertainty, doubt, and unconscious fear of defeat. He spoke to his colleagues of his disappointment with party politics:

> There are no more parties, only committed opinions. The Communists are tired civil servants, long past the retiring age: the Socialists have been dead since Jaurès; the Radicals don't exist; the M.R.P. has denied everything; the Independents aren't independent any more; as for the U.N.R., it's the R.P.F. without de Gaulle! . . . All that's left is the army, and of course, de Gaulle, to stop everyone making bloody fools of themselves.[16]

After the difficult elections of 1962: "Four years in power and you're thrown on the scrap heap." And after a long series of disappointments in internal politics: "De Gaulle was made to rule Russia or the United States." [16]

The General felt confusedly that such a series of successes could only be followed by a violent reversal. Caesar's end was tragic, Bismarck's not less so. The one who has prophesied and cursed knows when his star begins to decline from its zenith.

FINE ARTS

If there is one area where de Gaulle can face problems without prejudice, it is in fine arts. His preferences are, of course, literary. The few souls who have been admitted sufficiently far into his friendship to glance at his library have noted that the complete bound works of Maurice Barrès occupy the place of honor on his shelves.

❧

Barrès is a writer of his youth; he was twenty-eight when the General was born, fifty-two in 1914. He is an author who uses the French language with great authority, preoccupied with his own self, but trying to situate it between mystic heights where men seek a Supreme Being, present but undiscoverable, and political depths where small men quarrel in painful debate.

It is easy to recognize this spiritual elevation in de Gaulle and this scorn for parliamentary quagmires, as well as the writers profession, the classic taste, the sudden flashes amid the strict layout of phrases, a fertile imagination applied to reality.

Barrès was a harmonious writer, exercising his profession with care and a touch of preciosity. He was violently patriotic and became an ardent nationalist. Chief editor of the newspaper *Le Drapeau*, he became the spokesman and also the guide of the most enthusiastic nationalists, the bard of a militant Catholicism which he led without actually joining its ranks. That Barrès should be the General's literary master is certainly significant.

On the General's table at Colombey is a medallion of Charles Péguy. This other instinctive Catholic, who avoided the inconveniences of the mass and confession, was also a heroic patriot. The man of the Paris–Chartres pilgrimage, whose life ended on the battlefield in the summer of 1914, had no features in common with his admirer, but in London, the General gleaned various *idées fixes* from his writings, in language at times confused and a thinking that was often recondite.

In August, 1914, de Gaulle carried in his knapsack several copies of the *Cahiers de la quinzaine* of Péguy. Did he reread them in Carlton Gardens, these "thoughts" which were written before World War I and republished so often between 1934 and 1940?

"Surrender is essentially an operation by which one begins to explain, instead of act."

"The area of land where French is spoken is determined by the French soldier and the French 75."

"In time of war, there is only one policy: that of the convention."

"Right doesn't make peace, it makes war. As soon as a point of right appears in the world, there is a starting point for war."

And later, did he remember these sayings of Péguy?

"The war against demagogy is the hardest of all wars."

"The cowardice of the crowd, particularly parliamentary crowds, is incalculable."

"The real and permanent majority is the heavy, cowardly mass of the ignorant populace."

These preferences: Barrès and Péguy, are those of his maturity. In his youth, de Gaulle most admired Edmond Rostand, a fashionable author whom he had imitated in 1904 by writing a short comic scene in verse (*la Mauvaise rencontre*). The General still remembers long passages and complete speeches from *Cyrano de Bergerac* which he had learned by heart.

But of Rostand, in the written and spoken works of de Gaulle, nothing remains, neither the panache nor the rhythm. Should we look in his prewar books or his BBC speeches for traces of false lyricism, or in his postwar political utterances for blusterings of hollow grandeur? Can we find in the morphology of the General or in the behavior of the duelist of Warsaw echoes of that Cyrano with whom he identified himself in his youth? In the heroes of Rostand there is a superficiality, a brilliant veneer which bears no relation to the literary personality or the character of the General. In addition, many of Rostand's texts are slapdash affairs, whereas the books signed by de Gaulle are chewed over, licked and sucked dry of all sap.

In the General's works, the authors most quoted are moralists or stylists. Among the moralists: Chamfort, a bitter, violent satirist, who defended the monarchy under the Revolution in cutting phrases, pitiless toward fools and the niggardly; la Roche-foucauld, a disappointed ambition who used a harsh language to coin maxims.

Should we note that these two masters of thought are anxious sensitives made aggressive by the fear of failure? Does the General use them in his search for a mirror?

Among the stylists: Musset, Flaubert, Valéry and Samain, all classic authors. Musset, an uncompromising spirit lost in romanticism; Flaubert, the undisputed master of style whose sustained effort repels at first sight but who holds the attention by the perfection of his art; Valéry, an introspective virtuoso of the language but haughtily chilling. Let us pause for a moment with Albert Samain, a poet from Lille who lived in Paris, where he died in 1900. This anxious bachelor had a delicate soul, a passion for meditation, a proud timidity. He lived within himself, sighing after inaccessible paradises, unable to hide the failures he feared, while at the same time inviting them. His works abound in references to death, and the General's writings often show this violent cerebral tension toward an ideal he fears and desires, perhaps hoping never to attain, for the struggle would lose its meaning.

We do not know if the General reads these authors at the Elysée or if he keeps them for his periods of meditation at "La Boisserie," but we do know he continues to read a great deal.

In Paris, the General must find it hard to think "in the narrow setting of a house closed on the outside world," whereas at Colombey he can say: "I think as I walk, my memory records it; when I get back to my desk, I have already completed half the work." [16]

What does he read at the Elysée? Almost everything, particularly any book he is sent. Novels, such as *les Pianos mécaniques* of Henri-François Rey, or *La dolce vita espagnole*, which Madame de Gaulle wanted to borrow. He told her: "It's not for you: if you want a modern novel, read Cesbron." Adventure stories such as *Le Secret du jour-J* by the excellent writer Gilles Perrault: "I prefer *Fantomas*; it's more real!" And particularly history books, which he skims rather than reads.

Among contemporary writers, the General prefers Malraux. André Malraux supported the communist revolution movement in the Far East, and the International Brigade in Spain. He went to Berlin in 1934 with André Gide to ask the Nazi court to acquit the secretary-general of the Komintern, George Dimitrov, accused of having set fire to the Reichstag. Taken prisoner in 1940 with the armored group he commanded, Malraux escaped to join the Resistance under the pseudonym of "Colonel Berger." He lived with the *Maquis* and commanded the Alsace-Lorraine detachment, which he led as far as Strasbourg. De Gaulle met him in Paris for the first time after an inspection of the First French Army. The General was very struck:

"At last, I have seen a man," he said at the time.

As soon as World War II was over, de Gaulle asked Malraux to join his government, where Malraux was put in charge of culture. The novelist summed up for a Swiss monthly *Labyrinthe* (April, 1945) his views on European culture and its future:

> There is no such thing as Europe. There never has been. There was Christianity. There was a vaguely European culture, turn by turn Franco-English and Anglo-French, during the seventeenth and eighteenth centuries, vast territories which could be defined by their own life.
>
> What we mean today by Europe can only be defined in the negative: Europe is not Asia (because if you mean that it isn't America, this is much more subtle). It is a fairly childish idea, born of a whole assembly of bits and pieces, mingling the continent printed in pink on the maps of our childhood with the portrait of William II on top of the Yellow Peril . . . a "German dada." Europe as an

⚜

organic unity has often been a "German dada": in the portrait of the emperor, Germany is given her proper place, for it was Marshal von Waldersee who commanded the European army which fought in China, and if there is no powerful European reality which demands to be given its form, there is at least in the cultural scheme a readiness among the countries of Europe to absorb the culture of one of them.

The Europe the followers of Hitler dreamed of in the cultural order was much less a federation or a pseudo-family group than a confused world in which Nazi thinking filled the place French thinking in the eighteenth century had occupied on the continent. But French thinking of the previous centuries and English thinking, or even that of Goethe, are universal and therefore assimilable. Hitlerian thinking is the opposite. It is hierarchic, culminating in German values and is at the same time subject to them, as a conquered Europe would have been subject to Germany.

We are reminded of the somewhat cautious predictions of Oswald Spengler after World War I, announcing the "decline of the West" and the birth of an Aryan civilization which would submerge Western civilization with the same ease with which the Hunnish hordes had swamped "the City of the Caesars."

"The Napoleonic adventure," says Malraux, "obviously hastened the rise of English power in Western Europe, and everything is happening as if the Hitlerian adventure was the most sinister and efficient method of hastening the rise of American power (and Russian power as well)."

The author of *le Temps du mépris* is impressed by the fact that the sea has always been at the origin of civilizations: "Mediterranean culture in Roman and even Byzantine times, far more than a European culture." The art of the Pacific is mentioned. This is an exaggeration, says Malraux, but it is not entirely false. For him, the Atlantic will be behind the next civilization.

"I will not mention the other side of the question, the question of the East. It is clear that the Slav world in its entirety, and Rumania, will become part of a Russian world. But I believe that the metamorphosis of France will be turned in the direction of the Atlantic, even in a France where communism plays an important part." And he quotes the subtle affinities which exist between the eastern states of America, England, France, Portugal, Belgium, Holland, Switzerland, and Scandinavia. He concludes: "Politics plays a great part in culture, but in unpredictable and somewhat irrational ways. I mean that France is afraid of American influence. . . . Influence has a double meaning (Greece on Rome, Persia on the Arabs), and above all, a new culture is not the sum of its predecessors, it is their metamorphosis."

Like the General, the author of *la Condition humaine* believes in decisive political action and thinks that this can stem only from a hero, an individual hero at the head of a collective adventure.[51] Malraux's admiration for Lawrence of Arabia is well known and he, the man who never laughs, enjoys telling the following story: at the end of World War II, Hitler disappears from Berlin, reappears at Potsdam before a Supreme Tribunal consisting of Churchill, Stalin, and Truman. In his defense, he explains that his actions have profited all three by considerably increasing the powers of their respective countries. The Big Three are almost convinced, when Hitler quickly tears off his forelock and mustache to show his real face, salutes and says: "Colonel Lawrence, gentlemen." Then he rushes out so quickly that no one has time to hold him back.

Asocial, a woman-hater, Malraux remains lucid without weak-ening, a volunteer, always committed. He tries to work out the governing lines of the future. In private, he stands back to survey the present, the better to place it in its proper perspective.

It is possible to like or not like the style of the American Army, but it is clearly that of the twentieth century. An army without substance and without standards, an army of mechanics—though victorious—where soldiers and officers could say: "We aren't soldiers, we're mobilized civilians": it isn't only because it provided them with uniforms that the Allied forces resembled them. They did not dress the English. But English battledress and the American blouse are related: beside them, an officer of the Wehrmacht looks like one of Napoleon's soldiers.

At the height of her power, Germany made no impression whosoever on the countries she occupied. Neither courage nor discipline is a virtue specifically German, but the German outline, the German press, German picture magazines, the German cinema, have made no permanent impression anywhere. It all bores Western Europe profoundly. The whole of tragic cinema still impresses, together with the early Russian films. What has resulted from the German cinema, even its finest works? Whereas everything in America that has been created or developed between the wars is important: the street layouts, the façades of houses with enormous windows, the motorcars, the cinema particularly, of course. It is the first time a country has been able to impose its sentimental myths on the entire world, including its underground world, its lovers, its thieves and murderers. And its comics. Could the whole world ever have laughed at the same man before Chaplin? The influence of the United States is the least important part of the question. The lines of civilization in process of being formed in the world is important. This last war was obviously the first real World War.

Should France also jump onto the American bandwagon? No, for she must exchange, give and receive: "Our greatest efficiency can only be insured by our greater desire for liberty."

Such is the man who for more than a quarter of a century has been the General's cultural adviser. Minister of information in the two de Gaulle governments, from October, 1945 to January 26, 1946, he was part of the *Comité de Direction* of the R.P.F. in 1947, then minister of information in 1958 from June 4 to July 7, minister of state of the de Gaulle cabinets from July 7, 1958 to January 8, 1959 (succeeded by Debré, from January 8, 1959 to April 14, 1962 and Pompidou since April 15, 1962), always in charge of cultural matters.

It was to Malraux (and Pompidou) that de Gaulle gave the first copies of his *Mémoires,* asking: "Does this deserve to be published?" [16] But it was Pompidou who dealt with the editors (Plon and *Paris Match*). Malraux is behind the cinema of creation, of the *Caisse des lettres,* a kind of state Maecenas: he is responsible for the refurbishing of the public buildings in Paris, of cultural exhibitions with political overtones, such as the Tutankhamen treasures. He also acts as special envoy from the president to Mao Tse-tung or Nasser, but that is another story. The General takes his enlightened counsellor's advice. Confronted by his capital washed white by his minister, he exclaims: "Since Malraux dipped Paris in chalk, I feel I'm living in Washington." [16]

He tolerates his whims and puts up with his mannerisms and calls him gently to order at the council table when the writer is obviously bored: "Malraux's absent," cries the president.

"But, *mon général,* I'm here. . . ."

⚜

"Monsieur le Ministre des Affaires Culturelles, I didn't say you weren't here, I said you were absent." [16]

He seldom includes him in his policy and went to Athens without him.

"This time, there'll be no stereophonics, or cacophony, or abstractions, only the figurative. I'm leaving the Acropolis to Malraux in exchange for the Parthenon!"

Why the Acropolis? Because Malraux had installed the French lighting *"son et lumière"* system then, and de Gaulle teases him: "What would you say to giving a *"son et lumière"* to Mao Tsetung?" [16]

In fact, de Gaulle's disdain of men is equal to Malraux's, and their cutting remarks match each other. After the electoral victory of the R.P.F., Malraux said: *"Mon général,* have you brought us to the banks of the Rubicon to fish?"

When he returned to power, de Gaulle decided to decorate Mauriac with the Grand Cross of the *Légion d'Honneur,* in spite of various unfavorable comments from his ministers. "Mauriac is our greatest French writer!" But after noticing Malraux at the council table, he added: "The greatest French writer—among others." [16]

To be sure, Mauriac carries little weight in comparison with Malraux. The tall bourgeois from Bordeaux, melancholy and venial, loves de Gaulle, who merely likes him and does not follow his cultural guidance.

Whether he likes it or not, perhaps even unconsciously, the General owes a good deal to Charles Maurras, of whom he has been known to say that he was an excellent journalist, and in his political and literary writings the memory of the master is always present: "We must begin at the beginning. We must begin by affirming, teaching and disseminating a positive doctrine which can attract both the mind and the heart. Discussion can follow. Begin by laying down our idea of France."

✼

"The nonexistence of power is like an empty field; there for the taking, and there for the holding."

"The idea that authority can be created from below would never have entered the heads of our grandfathers, who were wise men."

Through these sayings of Maurras, it is easy to see the sense of "occasion" which obsessed the old master aiming at the conquest of power. But de Gaulle, a legitimist like Maurras, does not like the Orleans family. When the press alluded to the possibility that the Orleans pretender might succeed him, he said: "Le Comte de Paris? Why not Prince Napoleon or the Queen of Sheba?" [16]

In spite of all these masters, Charles de Gaulle remains a first-class man of letters. He has profited from his serious reading, but the synthesis is his alone, bears his mark and his personal style. If he had not been a statesman, his literary activity would have brought him to the fore, in the tradition of Chateaubriand or Lamartine, two French statesmen who were also great writers. Besides, *belles lettres* are a tradition in the de Gaulle family. His grandmother published no fewer than eighty somewhat-affected volumes, though these included a biography of Chateaubriand; his grandfather wrote a history of Paris.

Since 1958, the General visits the opera or the *Comédie Française* only in company with foreign guests, but he watches comedies on television. He visits the art expositions arranged by Malraux, but prefers the Impressionists, notably Renoir. In music he likes Beethoven, but he allows his grandchildren to play Johnny Halliday's records or the Beatles. In short, the General is deeply attracted to the fine arts, but pays them only a minimum of attention, as his taste has not been sufficiently formed.

PART II ✤ THE LIFE

A Brief Biography

1890: born Lille. Until 1907: secondary education in a Jesuit college in Paris. 1907–1908: *baccalauréat* at Antoing (Belgium). 1909: preparation for Saint-Cyr at the Ecole Sainte-Geneviève in Paris. September, 1909: military service in the Thirty-third Infantry Regiment at Arras. October, 1910: enters the Special Military School at Saint-Cyr. October, 1913: lieutenant in the Thirty-third Infantry Regiment at Arras.

The first years of Charles de Gaulle's life were spent under the gray skies of the northern regions of France. On the day he was born, November 22, 1890—seven months after the resignation of Bismarck, the man who imposed peace on the world— rain was falling on the whole of northern Europe. The president of the French republic, M. Sadi-Carnot, opened an exhibition of chrysanthemums by the Horticultural Society of France at 3 o'clock. In the provinces, preparations were being made for the elections to the French senate, due to take place on January 4, 1891; the Dutch were mourning their King, William III, who died the same day, leaving the throne to Princess Wilhelmina, a child of ten, who would reign from 1898 to 1948. A storm raged over England, and a mistral was blowing in Provence.

His memories of a childhood spent in Paris, at 3 Place Saint-François Xavier, and at the College of the Immaculate Conception, 389, rue de Vaugirard, were dull, but enlivened by visits to the Versailles of Louis XIV and Napoleon's tomb.

The first widening of his horizon took place at the chateau d'Antoing, in Belgium, where Charles spent two years at boarding school. It was here that the Jesuits, expelled from France, had been received by the Prince de Ligne in a fifteenth-century fortified castle, originally a summer residence, but now converted into the College of the Sacred Heart.

> We spent two years in this temporary college preparing for the senior school.[1] There were about a hundred pupils and life was very hard. The majority of pupils belonged to the aristocracy and came from the four corners of France. . . . We slept in the stables, converted into a dormitory, and it was very cold all through the winter.
>
> Wednesdays and Sunday afternoons, we went for long walks, as far as the battlefields of Fontenoy and Bouvines, for instance. Every other Sunday, we were allowed to go home. We had to walk from Antoing to Tournai (6 kms.) and take the train to Lille. We spent the day with our families and came back to Antoing the same evening.

Charles de Gaulle spent his free Sundays with his grandmother, Julia Maillot-Delannoy, in her house in Lille, 9, rue Princesse, where seventeen years earlier he had been born. It is an upper middle-class house, for whatever he may say, de Gaulle was born into a bourgeois family; his home and his ancestry betray it.[2]

"I was never middle-class. My family and I have always been poor," [3] he says.

Beyond the carriage gate was a courtyard, where the cabriolet was kept that the Maillot-Delannoys used for their various excursions. Along the route from Lille to Antoing is Lannoy, the smallest township in France, founded in 1458; it was from this town that in 1630 the Delanos, the maternal ancestors of President Roosevelt, set out for Holland and the United States.[4]

Across the Belgian frontier is Templeuve, whose chateau sheltered the Duke of Marlborough, the ancestor of Winston Churchill, in the eighteenth century. Finally, Tournai, an old French city, dear to the heart of Joan of Arc.

Thus, it is a road impregnated with history, particularly for the young son of a history professor and the grandson of two historians.

Charles de Gaulle's adolescence was spent in Paris in an apartment of the Place Saint-François Xavier, and at the Ecole Sainte-Geneviève, rue des Postes, where he completed his studies for the Ecole de Saint-Cyr, his father, Henri de Gaulle, being the history professor.[5]

At Saint-Cyr he did reasonably well, and graduated thirteenth out of 212. The head of the class ended as a marshal: his name, Alphonse Juin.

In 1912, de Gaulle chose his regiment: the Thirty-third Infantry stationed at Arras, midway between Paris and Lille, in other words, between his father's and his mother's families. The colonel commanding this regiment was called Philippe Pétain. Roosevelt, Churchill, Juin, Pétain, so many great names on the road of this young officer. Chance, coincidence, predestination?

When he was ten, Charles de Gaulle was sliding down the

banister rail of the Paris apartment, when he fell. As he was
picked up he was asked: "Weren't you afraid?"

"Afraid? Haven't I got a lucky star?" [6]

The way ahead at that time seemed quite plain.

THE "Connétable"

August 15, 1914: first wound at Dinant. March 15, 1915: second
wound in Champagne. September 4, 1915: promoted captain.
Second March, 1916: third wound at Douamont. 1916–1918:
prisoner in Germany. May, 1919: seconded to the Fourth Division
of Polish *chasseurs:* campaign in Poland. October, 1921: professor
at Saint-Cyr. November 1922: Ecole de Guerre. 1924: headquarters staff of the army of the Rhine at Mayence. 1925: attached to
the personal staff of Marshall Pétain, vice-president of the *Conseil
de Guerre Supérieur.* December, 1927: promoted commandant,
posted to the Nineteenth Battalion of *chasseurs à pied* at Trèves.
1929: posted to the headquarters of the army of the east at Bey-
rout. 1932: attached to the general secretariat of the *Conseil Supérieur* of National Defense. December 25, 1933: promoted
lieutenant-colonel.

There are no eyewitness accounts of Charles de Gaulle during
the 1914 war. Nothing from Dinant, nothing from Verdun, but
there are descriptions of the battles in which he played his part:
". . . the Thirty-third Infantry Regiment was engaged in the
battle of the Meuse from August 15 to 23, 1914, and shared in
the terrible struggle for the bridge at Dinant. While the Belgians
protected the approaches, the French attempted to reach the
right bank to attack the citadel which had been captured by the
Saxon troops of General von Hausen. But as soon as they set
foot on the bridge, the Germans, from the fortress, had fine sport
shooting down the French like rabbits. Bodies began to pile up,

and were pushed toward the Meuse by the cavalry. The slaughter was appalling, and only ceased when the order to retreat was given on the August 23 after the fall of the citadel of Namur." [7]

Charles de Gaulle had been wounded at the outset of the fight. He was wounded again in Champagne, then at Douaumont.

On March 2, 1916, Captain de Gaulle led the Tenth Company of the Thirty-third Infantry Regiment in a fight before Douaumont which was to last six days. The sixth day, an intense bombardment decimated the battalion, but just as the enemy was about to encircle the survivors, de Gaulle led his men in a furious attack, and a savage hand-to-hand battle followed. He fell in the melée, his thigh transfixed by a bayonet. He was taken prisoner, and remained in German hands until the end of the war. After three attempted escapes, he ended up in the punishment camp at Ingolstadt, where he met the future generals Catroux and Tukhachevsky.

In 1919 and 1920, he served in Poland with the French mission who helped the Poles to oppose and beat the newly formed Red Army. Then he returned to France, in October, 1921, to teach military history at Saint-Cyr. He was appointed to the Ecole de Guerre Supérieure in 1922. A colleague describes him at this time:

Until he arrived at the war school, in November, 1922, I had never met him. At the opening assembly, in the conference hall, I saw a tall, very tall captain in horizon blue coming down the stairs to take his place on the bench below mine. He walked very straight, very stiffly, very seriously, strutting like a statue. The face struck me, and I couldn't help thinking to myself: "Well! there's somebody who doesn't think he's nobody." First impressions, they say, are always right. The two years I spent with Charles de Gaulle went to disprove that slightly unfavorable first

impression and made me ashamed of having felt it. . . . I
still keep the warmest memories of our association.[8]

Another opinion came from a foreign pupil:

> He was perfectly like his own legend: a little distant and
> superior. . . . He excelled in teaching. He was a man
> who liked to talk, and knew how to present his ideas
> clearly and succinctly with perhaps a touch of the dog-
> matic. He remained likable, in spite of his occasional
> brushes with our superiors.[1]

During this time, de Gaulle worked on his theories on the
autonomous infantry armored division, which he presented in his
book *Vers l'armée de métier*.

"COLONEL MOTOR"

December 25, 1937: promoted colonel commanding the 507th
Tank Regiment at Metz. 1939: commanding the tanks of the Fifth
Army: May 16, 1940: commanding the Fourth Armored Division.
June 5, 1940: appointed undersecretary of state for war.

The prophet of mechanization preached in the desert. Then
the *anschluss*, then Munich, then the war.

Colonel de Gaulle commanded the tanks of the Fifth Army,
and tried unceasingly to get his views on the autonomous organization of armored divisions accepted. In Paris no one would
listen. He talked to his officers, complained of the standing of
tanks, of the state of mind of the administration. He banged the
table: "When I am master!" The officers are all ears. The colonel
looked at each of them in turn, sighed, laughed: "When I am
master, shall I use a big or a small broom to sweep the donkeys'
stable?" [9]

On May 16, "Colonel Motor" took command of the Fourth Armored Division . . . too late. The French President Lebrun reviewed the tanks and said to de Gaulle: "Your ideas are well known. But it seems a little late for the enemy to apply them."

We know what happened and the resulting disaster. Called to the war office, de Gaulle remained powerless, blocked by Pétain and also Weygand, who was then commander-in-chief of the French Army. But de Gaulle's strength was still apparent to those who could see.

I, GENERAL DE GAULLE

June 18, 1940: call to rebellion. September 23, 1941: formation of the French *Comité National*. December 24, 1941: liberation of Saint-Pierre and Miquelon.

Installed in London in a small apartment in Seymour Place, then in an office in St. Stephen's House, de Gaulle organized Free France. It began with his "summons to rebellion" broadcast on June 18, 1940.[10] He tried to rally political and military opinion to his side, together with officers and soldiers. But only a few answered his call. The total strength of the Free French forces numbered only 7,000 at the end of July, 1940. When the General visited the transit camps of the French troops returning from Norway, the British Colonels de Chair and Williams, sent by the war office, made the following short speech after the General had gone: "You are completely free to serve under the orders of General de Gaulle. But we feel we should tell you, as man to man, that if you do so decide, you will be rebelling against your own government." [11]

Among the first recruits was an officer, Captain André Dewavrin, who saw de Gaulle like this:

Two big windows overlooked the Thames, whose gray-
ish waters carried a ribbon of barges and tugs. The General's office was on the left. I introduced myself in accordance with army regulations, and his immense body
uncoiled and rose to meet me. He asked me a series of
short questions in a clear, incisive, slightly rough voice.
The conversation ended, I saluted and left the room. The
reception had been icy, and my only impression of the
General was of his piercing gray eyes, his iron will, even
more apparent in his words than in his gestures, perhaps
also a touch of pride or disdain, but which might also
have been a touch of shyness. We need not be surprised
that many officers, lost in the agony which followed the
armistice, were completely chilled by their first and often
only meeting with General de Gaulle.

Captain Dewavrin also saw the General make the great political
decision which led to the construction of a state:

In July, 1940, the General said to us more or less as follows: The war will be long and difficult. We must bring
France back in so that she can share in the victory. I can
see three choices:

1. Let Frenchmen volunteer individually in the British
army.

2. Create a kind of legion which will be integrated completely or piecemeal with the British forces.

3. Or else, declare that France continues to fight. This
last solution, which involves tremendous political consequences, is the only one which will enable the nation as a
whole to return to the fight.

"Besides, it is certain that the Germans, sooner or later,
will be forced to invade that part of France which, for the

moment, is so-called free. It will be a vital necessity for their defense, for this war must become worldwide, and whether we like it or not, North Africa will be a strategic center so important that each of the adversaries will have a vital interest in having it under their control. . . . But if we want to bring France back into the war, if we want to represent our country's interests worthily, as much to our Allies as to the Frenchmen of France and overseas who are watching our movements, it is of the greatest importance that the seat of the French government which continues the fight should be situated on French territory." [12]

Muselier, a retired admiral, older, more critical, expressed himself with more vigor:

I was immediately struck by the man's physique: very tall, with a disproportionately small head, his forehead too low. His eyes, which were small and gray, did not meet your own frankly, and always slid away before answering direct questions. The chin, of a very individual shape, did not indicate much will power. The speech was slow, as if he were listening to his own voice; and the mouth, of medium size, often opens wide, showing irregular teeth. The nose is powerful, almost Bourbon, his ears badly shaped, and standing well away from his head. The first physical impression is not good, but the kind words, the determination very clearly expressed to continue the fight at all costs by relying on the forces of the empire, and without ever taking arms against France, a mixture of simplicity and good sense in general conversation, an easy eloquence, made me change my first impression.

De Gaulle congratulated me on my escape and compli-

mented me on the energetic way in which I had rallied
airmen, sailors, and ships at Gibraltar. He asked about
the conditions in which I had left my family, and spoke
of his own that he had the happiness to have them with
him. He spoke of Madame de Gaulle, of his son who
wanted to be an officer in the navy, in spite of delicate
health and the gaps in his education; of his daughter
whose permanent bad state of health obliged Madame
de Gaulle to live in the country. He added that his financial situation was very adequate and offered me money,
which I refused. He ended by saying: "Very well. It is
agreed. In the legion I am trying to create you will command the navy and the air force. Get back into uniform.
We'll have a longer meeting tomorrow."

Next morning, I saw him . . . and received the following order:

London July 1, 1940

Vice-Admiral Muselier is appointed to the
commandment of the Free French martime forces
whatever and wherever they may be. He will
also assume the provisional command of the
French air forces in the same conditions.

C. de Gaulle.[13]

Soustelle came to the new headquarters of Free French Forces
at 4 Carlton Gardens at the end of the summer of 1940. It was
during the Blitz:

The General had taken me to dine at a small two-room
apartment where he was living, not far from the Con-
naught Hotel. Also with us was his *aide-de-camp*, Seur-
relles. I was much less moved than curious, passionately
curious, and immediately I had the feeling that this man

was not "acting." He was being himself and was not thinking of creating an impression. He was not familiar, but natural, neither vulgar nor precious, but in short, made to offend fools. He likes to ask questions and knows how to listen. He is interested in what is said, and stores it away in his astounding memory. Small human failings can arouse his sense of humor, and although he laughs rarely, he can laugh heartily. Instinctively, he is concerned with wider matters in space and time, in current opinion, in the changing shape of civilizations, in the tendencies of an age or a country. He appreciates the present and the immediate future with a prodigious intuition; he never prides himself on the success of his forecasts (he isn't a man to say "I told you so") but draws lessons for himself. He is capable, during long periods, of submitting everything to a central idea, of turning all the implications over and over in his mind, and only making a decision when he judges the moment right, with the speed of lightning. He is a man of thought who is only driven to action by the evidence of his own thoughts. When his action is that of a soldier, he is strictly military, but only does so within the framework of his profession—outside, he is a philosopher of history who applies his philosophy to reality—a little like a doctor who is at the same time an engineer.[14]

On September 23, 1941, de Gaulle created a first embryonic government: the *Comité National Français* (French National Committee). But the first major enterprise of this committee nearly destroyed it: the decision to liberate the islands of Saint-Pierre and Miquelon. On December 24, in spite of advice to the contrary from the American government and the unconfirmed announcement of an imminent landing by Canadian forces in the islands, de Gaulle ordered Muselier to proceed to win over the islands. The operation was completely successful, without a blow being struck.

Secretary of State Cordell Hull immediately loosed a diplomatic storm. Washington always sided with Pétain, the head of the Vichy government, and did its best to bypass and ignore de Gaulle.

THE "PRIMA DONNA"

November 8, 1942: Allied landings in North Africa. March 24, 1943: de Gaulle–Giraud meeting in Casablanca. May 30, 1943: arrival of General de Gaulle in Algiers. June 3, 1943: constitution of the *Comité Français de Libération Nationale*, (French Committee of National Liberation). September 17, 1943: creation of the provisional Consultative Assembly of Algiers.

Under these conditions, it is not surprising that Roosevelt should personally have seen that de Gaulle was not given notice of the plans for a landing in North Africa. On November 7, in the evening, a grand reception was given as the Soviet Embassy in London to mark the twenty-fifth anniversary of the October Revolution. Bogomolov exchanged a few words with Jan Masaryk, the Czechoslovakian minister for foreign affairs. Then the latter had a drink with Pleven, one of de Gaulle's commissioners, and whispered to him: "It's for tonight." The General was immediately informed.

At eight minutes to one in the morning, Colonel Billotte, chief of the General's headquarters, received a telephone call from General Ismay: "The Americans insisted we keep the secret from you because they were afraid of complications that might result for the Free French. I appreciate your bitterness, but ask you to master it." Billotte woke the General at 6 o'clock. The General grumbled: "I hope the Vichy people fling them into the sea. You can't break into France like a burglar!" [15]

Charles de Gaulle as a child

Charles de Gaulle as a Saint-Cyrian cadet.

ich Embassy Press and Information Division

1941. London.
General and Mrs. de Gaulle
sitting on their terrace steps.

French Embassy Press and Information Division

March, 1944.
General de Gaulle visiting an
outpost on the Italian Front
accompanied by General Juin.

August, 1944.
General de Gaulle, flanked by members of the Resistance,
marching down the Champs Elysées on the day of the Liberation of Paris.

April, 1945. Ceremony of the
awarding of the Cross of the Liberation
to the City of Paris.

...ember, 1944. General de Gaulle
...ng in a car with Winston Churchill .

...OM LEFT: 1944. Washington, D.C.
...ident Roosevelt clasps the hand of
...eral de Gaulle in the White House.
...Anna Beottiger, daughter of
...President, stands behind him .

June, 1945. General Eisenhower
as he thanks General de Gaulle for the
presentation of Napoleon Bonaparte's sword
which the Conqueror had carried during
the time of his first consulate,

French Embassy Press and Information Division

September, 1958.
General de Gaulle in Rennes.

French Embassy Press and Information Division

The crowd bath. April, 1960.
General de Gaulle on his
visit to the U.S.A. and
Colonel Bonneval in the
middle of the crowd.

G. Oriol

April, 1960. Washington, D.C. Mrs. John F. Kennedy,
wife of then Senator Kennedy, chats in French with
President de Gaulle at a reception given by the
President and Madame de Gaulle at the French Embassy.

G. Oriol

TOP RI

April, 1960. Washington,
The President of the United States
Mrs. Eisenhower are welcome
the President of the French Rep
and Madame de G
at the French Emb

A community of views. June, 1961.
President Kennedy and General de G
leave the Elysee Palace afte
last of their series of six meet
Along with a broad range of ge
problems, the leaders confirme
identity of their views on
committments towards E

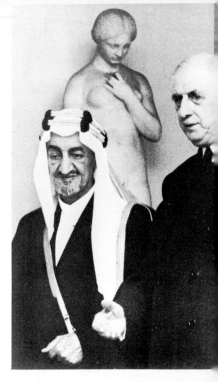

G. Oriol

The Lion's portion. July, 1963.
General de Gaulle with African Delegations.

June, 1967. French President Charles de Gaulle
escorts his guest,
King Faisal of Saudi Arabia, from
a luncheon at Elysee Palace in Paris.
Statue in background is "La Colombe D'Or
(The Golden Dove)" by Jouffroy.

July, 1962. Charles de Gaulle receiving the
African Delegates at the Noirmoutier Hotel.

French Embassy Press and Information Di

December, 1966.
Soviet Premier Alexei N. Kosygin
and General de Gaulle
pose for photographers
after official luncheon
offered at the Elysee Palace.

World Wide Photos

June, 1965. Bonn, Germany.
De Gaulle shakes hands with
former West German Chancellor
Konrad Adenauer as they met at
the Parliament Building, during
a visit by General de Gaulle.

TTOM LEFT:

ly, 1965. General de Gaulle
d M. André Malraux visit the
ening of a Cultural Center.

BOTTOM RIGHT:

July, 1967. De Gaulle stands
ith West German Chancellor
Kurt Georg Kiesinger
before they entered the
Palais Schaumburg in Bonn.

French Embassy Press and Information Division

World Wide Photos

Jacques Soustelle

Admiral Muselier

Christian Fouchet

Georges Pompidou

FRENCH
LEADERS

(Gaullists)

G. Oriol

André Malraux

Maurice Couve de Murville

Gaston Palewski

𝓕rench Embassy Press and Information Di

General and Mrs. de Gaulle
in their garden at Colombey-les-Deux-Eglises

The American radio and the BBC put out the famous message: "Allo Robert! Franklin arrive! Franklin arrive!"

At noon, de Gaulle answered an invitation to lunch with Winston Churchill and Anthony Eden, the British foreign secretary. As de Gaulle related:

> During the conversation, the prime minister showed me endless signs of friendship, without hiding from me that he felt a certain embarrassment. He told me that if the fleet and the Royal Air Force were playing an essential part in the operation, British troops were only acting as makeweights. For the moment, Great Britain had had to leave the entire responsibility to the United States. Eisenhower was in command. The Americans had insisted that the Free French should not be included.
>
> "We were forced," declared Churchill, "to agree. Be assured that we will not in any shape or form revoke our commitments to you. Since June, 1940, we have promised you our support. In spite of incidents that may have taken place, we intend to continue. Besides, according to the way the affair develops, we, the English, are expected to come into action. Then we shall have our own say in the matter, and it will be in your favor.
>
> "And," Churchill added, showing signs of emotion: "You were with us during the worst moments of the war. We will not abandon you when the horizon is beginning to clear."

Churchill announced the simultaneous presence in Algiers of Darlan and Giraud. He asked de Gaulle how he saw "the sequel as it concerned the relations between Free France and the authorities of North Africa." De Gaulle answered that, for him, it was only a matter of achieving unity.

De Gaulle saw no reason to give way at once and without conditions. For the French Resistance, at home, he had become "the symbol." As such, he was seen by one of the great leaders of the Resistance, "Bernard" (Emmanuel d'Astier de la Vigerie), on his way through London in October, 1942:

> It was at the Connaught Hotel, the most old-fashioned of London hotels. A porter, as silently efficient as the carpets and the lift, showed me to a sitting room, where a table had been laid for two. I stood waiting. The Symbol entered. He is even taller than one might think. His gestures are as slow and heavy as his nose. His head is small, his face shiny, carried by a body that has been loosely put together. His most usual gesture consists in raising his forearms, while keeping his elbows at his sides. Then, at the end of these arms, connected to thin wrists, his slack hands, very white, slightly feminine, with upturned palms, seem to be raising a world of abstract burdens. He asks no questions. We dine. He doesn't like men: he likes history, particularly the history of France, for which he is forever creating a chapter that he seems to be writing in his head. I said things that were much too exact, much too confused, or where concrete details and utopian sentiments were mixed. He only picked up a few odds and ends which will probably go into his memoirs. Like so many others, since this morning I have lived in a state of mounting incredulity—the incredulity in which I have been wrapped for the last eighteen months, like a cloud of cotton wool. But why should he be incredulous? Suspicious? Yes, because he despises too many men and things in this world. Incredulous? No, because I am a French ant, who is bringing him a scrap of straw. I leave with my head spinning.[17]

✤

From January 14 to 27, 1943, Roosevelt and Churchill held meetings at Casablanca, where they decided to demand the unconditional surrender of the Axis Powers. They also tried to reconcile de Gaulle and Giraud.

"Your *enfant terrible* must come down here," said Roosevelt to Churchill.

"De Gaulle is on his high horse," the prime minister said. "Refuses to come down here. Refuses point-blank." He seemed to be enjoying his description of his own difficulties. "I can't move him from London," Churchill would say, cheerfully. "He's furious over the methods used to get control in Morocco and Algeria. Jeanne d'Arc complex. And of course now that Ike has set Giraud in charge, down here. . . ." And he wagged his head sadly.

Gently at first, but firmly, and later with real insistence, says Elliott Roosevelt, his father demanded that de Gaulle had to be brought down, insisting that a provisional government could not be left to one man, whether it was de Gaulle or Giraud, that the good offices of both Frenchmen would be required to set up the structure which would govern France until she had been completely liberated.

> I got the impression that Churchill and Anthony Eden must at some time in the desperate past have promised de Gaulle—tacitly if not contractually—that his would be the only say in the reconstitution of France. The prime minister was moving very cautiously throughout this conversation. . . . Well, after midnight, the prime minister took his leave. Father was tired, but still in a talkative mood, and happy to see me again. I sat with him while he got into bed.
>
> 'Was I just imagining things,' I asked, 'or isn't the P.M. really worried by de Gaulle's pouting?'

Father laughed. 'I don't know. I hope to find out, in the next few days. But I have a strong sneaking suspicion that our friend de Gaulle hasn't come to Africa yet because our friend Winston hasn't chosen to bid him come yet. I am more than partially sure that de Gaulle will do just about anything, at this point, that the prime minister and the foreign office ask him to do.'

'How come?'

'Their interests coincide. The English mean to maintain their hold on their colonies. They mean to help the French maintain *their* hold on *their* colonies. Winnie is a great man for the *status quo*. He even looks like the *status quo*, doesn't he?'

On January 25, Giraud and de Gaulle were at Casablanca. Roosevelt saw Giraud first, who talked of nothing but the equipment of his troops.

To his son, Roosevelt said: "The Allies are bringing pressure to bear on de Gaulle."

To Churchill's delegate in Algeria, he declared: "Nothing stands in the way of unity around General Giraud. If General de Gaulle refuses the hand held out to him, you should know that America and Great Britain will drop him completely and he will be nothing any more."

De Gaulle prepared the unification and brought Algiers round to his views. The agreement was made by the *Comité Français de Libération Nationale* on June 3, 1943. Afterward, Giraud was progressively eliminated by de Gaulle from the political scene.

THE LIBERATOR

June 6, 1944: Allied landings in Normandy. August 15, 1944: Allied landings in Provence. August 25, 1944: arrival of Gen-

⚜

eral de Gaulle in Paris. September 2, 1944: first meeting of the provisional government. November 23, 1944: liberation of Strasbourg.

The time for the great landings drew near. There was no French government assigned to carry out the government of the liberated country. In the United States, an Allied Military Government (A.M.G.O.T.) had been set up which, with the help of innumerable "specialists" in French affairs, was to take control on D-Day. The situation was confused and complicated by the elimination of Giraud, on whom, in spite of everything, Roosevelt had particularly counted.[19]

On December 30, on leaving Algiers in order to take up the Supreme Command, Eisenhower went to see de Gaulle at the Villa des Glycines. De Gaulle had promised to provide five or six infantry divisions, three armored divisions, and three army corps by April 1, 1944.

De Gaulle: General de Lattre will proceed with the organization. It has to be done carefully and in depth.

Eisenhower: Can you give me the exact strength of your land forces in Great Britain?

De Gaulle: To all intents and purposes, nil. Let us say, 2,000 men.

Eisenhower: I must be able to use French forces in the northern operations. I don't think it possible to transfer large units from the Mediterranean theater of operations, which is the principal zone of action of the French forces. Besides, it would be very difficult to transport them to England, particularly if we're talking about an armored division.

De Gaulle: Yes, but we must have at least one French division in England. Our infantry includes a good many colored troops, and the English will object to their presence, whereas our armored divisions consist entirely of French elements.

Eisenhower: There may be a solution. I don't know what I shall find in England. But it may be that I shall unearth the necessary equipment, in which case, we merely bring the troops over, which will simplify the problem a good deal.

De Gaulle: You can go into that when you get there, but I repeat: do not arrive in Paris without French troops.

Eisenhower: I assure you I would never contemplate entering Paris without your troops. Now I would like to explain my personal feelings. I have a reputation for being blunt and I think, *mon Général,* that when you arrived in Algiers, you more or less acted on this reputation in your dealings with me. At first, I got the impression that you were judging me without taking sufficient account of the problems I had come up against in the course of my mission and in my dealings with my government. I have only one object in view; to bring the war to a successful conclusion. I got the impression that you weren't prepared to give me your full co-operation. I can understand that you and the *Comité Français de la Libération Nationale* must, on a governmental level, be faced with grave problems. But the responsibilities of the commander-in-chief of the Allied Forces for the direction of the operations in this theater seem to me to be all-important. I realize now that I did you an injustice, and I wanted to tell you so.

De Gaulle: (In English) *You are a man.* None of that matters. Let us look at things as they are. I assure you that I myself, the French government, the French army, are pleased to see you called to command this decisive operation. We will do everything we can to help you. When difficulties arise, I ask you to trust me and get in touch with me. For instance, I can see what must be done when the question of Paris comes up.

❦

Eisenhower: We must smooth out all difficulties as soon as they appear. I doubt that I shall be able to keep our meetings secret in the United States. In the same way as your Committee has responsibilities to French opinion, we have to reckon with public opinion in the United States. Public opinion can win wars. If I see an opportunity, I am prepared to make a declaration expressing the confidence I place in our meetings, acknowledging the injustice I did you, and adding that you have declared yourself ready to help me, to the best of your ability. For the forthcoming campaign in France, I shall need your support, the assistance of your administrators, the co-operation of French opinion. I don't know what theoretical position my government will advise me to accept in my contacts with you. But, apart from principles, there are facts. I want to tell you that, in fact, I recognize no authority in France except yours.

De Gaulle: If we have experienced any difficulty in our relationship, it is neither your fault nor mine. It stemmed from conditions arising from the very complicated situation in our two countries, in relation to each other, whilst France is no longer established as a Great Power. But all this is only momentary. When the war is won, no trace of it will remain —except, naturally, for the historians.[20]

De Gaulle never forgets history; it is his major obsession.

The tension with Churchill was not less acute. The General did not see the British prime minister for six months. Pressure was brought to bear on de Gaulle, and in the course of a stormy encounter, the prime minister said (June 2, 1944) : "Every time I have to choose between Europe and a wider horizon, we will always be for the wider horizon. Every time I have to choose between you and Roosevelt, I will choose Roosevelt."

At Eisenhower's headquarters, de Gaulle discovered that the

date for the Normandy landing was imminent. Ike showed him the proclamation to the peoples of Europe prepared for D-Day. It had been arranged that Eisenhower would speak after Haakon VII of Norway, Wilhelmina of Holland, Charlotte of Luxembourg, and M. Pierlot, and before General de Gaulle. The text made no reference to the French Committee and placed part of the French Army under Eisenhower's command. De Gaulle refused. Churchill was furious, but de Gaulle would not give way. He insisted on speaking on the BBC alone on June 6 at 18 hours, independently of Eisenhower.

De Gaulle's triumphant visit to Bayeux, the first big town liberated at the head of the Allied advance, enabled Churchill and Roosevelt to cut their losses and forced them to accept the General.

On July 6, on the insistence of Roosevelt, de Gaulle went to Washington to settle the question of administrative co-operation between the Army of Liberation and the French authorities. On August 25, he received the text of the Franco–American agreement on civil affairs, with the proviso that this document was not a recognition of his government.

During this time, in the Italian theater of operations, the French expeditionary forces, commanded by General Juin, covered themselves with glory as they opened the gates of Rome to the Allies.

On August 20, de Gaulle was again on the Normandy front at Eisenhower's headquarters, complimenting him, but adding:

> From the strategic point of view, I don't understand why, when you have crossed the Seine everywhere, you have only failed to cross it at Paris. It is the center of communications, which you are going to need, and which you must establish as soon as possible. If it were a question of anywhere else, and not the capital of France, my advice

⚜

would not concern you, for you are directing the operations. But the fate of Paris concerns the French government vitally, which is why I feel obliged to intervene and ask you to send troops there. It goes without saying that the Second French Armored Division should be at the head of any such move.[21]

This advice was accepted and the Second French Armored Division, supported by American elements, was launched in an attack on Paris, which had already been partially liberated by the Resistance.

On August 26, General de Gaulle walked down the Champs Elysées and went to the Hotel de Ville. To Bidault he said: "One pace behind me."

Since August 15, the troops of Generals Patch and de Lattre had been working their way northward from Provence, and made contact with Eisenhower's forces (including the French Second Armored Division) near Dijon, on September 12, 1944.

In the final reckoning, France provided one quarter of the fighting strength of Eisenhower's army, and yet she was given no place at the conference table deciding her future.

De Gaulle fought one more battle in this Second Battle of France.

Although Strasbourg had been entered by General Leclerc's troops on November 23, orders were given for it to be evacuated for strategic reasons.

General de Lattre de Tassigny relates: "On January 2, 1945, at exactly 21:47, I received a telegram from General Devers commanding the Sixth Army Group, informing me of the order to retreat given by the Supreme Commander. The telegram read:

YOU MUST ACCEPT THE LOSS OF TERRITORY EAST OF THE VOSGES ON YOUR LEFT AND FALL BACK ON THE VOSGES POSITION, ARRIVING ON THE MORNING OF JANUARY 5.

✥

"Ça, non!" exclaimed de Lattre. *"Non possumus.* In theory, this strategic withdrawal might be justified in military terms. But there are circumstances where instinct is worth more than reason. Not only will I not withdraw my left, but I take it on myself to defend Strasbourg." [22]

In Paris, de Gaulle had already been informed. He wrote:

> On January 1, General Juin told me of the immediate peril threatening Alsace. He had been warned by G.H.Q. at Versailles that it was vital to despatch all the reserves to the Ardennes immediately. Consequently, the German attack developing in the region of Saverne would create grave risks for the Devers army group, and General Eisenhower himself had ordered the falling back on the Vosges in order to shorten his front. It was time for me to intervene. Strasbourg must be defended. In order to make sure it would be done, I had no other recourse than to send my own orders to the First French Army. On January 1, in the afternoon, I sent the following orders to General de Lattre: "It goes without saying that the French Army will not consent to abandon Strasbourg. I order you to take command of its defense." [22]

General de Lattre had already ordered the Guillaume division to take over from the American troops in retreat, and to defend Strasbourg. De Gaulle went to Eisenhower's headquarters, where Churchill joined him.

"On the strategic level," said de Gaulle, "this is nothing but a maneuver . . . but for France, it would be a national disaster, for Alsace is sacred."

"All my life," said Churchill, "I have been aware of the place Alsace holds in the hearts of Frenchmen everywhere."

Eisenhowever gave way. He telephoned to General Devers to

❧

suspend the retreat provisionally. French troops defended and saved Strasbourg.

THE INCONVENIENT ALLY

December 1 to 10, 1944: de Gaulle–Stalin meetings in Moscow. December 10, 1944: Franco–Soviet alliance. February 4, 1945: Yalta. May 7, 1945: German surrender at Rheims. May 8, 1945: signature of the surrender at Berlin. July 17, 1945: Potsdam. August 21 to 25, 1945: de Gaulle–Truman meetings in Washington. November 13, 1945: elected president of the provisional government. November 21, 1945: first de Gaulle government. January 20, 1946: resignation of President de Gaulle.

As soon as the provisional government was recognized by the Allies, despite Roosevelt's opposition (October 23, 1944), de Gaulle stepped into Marshal Foch's shoes.[23] He went to Moscow to defend his plan for the dismemberment of Germany. He wrote:

> During the fifteen-odd hours my conversations with Stalin lasted, I was able to appreciate his plan, which was secret and grandiose. A communist dressed as a marshal, a dictator crouching over his own cunning, a conqueror with a friendly expression, he did his best to put me off the scent. But so violent was his passion that it often broke through, not without a kind of black charm.
>
> Our first conversation took place at the Kremlin, on the evening of December 2. A lift carried the French mission to a long corridor, where an imposing number of policemen were on duty. This opened out into a large room furnished with a table and chairs. Molotov showed us in, and the marshal appeared. After the usual exchanges, we sat down round the table. Whether he was speaking or not, Stalin, with lowered eyes, scribbled hiero-

glyphics. We discussed the German business immediately. None of those present doubted that the Reich must collapse shortly under the attacks of the Allied armies, the marshal stressing that, of these attacks, the heaviest had been struck by the Russians.

We were immediately in agreement that Germany must be disarmed and rendered harmless forever.

I pointed out how much the separation between Russia and France had contributed to the unleashing of German ambitions, the French disaster, and the invasion of Soviet territory. I sketched the outlines of a direct entente between the governments of Moscow and Paris as the basis of a settlement which they could jointly propose to the other Allies, but Stalin became evasive.

On the contrary, he insisted on the necessity of examining each question with the United States and Great Britain, from which I inferred that he had already good reason for discounting Roosevelt's and Churchill's agreement as to what he wanted to obtain. Nevertheless, he asked me what guarantees France would like in the West, but when I spoke of the Rhine, the Saar and the Ruhr, he declared that the solutions to those problems could only be discussed on a four-handed basis. When I mentioned the eastern frontiers of Germany, he replied categorically:

"The former Polish lands of Eastern Prussia, Pomerania, and Silesia must be given back to Poland."

"In effect," I said, "the frontier of the Oder?"

"The Oder and the Neisse," he agreed. "In addition, there are rectifications to be made in favor of Czechoslovakia."

I remarked that we raised no objection, in principle, to these territorial changes which, in addition, would include the settlement of the eastern frontier of Poland. But I added:

"If you feel that the question of the Rhine cannot be solved at the moment, that of the Oder is already settled." Stalin was silent, still drawing lines and circles. After a moment, looking up, he proposed a Franco–Russian pact, "so that our two countries can take sides against any fresh German aggression." [24]

The pact was signed on December 10, 1944. But its contents were very vague, and Stalin attached no importance to it. On the other hand, he had realized that de Gaulle did not share his views on Eastern Europe, particularly with regard to Poland.[25]

France was not invited to the Yalta conference. Roosevelt, as soon as he arrived, asked Stalin about his conversations with de Gaulle. The marshal replied "that he had found de Gaulle without subtlety and without any realistic judgment of the contribution made by France to the victory, since he demanded the same rights as the Americans, the British and the Russians, who had carried the whole weight of the war." [26]

Four months later, the Germans were forced to capitulate.

Eisenhower set up his headquarters in a school in Rheims, which became the nerve center of the war in Europe.

On May 4, 1945 at 11 o'clock in the morning, Montgomery announced that the Germans were ready to sign. On May 5, at 17 hours, the delegation, consisting of Admiral von Friedeburg and Colonel Polek, arrived in Rheims, but they were authorized by their commander, Admiral Donitz, to negotiate only, not to sign. Eisenhower had very little patience. With his own eyes, on April 5, near Gotha, he had seen a concentration camp, and he remembered the corpses of men who had died of hunger and ill treatment. He had forced himself to look at the bodies to be able to bear personal witness to those who pretended that the accounts

of those atrocities were mere propaganda.[27] Since then, he had
hardly been able to hide his repulsion for the Germans. Surrender
must be unconditional. This time the German Army must know it
had been beaten in the field, utterly and completely. There would
be no repetition of the German World War I legend that the
civilians had backed out, and not the army.

On Saturday, May 5, during the afternoon, Butcher, Eisenhower's naval attaché, asked Ike if he didn't think "the French
should have a representative present for the signing, this being
their country." Ike agreed and said that the omission was a complete oversight. He sent word to invite someone from the de
Gaulle government to be on hand to sign as a witness.[27]

The message from G.H.Q. arrived in the Paris office of de
Gaulle's Commander in Chief headquarters. General Juin was
away in San Francisco. His assistant, General Sevez, was told
that an airplane sent by Eisenhower would be coming to fetch a
French delegate for an important mission at a place that would
be kept confidential until the last minute. Sevez asked for a war-
rant from General de Gaulle, who tore a page from his notebook
and scribbled eight lines rapidly in his quick and nervous handwriting. Then, armed with his precious document, Sevez left for
Rheims on the morning of Sunday the 6th. At the same time,
General Jodl, the most recent commander of the German Army,
arrived in Rheims with plenary powers.

The act of surrender was signed on May 7, 1945 at 2:41 in
the morning, on the first floor of the school in Rheims, in the
war room, which was the map room of the Allied headquarters.

Jodl was in *feldgrau* uniform, trousers with a red seam, dazzling boots. Friedeburg, bare-headed, carried his gold-laced cap
in his hand. A third German, Commander Oxenius, small and
pale, followed at a respectful distance.

After the regulation salutes, Jodl signed with General Bedell
Smith (for Eisenhower) and the Russian General Susloparov in

the names of the two Allied armies (East and West); Sevez (for France) initialed the document as witness.

Next morning, May 8, the same ceremony was repeated in Berlin. Marshal Keitel headed the German delegation, supported by Admiral von Friedeburg and the Luftwaffe General Stumpf. Eisenhower was represented by his English deputy, Air Chief Marshal Sir Arthur Tedder; the Russian General Zhukov presided over the meeting, supported by Vishinsky, also the American General of the Air Force Spaatz and the French General de Lattre de Tassigny.

When de Lattre took his place, Keitel was surprised. *"Ach! The French too!"* The document was signed by Keitel and Zhukov, and by Air Chief Marshal Sir Arthur Tedder, and initialed by Spaatz and de Lattre.

As soon as the Allies had signed, Zhukov rose and peremptorily ordered the Germans to leave the room. Keitel rose, clicked his heels, saluted with his marshal's baton, wheeled round and left the room with long strides, followed by the other German representatives. As soon as they had gone, the various Allied representatives rose and moved into the adjoining rooms.[27]

That night, three Allied generals had to be carried out of the dining-room.

At Rheims, as in Berlin, a small French flag had finally been found and hoisted alongside the Allied flags. On September 2, 1946, General Leclerc, in the same terms, initialed the Japanese surrender at MacArthur's side, on board the battleship *Missouri*. On May 8, 1945, the number of French dead in the Second World War amounted to 355,422 against 338,410 for Great Britain and 298,150 Americans. France had lost half a million houses, whereas England reckoned that she had had 175,000 destroyed. The French national exchequer had decreased by more than 6,000 billion francs, whereas American trade had been able to increase.

Nevertheless, de Gaulle was not invited to the Potsdam Conference. Stalin confirmed the Yalta decisions with Truman, who gave a piano recital one evening, and found time to explain the rules of baseball during a plenary session. Speaking of French Indochina, the American president repeated the opinions he shared with the last president, Roosevelt: to bypass the French and put the country under the jurisdiction of the United Nations. At Yalta, Roosevelt had said to Stalin:

> France has done nothing to improve the conditions of the natives since she has possessed Indochina. But the British are against my proposals because they are afraid I may insist on the same solution for Burma. General de Gaulle has asked me for ships to transport his troops for the reconquest of "his Indochina."
>
> "Troops," interrupted Stalin, "where will he get them?"
>
> "I've no idea," replied Roosevelt. "De Gaulle told me he would find his troops when I had found the ships. Up till now, I haven't been able to find any."

Which made both statesmen laugh heartily.[28]

After Potsdam, Stalin said again and again, "France is no longer a Great Power." The Truman–de Gaulle conversations on August 22, 1945, did not affect the situation.

De Gaulle stabilized his position in France. On November 21, 1945, he formed his first government, of which he was unanimously elected president by the 555 votes of the Constituent Assembly: four communists, among them Maurice Thorez, were included in the cabinet.

This government lasted for sixty days. There was too much opposition, and de Gaulle would not put up with it. After a short interval, he called his ministers together on January 20, 1946, at noon.

⚜

My mission is accomplished. The party system, which
I deplore, has reappeared. But short of establishing a military dictatorship, which I don't want, and which would
probably be disastrous, I have no way of preventing this
happening. Your ideas of how a government should work
do not correspond with mine. I have told you over and
over again, you spend your time eating the wool off your
own backs. You champion the causes of your respective
parties. That is not the way I see how things should be
done. Therefore I have decided to resign. My decision is
irrevocable.[29]

He shook hands and left the room. Nobody called him back.

THE *Rassembleur*

June 16, 1946: speech at Bayeux. April 7, 1947: creation of the
Rassemblement du Peuple Français (R.P.F.). March 16, 1949:
Atlantic pact (NATO). April 18, 1951: creation of the European
Coal and Steel Plan; treaty ratified June 16, 1952 (European Coal
and Steel Community, ECSC). August 28, 1954: the European
Community of Defense (CED) rejected by the French parliament.

As the world conflict which de Gaulle had foretold showed no
signs of breaking out, the General chose to intervene in the debate
which divided the parties on the project of the Constitution of
the Fourth Republic, and spoke at Bayeux on June 16, 1946. He
defined the functions of the head of state, leader of the executive,
assisted by a prime minister and a government, and advised by
parliament. This speech followed on the rejection of a preliminary
outline of a Constitution which would give supreme powers to the
Assembly. He made a fresh declaration on the eve of the referendum on the second revised project: "In spite of appearances, this

project is, in reality, the same the country refused to accept, and rightly so, on May 5 last: an all-powerful Assembly, government by the Assembly, a head of state as a mere figurehead, no organization of the French union."

Nevertheless, the Constitution was adopted on October 13, 1946. De Gaulle no longer had any influence over the French people.

He returned to the political battlefield on March 30, 1947, at Bruneval. "The day will come when, throwing off the sterile interplay of party politics, and rebuilding the badly constructed framework within which the nation is losing its way and the state is losing its grip, the immense mass of the French people will rally around France itself."

On April 1, the prime minister, Monsieur Ramadier, went to Colombey to inform the General that he would be deprived of all military honors and would not be able to use the radio for nonofficial pronouncements. Reacting to this opposition, de Gaulle announced in Strasbourg on April 7: "It is time for a *Rassemblement du Peuple Français* to be formed and organized which, within the framework of the law, will promote a great effort toward public safety and a fundamental reform of the state and cause it to triumph over differences of opinion."

The movement was born. By May 1 it had 800,000 members. Its leader held meetings throughout France and, on October 26, 1947, the R.P.F. won 38 percent of the votes in the municipal elections and a majority in most of the large towns. Social unrest was at its height. Strikes were breaking out all over France. Government succeeded government more and more rapidly: one Socialist ministry, four Radicals, two Christian-Democrats before the elections of 1951.

The General made a praiseworthy effort to "reassemble" opposing views. He wrote personal letters by the thousand to correspondents of all shades of opinion, expressing his sympathy to

⚜

those who followed the Munich line, received former friends of Marshal Pétain, made payment in kind to the relatives of former collaborators, and forced himself to listen rather than talk. The effort probably paid off.

The R.P.F. made its mark on the electorate, stressing the dangers of communism, the red peril which forces governments to moderation, but at the 1951 elections only collected 20.85 per cent of the votes, and returned 118 deputies.

"A great success," said the directors of the R.P.F.

"A disaster," pronounced Georges Pompidou, the General's closest adviser.[30]

To begin with, there was a deficit of 80 million francs in the coffers of the R.P.F., which Pompidou undertook to wipe out in a few months. The General continued to fight for his grand design. Just as he attacked the London agreements which accepted the reunification of Germany (1948), he criticized the organization of the Atlantic Pact and its forces, which were too weak compared with those of the Soviet Union (1951), and also the coal-steel pact which, without any guarantees, allowed German heavy industry to be reconstituted (1951).

His main attack was launched against the European Defense Community (CED), conceived by René Pleven, the first prime minister of the new legislation (1951). But the General could not prevent the signing of the treaty (May 27, 1952), and after a pause for reflection, he decided to retire once more from active politics and, after a final press conference, February 25, 1953, directed entirely against the CED, the General gave the following statement to the press on May 6: "The efforts I have made since the war, supported by determined Frenchmen, to let our country find its unity again and place a real government at its head, have not been successful. I recognize the fact clearly. I see the forthcoming bankruptcy of my illusions. I must work for the remedy."

And he went into exile once again and, in the tower room at

Colombey, settled down to write his memoirs. The first volume appeared on October 5, 1954.

THE CONQUEROR OF MAY 13, 1958

July 20, 1954: Geneva agreements ending the war in Indochina. October 3, 1954: London agreements on German participation in the union of western Europe. October 13, 1954: meeting de Gaulle–Mendès-France. November 1, 1954: outbreak of war in Algeria. April 28, 1955: meeting de Gaulle–Edgar Faure. June 3, 1955: independence of Tunisia. August 7, 1956: General de Gaulle's visit to the Antilles. March 10, 1957: General de Gaulle's visit to Africa. March 25, 1957: European Treaty of Rome which established European Economic Community and Euratom. May 13, 1958: rebellion in Algiers. June 1, 1958: de Gaulle's government (329 votes to 224).

From time to time, General de Gaulle emerged from his retreat to inveigh against party politics or meet this or that prime minister. There were seven in the second legislature (five Radicals and two Christian-Democrats), and three (two Radical and one Socialist) in the third legislature of the Fourth Republic.

At the legislative elections of January 2, without their leader, the Gaullists obtained only 840,000 votes as against 4,125,000 in 1951. Only twenty deputies still proclaimed themselves Gaullists.

On May 29, 1956, de Gaulle published the second volume of his *Mémoires*, then visited the far-flung territories of the Antilles and Africa. He remained their hope.

Meanwhile, conspiracies flourished in "metropolitan" France, the most important being that of General Cherrière. This handsome officer knew Algeria well, where he lived through the early stages of the rebellion. "If we'd been left alone . . . we wouldn't be where we are." He knew the French Army even better. Trusted by Weygand, he was obsessed with the fear of communist infiltration into the army. The "republican politicians" were trying to destroy the army, which alone could maintain the prestige of France.

Cherrière, a retired general for whom inactivity was unbearable, had numerous political conversations during the years 1956–1957, and quite naturally became the center of a conspiracy against the republic. Around this future "head of state" were grouped the veterans of Indochina, many of the returned soldiers who had been unable to find a place in the homeland which had forgotten them and could not appreciate the reasons that led France to put an end to the fighting after so many heroic sacrifices. "We were betrayed by the politicians," they claimed, and did not want to see this happen all over again in Algeria. Their president, General Salan, was affectionately nicknamed the Mandarin," and when he was posted to Algeria, General Chassin, a friend of Cherrière, succeeded him. A distinguished officer of fifty-six, general of the air force, stiff with diplomas, Chassin was also a remarkable military historian.[31]

Another born organizer was recruited, Yves Gignac, general-secretary of the Veterans of Indochina, together with Dr. Martin, who had taken part in all the antirepublican conspiracies for more than twenty years. A card-index specialist, knowing always where to find money, men who had been compromised and wanted to clear themselves, or guns and gun runners, Dr. Martin made himself indispensable, and under multiple identities, provided the link between Paris and Algiers. Chassin also recruited his friend General Miquel head of the military district of Toulouse; Martin brought in Robert Martel, a man of the Vendée, living in Algeria, where either in the open or from his prison cell, he had been directing an active movement.

While this conspiracy developed, the social republicans, heirs of the R.P.F., had been working for the return of General de

Gaulle. They worked with no undue haste, and without any great enthusiasm. They merely allowed the régime to rot.

Michel Debré, in the *Courier de la Colère*, untiringly attacked the "princes who govern us," but he approved of some of the actions of Robert Lacoste. Jacques Soustelle defended *"Algérie Française,"* preserving a dazzling souvenir of his stay in Algiers, and above all of his triumphant departure. With a few other Gaullists, this cold and astute man created the *Union pour le Salut et le Renouveau de l'Algérie Française*—USRAF—rue Louis le Grand in Paris, and wove his own plot which should simultaneously restore General de Gaulle and Algeria to France. Maxime Blocq-Mascart, an expert in the corridors of power, was alone in seeing the two plots developing on parallel lines without any prospect of their meeting.

It was he who took the initiative in organizing a meeting between Soustelle and Cherrière at USRAF headquarters. The two men agreed to overthrow the republic, but Soustelle, much more devious than Cherrière, did not reveal his determination to call on General de Gaulle. Both of them were in agreement as to the necessity of acting quickly and basing the revolutionary movement on Algiers, the republic's weak spot. Soustelle sensed that the other's plot was ripe and he must speed up the preparations for his own attack.

Anxiety increased among the French population. Public opinion felt that the governments which followed hard on each other's heels (seventeen in eleven years) were incapable of resolving the problems created by the decolonization, France's entry in to the Common Market, and her share in the Atlantic Pact. Soldiers were being killed in Algeria, no one quite knew why, but they were being killed. Prices were rising, but wages never seemed to catch up with them. Political maneuvering eliminated Mendès-France, but the maneuvers continued. France was afraid, and was waiting for a heaven-sent leader. People were saying it, journalists were writing it. The two conspiracies elaborated their schemes, but only the Gaullist plot made progress.

The Cherrière group prepared a *coup d'état* in Algiers. On D-Day, Cherrière was due to take command of a Committee of Public Safety, then send troops to France to re-establish order. The *"paras"* (paratroopers) would be launched against nerve centers. Veterans of Indochina, the Students Union of Algeria (around their president, Lagaillarde), would occupy key points in Paris. This plot remained secret enough for the main threads to be ignored by the Gaullists, since a mutual distrust separated the two groups of conspirators. The D.S.T. (*Direction de la Sécurité du Territoire*) was, however, informed, and did nothing; it could not believe in the realization of such bold plans.

The Gaullists' discussions were based on the organization of a coup in Algiers, followed by a landing in France. At USRAF, the coming to power would be achieved by legal means at the time of the coup in Algiers. These contradictions did not worry the conspirators—some of them even belonged to both plots, while General de Gaulle took up no position. He awaited his hour at Colombey les deux Eglises.

The D.S.T. also followed the Gaullist plot and seemed convinced that these contradictions showed proof of lack of power. Its leaders were playing their own game and the government was only partially informed.

A great step forward was made when the two plots nominated their representatives in Algiers. The Cherrière action committee chose Robert Martel, flanked by Crespin, while Léon Delbecque represented the Gaullists, assisted by Guy Ribeaud.

The moment for action came with the fall of the Gaillard government. Pacification had made no progress. A thousand "rebels" had been captured, as they had been every month, but the Moroccan and Tunisian frontiers were still not closed. No negotiations were contemplated, but the Americans were urging France

to make use of the good offices of Monsieur Bourguiba. Jean
Monnet even acted as a go-between between the United States
embassy and the Elysée.[32] The number of assassinations in Algiers continued to increase.

Faced by this deadlock, France was without a government.
The ministerial crisis lasted for twenty-three days. The courtyard
of the Elysée saw a fresh procession of hopefuls. Monsieur Bidault, very sure of himself, very confident, thought he could
succeed, and failed. Monsieur Pleven, supported by the *"petit
bleu"* of the north coast, tried to wipe out the memory of Dien
Bien Phu, with which his name remains forever linked in the
memories of the soldiers, by preparing a coalition which would
link both the principle of negotiation and that of an armed victory. He was not successful either.

It was Monsieur Pflimlin, the energetic defender of the price
of beetroot, who settled the crisis. Pale, but verbally resolute, this
deputy for Strasbourg announced the pursuit of pacification and
the opening of discussions with a view to a cease fire at the right
moment. No one could be less imaginative, less provocative. The
new prime minister was the final incarnation of the system. To
continue the war represented the opinion of the right, the negotiations the opinion of the left, and both together composed a
majority.

But in Algiers everything was going wrong. The Committee of
Veterans, roused by the Gaullists and Delbecque, on April 26,
during a great demonstration, demanded the formation of a government of public safety, and handed the *prefet* of Algiers a note
intended for President Coty:

"All the French of Algeria swear before their dead to oppose
by every possible means the formation of any government based
on desertion. It insists on the constitution of a government of
national safety, alone capable of restoring grandeur and independence to the country."

⚜

The choice of Pflimlin was the signal for revolt. Robert Lacoste flew to Paris on May 10, more or less in secret, and set up shop at the *brasserie* Lipp. In between the rush hours, he gossiped with the waiter sweeping the floor. To Monsieur Pflimlin who asked him to go back to his post in Algiers, he replied: "Go back there? Not bloody likely."

Léon Delbecque returned to Paris on May 9 to make his contact with the Gaullists, a stormy meeting at which Debré, Guichard, and General Petit were present. As he left, Delbecque said to Alain de Serigny who accompanied him in this rapid to and fro: "We've got the green light for the 13th." [33]

On the 10th, Delbecque was again in Algiers. He speeded up the preparations, intensified the suspense. On the 11th, in the evening, he caught the plane for Paris, and on the morning of the 12th, appeared in Soustelle's apartment, where he met Debré, Guichard, and Frey. Delbecque's main concern was to persuade Soustelle, the "boss," to come back to Algiers as soon as the coup began.

"What am I to do, all by myself, with Chassin and Cherrière on my back?"

Soustelle must chair the Committee of Public Safety. Fresh consultations were held during the afternoon, and a suggestion was made to stir up trouble in Paris and call in troops from Algeria to re-establish order. De Gaulle would settle everything.

Delbecque left for Algiers after obtaining the decision, but Soustelle planned to speak during Pflimlin's opening debate during the afternoon of May 13 and make the crisis insoluble. Delbecque was not wrong. Martel had telegraphed very irreverently on the morning of the 12th: SEND OVER THE GOODS, the signal for the start of operations. As soon as he arrived in Algiers, Delbecque telegraphed to Paris: IF SOUSTELLE CAN'T COME, SEND DEBRÉ. Soustelle confirmed that he would arrive after his speech in the National Assembly. But the "goods" (Cherrière), no more than Soustelle, could arrive in Algiers on May 13, for all the French airports had been closed. Robert Martel and Lagaillarde, at the head of their team of activists, seized the buildings of the general government and asked General Salan to form a Committee of Public Safety under the presidency of General Massu, quite surprised to find himself there in company with Martel, Lagaillarde, and Delbecque.

May 14 was a day of waiting, full of uncertainties and anxieties. Pflimlin, nominated in spite of everything, dared not leave the Matignon building, afraid of being kidnaped. Salan, shattered, would not set foot outside his office. Delbecque won a brief respite by announcing the arrival of Soustelle. Martel tried to eliminate Delbecque.

During the night of May 13 to 14, Chassin slipped off to the Loire to take command of his *Maquis*. Cherrière had driven off in the direction of Switzerland. Soustelle, delayed and under surveillance, managed to escape to Switzerland, hidden in the back of a car.

On May 14, de Gaulle arrived in Paris for his usual Wednesday visit and settled in his usual room, No. 11, at the Hotel Lapérouse. His visitors arrived as usual. That day they included Georges Bonnet, a former minister, Pierre Closterman, a Gaullist deputy, and Charles Arengo of Librairie Plon, de Gaulle's publisher—three well-informed men whose conversation sparkles with intelligence and whose opinions are just and pitiless.

Outside France, everyone was expecting the return of de Gaulle. I was in Brussels, at the International Exposition, with a group of historians specializing in colonial affairs. Hundreds of people congratulated Pierre de Gaulle, who was in charge of the French pavilion.

The chips were down on May 15. Salan, after consulting his friends in Paris and his collaorators in Algiers, prodded on by Delbecque, made a speech to the crowd and ended it with *"Vive*

❧

l'Algérie française! Vive de Gaulle!" The position of the army was thus established. Six hours later, de Gaulle replied:

"I am ready to assume the powers of the republic."

Minister of the Interior Jules Moch expected civil war. He wanted to take security measures against probable troubles, but the police and administration hesitated. Nevertheless, Jules Moch told me a year later, in Lausanne, the risks of airborne landings were very real, and the communists were ready at the first opportunity to install a people's democracy in Paris.

On the 17th, Soustelle emerged from a Swiss airplane at the Algiers airport, Maison-Blanche. Cherrière only reached Oran on the 18th in a Spanish plane, having wasted three days, and could do nothing except side with de Gaulle.

On the 19th, the General held a press conference in Paris: he was waiting to be called. Monsieur Pinay, then others, made the pilgrimage to Colombey. On the 24th, the deputy Arrighi pledged the support of Corsica to the Algiers movement. On the 26th, de Gaulle met Pflimlin at Saint-Cloud, and the following morning announced:

"I have set up the process necessary to establish a new republican government."

At the same time, de Gaulle asked Salan to send him a representative. General Dulac, Salan's chief of staff, and three other officers arrived at Colombey on May 28, expecting to be asked for details on the plans for landing airborne troops. After listening to them, de Gaulle said:

"What General Salan has done and will do is for the good of France."

The following answer was sent to General Miquel, with whom Salan had kept in touch:

"General de Gaulle does not desire a landing in Paris, but he will deal with the situation as it develops."

Yet it was not until June 1 that General de Gaulle was asked to form a government (329 votes to 224), a semi-victory which prompted a phone call from Guichard to Salan:

"Things are going badly for us, it's your turn now, be prepared."

On June 2, General Miquel flew secretly from Toulouse to Algiers to consult Salan and his collaborators:

"Fine, we do the same thing again."

Salan cut short the discussion:

"The people have asked for de Gaulle. We must trust him."

Miquel returned to Toulouse.

On June 4, de Gaulle spoke in the Forum of Algiers:

"I understand you!"

Stalemate was to be succeeded by cross purposes.[34]

THE EMANCIPATOR

August 20 to 27, 1958: journey to Africa. September 28, 1958: acceptance by referendum of the Constitution of the Fifth Republic. Adherence to the French community and proclamation of indepence in Madagascar (October 14, 1958); Sudan, (November 24); Senegal (November 25); Gabon, Tchad, Congo, Mauritania (November 28); the Centrafrican Republic, the Ivory Coast, Dahomey (December 4); the Haute Volta (December 11); Niger (December 18). December 21, 1958: de Gaulle elected president of the republic and the community.

Armed with Constitution and plenary powers for six months, General de Gaulle was finally able to create "his" Constitution. The plan was ready by September, 1958, and approved by referendum on the 28th by 79.25 per cent of the electorate. Among those who voted against it: Mendès-France and Mitterrand. The question now arose of constructing the French community.

During the summer, from August 20 to 27, under a blazing

⚜

sky, the General offered all the countries of French Africa the choice of belonging to the community and secession, in other words, independence. In Brazzaville, he said: "I must offer this community to each and every one, wherever they may be. People say: we have a right to our independence, and of course they have. Besides, whoever wants his independence can take it immediately. The metropole (France) will not stand in their way." And he clarified his proposition:

"Inside the community, if any country, as the days go by, feels that I have not been clear enough regarding the exercise of all the duties of independence, it is up to that country to make its decision through its elected assembly and, if necessary, by a referendum of its inhabitants."

In Abidjan, he said: "Africa, as you all know, is particularly concerned with the circumstances in which we find ourselves. There are in the world countless men who leave their homes and conquer other lands. Africa is exposed to this coveteousness which, naturally, is disguised by ideologies."

All the countries agreed to join the community, except one, Guinea, which chose immediate independence. At Conakry, Sékou Touré declared:

"We have a first and inescapable duty, dignity. There is no dignity without liberty, for all surrender of authority, all constraint, imposed and accepted, degrades those on whom it weighs. . . . We prefer poverty in freedom to riches in slavery." [35]

Yves Guéna relates that General de Gaulle replied with great nobility, without making a move to open the door Sékou Touré had just slammed so firmly.

The community solution was accepted by referendum, 99 per cent by the Ivory Coast, Haute Volta, and Moyen Congo, 98 per cent in Dahomey, Sudan, Oubangui-Chari, Senegal, and Tchad, 94 per cent in Mauritania, 92 per cent in Gabon, 78 per cent in Niger and Madagascar. Immediate independence was voted by

95 per cent in Guinea. The day after the referendum, French credits and administrative aid in Guinea came to an end. President Sékou soon afterward was received by Khrushchev, Kennedy, and the Queen of England. For the other countries, the period of the community was only temporary and, in 1960, all the states attained total independence, their relations with France being henceforth solely that of willing co-operation freely given.

THE DECOLONIZER

June 4, 1958: de Gaulle in Algiers. July 1 to 4, 1958: second visit to Algeria. September 19, 1958: creation in Cairo of the provisional government of the Algerian Republic (G.P.R.A.). October 2 to 3, 1958: third visit to Algeria (Constantine plan). October 23, 1958: de Gaulle offers "peace of the brave." December 3 to 6, 1958: fourth visit to Algeria. August 27, to 31, 1959: fifth visit to Algeria (military inspection). September 16, 1959, de Gaulle recognizes the right of Algerians to self-determination. January 24, 1960: insurrection and barricades in Algiers. March 3 to 7, 1960: sixth visit to Algeria ("mess tour"), "Algérie Algérienne." June 14, 1960: de Gaulle proposes an "honorable end to the fighting." June 25 to 29, 1960: conference at Melun. December 9 to 13, 1960: seventh visit to Algeria. April 22, 1961: generals' coup in Algeriers. May 6, 1961: de Gaulle offers Algeria the choice between association with France and complete independence. March 18, 1962: agreement at Evian and cease fire in Algeria. April 8, 1962: referendum on self-determination in Algeria (90.70 percent affirmative). July 3, 1962: proclamation of the independence of Algeria.

When General de Gaulle took power, the war in Algeria had lasted for forty-three months. The cease fire was signed forty-six months later. Why this long delay? Because France was deeply divided.[36] Certainly, the majority of the people supported the General, but their objectives were contradictory; the conservatives were for the maintenance of French control in Algeria, the progressivists for withdrawal. To come down on one side or the other would split the nation into two unequal parts, but opposing opinions might drive them into civil war.

The General's aim was to put an end to colonial government in Algeria without unleashing these warring elements. Numerous witnesses show that de Gaulle was always in favor of ending colonial rule,[36] but he wanted to establish the conditions himself. When Christian Pineau asked him, in 1957, what he thought of the future of Algeria, he said:

"There is only one solution for Algeria, independence."

"But, *mon général*, you should say so; it would change everything."

"No, Pineau, this isn't the moment."

In fact, de Gaulle acted empirically. His plan was to bring Algeria into the framework of a grand ensemble: the French community, that is to say, a confederation of African states and France. But just as the community was unable to contain the African states, it could not satisfy the ambitions of the Algerian nationalists. De Gaulle made a move toward the community in the plan of development launched in Constantine on October 3, 1958, followed by an offer of "peace to the brave." Then, faced by the defeat of these peace proposals, he recognized the Algerians' right to self-determination on September 16, 1959. But the French population of Algeria, supported by elements of the army, showed itself very reluctant. First there was the rising of the barricades, then the generals' coup, encouraged by the C.I.A. During this time, the partisans of *Algérie Française* organized demonstrations in France, even while the left was demanding immediate peace. Multiple attempts to make peace did nothing to speed up the negotiations.[37] In 1961, after the failure of the generals' coup, the conference of Evian ended with a cease fire and a signed peace.

Algeria, an independent country, will maintain her relations with France on the sole level of co-operation freely given.

HEAD OF STATE

June, 29, 1958: Macmillan–de Gaulle in Paris. July 4, 1958: John Foster Dulles–de Gaulle in Paris. September 14, 1958: Adenauer at Colombey. March 23 to April 3, 1959: Khrushchev in France. September 2, 1959: Eisenhower–de Gaulle at Rambouillet. July 29, 1960: Adenauer at Rambouillet. Proposals for a political Confederation of Europe. May 31, 1961: Kennedy in Paris. April 17, 1962: failure of the plans for a political Confederation of Europe. June 12, 1962: Macmillan–de Gaulle at the Château de Champs. December 15, 1962: Macmillan–de Gaulle at Rambouillet. December 17, 1962: Macmillan–Kennedy in Nassau. January 27, 1964: recognition of Communist China. September 1964: visit to South America. December 19, 1965: de Gaulle elected president of the republic by universal suffrage. June, 1966: visit to the U.S.S.R. August, 1966: visit to the Pacific. July, 1967: visit to Canada. September, 1967: visit to Poland.

Internal difficulties and the dramas caused by the war in Algeria did not prevent de Gaulle playing an important part in European and world politics. As soon as de Gaulle returned to power, John Foster Dulles (who had not long to live), discussed with him the question of the revision of NATO suggested by de Gaulle, who stressed his rights to a decision regarding nuclear armaments (June 29, 1958). But it was to his "good, wartime friend," President Eisenhower, that he proposed the creation of a tripartite directorate of nuclear arms (September 2, 1959). Ike avoided the question in order to gain time.

Concurrently, de Gaulle had nine meetings with Chancellor Adenauer, notably at Colombey, then at Rambouillet. Together,

❧

they projected a political Confederation of Europe which, in spite of various oppositions, made progress. De Gaulle advocated the project during visits he made to the Germans and Italians. He received Dr. Adenauer in France (July 2 to 8, 1962) and paid a triumphal visit himself to Germany (September 4 to 9, 1962). The idea made slow progress, and the Fouchet Commission endeavored to reconcile divergent opinions (Bad Godesberg, July 8; Paris, September 5 and November 3, 1961). But the whole operation collapsed during a conference of foreign ministers (Paris, April 17, 1962), faced by resolute opposition from Monsieur Spaak and Mr. Luns, who advocated a federation and not a European confederation. The General also saw the British prime minister, Mr. Macmillan, to whom he barred the door of the Common Market because England wished to impose conditions before joining.

The meetings de Gaulle–Kennedy were cordial, and the presidential couple was acclaimed by the French population.

"You know, I come from an old French family," said Jackie Kennedy during a state banquet.

"Really," said the General, with an air of interest. "So do I."

The two heads of state found themselves in agreement over Berlin, Laos, and even their own particular "grand design": a European–American agreement. Kennedy had supported de Gaulle at the time of the generals' coup. De Gaulle backed up Kennedy over Cuba. But a clash of interests occurred during the Kennedy–Macmillan meetings in the Bahamas. De Gaulle disapproved of the American nuclear monopoly and English acquiescence. The two presidents had planned to meet again and would certainly have come to an agreement, but the dramatic events in Dallas put an end to this project.

The Americans hardened in their position after Kennedy's death. De Gaulle made his point again: America is too powerful on the map of the world. A Washington–Moscow *rapprochement* would consolidate the Yalta agreement, which the General would like to see revised.

A special emissary from the General, M. Edgar Faure, investigated the conditions of recognition by France of the Chinese People's Government. Perhaps de Gaulle hoped by a Peking–Paris agreement to counterbalance the Moscow–Washington association in order to emphasize the French point of view. In any case, he established diplomatic relations with Mao Tse-Tung.

In France itself, by an anti-constitutional *coup d'état*, after the attack at Petit Clamart, de Gaulle had had himself elected president of the republic by universal suffrage. He confirmed France's position in distant countries: Latin America, the Soviet Union, the Pacific, then in Canada.

The Moselle canal, the Mont Blanc road tunnel, the tide power plant of la Rance will keep his name alive for future generations.

PART III ✤ THE WORK

Domaine Réservé (The Private Preserve)

In taking office, Charles de Gaulle twice found himself—between 1944 and 1946, and after 1958—supported by such an enormous majority of the electorate that he was able to set his personal mark on the direction of the state. He did this with the help of a restricted cabinet in 1944, and an "establishment" after 1958. His closest collaborators were mostly his wartime companions.

In 1944, the General was supported by Gaston Palewski, leader of the cabinet, a former colleague of Paul Reynaud, replaced by the Comtesse de Portes, who had gone to London with the General. He was flanked by two very dissimilar assistants: Louis Vallon, a colorful graduate of the Polytechnique, an independent socialist, talkative and witty, unconventional and gay, who took charge of economic and social affairs; René Brouillet, another assistant, from the Ecole Normale, courteous, discreet, and a deep thinker, a former colleague of Georges Bidault in the Resistance. It was Brouillet who recruited a professor from the Lycée Henri IV, Georges Pompidou, like himself from the Ecole Normale, who was made responsible for cultural affairs. Etienne Burin des Roziers, a professional diplomat, one of the General's staff officers in London, took on diplomatic affairs. Elizabeth de Miribel, throughout, was the General's faithful secretary, dating from his London days.

Such were the official channels between the General and the provisional government.

1944–1946: THE PACIFICATION OF FRANCE

Among the troubled events which accompanied or followed the Liberation, General de Gaulle was faced with two vital problems: political amalgamation and economic austerity.

Political amalgamation: in other words, to re-establish unity between the French people, pardon offenders, and assure a peaceful transition, at least the most peaceful possible, between the government of Vichy and that of Free France.

Marshal Pétain had taken the first steps. One of his trusted followers, an undeniable patriot, Admiral Auphan, on August 11, 1944, was charged with a mission, in very precise terms:

> I empower Admiral Auphan to represent me with the Anglo-Saxon High Command in France, and afterward to make contact on my behalf with General de Gaulle or his qualified representatives, with the object of finding a solution to the French political problem, at the time of the liberation of our territory, of a nature to prevent civil war and to reconcile all Frenchmen of good faith. If circum-

⚜

stances permit, Admiral Auphan will refer to me before any decision regarding the government is taken. If this is impossible, I trust him to act in the best interests of the country, provided that the principle of legitimate government which I represent is safeguarded. If I am no longer free, Auphan will open the document which I myself gave in 1943 to the vice-president of the *Conseil d'Etat* and to the public prosecutor at the court of appeal. Signed: Philippe Pétain.

On August 20, in a message to the French people when he left Vichy, Pétain made known his last political wishes:

> Order must be maintained, and because I represent it lawfully, I am and I remain your leader. Obey me and obey those who bring you the means of social peace, without which no order can be established. Those who speak to you in terms which will lead you to a reconciliation and a rebirth of France, by a reciprocal forgiveness for our sins and the love of our fellow men, those are the true French leaders. They will be carrying on my task and following my disciplines. Rally to their side.

Admiral Auphan did everything he could to contact de Gaulle. By indirect means, with the help of his collaborators, he endeavored to transmit his message to the president of the provisional government. He tried to reach Léon Noel, who was worried in case Auphan had been followed, and dismissed him as soon as possible. He saw Pierre-Henri Teitgen and Michel Debré, two leaders of the Resistance. These in turn reported to Bidault, president of the National Council of the Resistance, who informed General de Gaulle. There was no reply.

Auphan did not lose hope. On August 27, 1944, he went to see

General Lacaille, General Huntziger's former *directeur de cabinet,* who invited General Juin to meet the admiral. Auphan pointed out the legitimacy of Marshal Pétain's powers, the dangers of internal revolution, the necessity of setting up a government of national unity.

Afterward, Juin said:

"I made no promises to Auphan, who I hold in very high esteem, except to pass on his documents without prejudice of any kind to the effect which they might produce."

General de Gaulle received Auphan's message from General Juin, and made no answer. On March 2, 1945, in the consultative assembly, he referred to it in a few scornful words:

"When I arrived in Paris, I was given a communication from a representative of Marshal Pétain. By virtue of a written order, dated August 11, the representative was given full powers to reach with us a solution which would avoid civil war. I dismissed him. Gentlemen, where is this civil war?"

This opinion was expressed mainly after the event, but what was the General's frame of mind when he originally received Auphan's[1] proposal?

We know that on August 19, 1944, when he arrived at the Hotel de Ville in Paris, Georges Bideault asked him to proclaim the republic. "No," replied the General, "the republic has never ceased to exist: Free France, Fighting France, the French Committee for National Liberation, each in turn incorporated it. The Vichy government was and always will remain null and void. I am the president of the government of the republic. Why should I have to proclaim it?"

His main care, therefore, was to maintain his power by taking its legality for granted. He refused in any shape or form to admit that the Vichy government had had a legal basis, or even that it had ever existed. In point of fact, the decision of August 19, 1944, was a genuine *coup d'état*. With the consent of a revolutionary movement, de Gaulle named himself president of the government of the republic. He behaved like the consuls of the year VIII, like Pétain on July 11, 1940.

Concluding the description of his visit to the Hotel de Ville, de Gau le wrote:

"Goi. g to a window, I waved to the crowd filling the square, which proved, by its cheers, that it wanted nothing else."

The order, signed in Algiers on June 3, 1944—which merely changed the name of the *Comité Français de la Libération Nationale* to that of the *Gouvernement Provisoire de la République Française*—was only binding on the members of that committee and could not be considered as representative of the opinion of the French people.

On August 19, 1944, Charles de Gaulle placed the crown on his own head. He knew perfectly well what he had done, since on September 12, at the Palais de Chaillot, he declared:

"As soon as control has been re-established in the persons of the elected representatives of the nation, the government will place in their hands the provisional powers with which they are at present invested."

Nevertheless, it was only on October 14 that a National Consultative Assembly of 248 members was appointed to take on part of the responsibility for government decisions. The first general elections took place on October 21, 1945, simultaneously with a referendum which gave constituent power to the first elected Assembly. The General remained in office for only sixty days under the new régime, which had been established by universal suffrage.

Nevertheless, during the thirteen months of the provisional government, all the main decisions for postwar France had been taken:

1. The nationalization of the main means of production.
2. The planning (for economic recovery).
3. The political purges.

These decisions were made by de Gaulle and by him alone, since he dominated the debates of the provisional government and acted on them in the sense that he made the choice:

"I have listened to your views. They don't accord with mine. The decision is unanimous."

We shall return to the orientation given to the economy, but de Gaulle's categorical refusal to consider any suggestion of political amalgamation must be remembered. Basically, he was disturbed by this decision, but reassured himself by autosuggestion.

In the annihilation of Vichy, Philippe Pétain turned to Charles de Gaulle, but there is no room for sentiment in affairs of state. Above all, the circumstance which made Pétain attempt an agreement with me was the very reason which made that agreeement impossible. The legality he claimed to personify, the government of the republic, denied him utterly, not because he accepted the surrender of a frightened parliament, but because he agreed to the submission of France, collaborated with the invader, ordered French soldiers to fight the Allies of the Liberation, and not for a single day allowed them to fire on the Germans.

A historical summons, then the country's instinct, led me to pick up the escheated treasure and assume French sovereignty. I am the legitimate authority. In its name I call the nation to arms and to unity, enforce law, order, justice, and abroad insist on respect for the rights of France. In that domain, I shall renounce nothing, make no concessions. Without misunderstanding the capital reasons

⚜

behind the marshal's message, without questioning the importance for the future morale of the nation of the fact that Pétain had turned to de Gaulle, I could make him no other reply than my silence.

So de Gaulle wrote ten years after the event, as counsel for the defense, but he also noted:

> In the provinces as in Paris, I had been able to measure the fervor I inspired. . . . No reservations were expressed regarding my authority, either by the administration, the legal and teaching professions, or by the armed forces. The council of state, with President Cassin at its head, set an example of complete loyalty. . . . There was no one, including all the representatives of previous régimes, who did not voice his adherence. The comte de Paris wrote announcing the arrival of a representative. Prince Napoleon, a model Resistance fighter and captain of Chasseurs Alpins, made a similar declaration. General Giraud, arriving from Algeria where he had escaped a fanatic's bullet, also came to me. The former Vichy supporters bowed before the evidence: Pétain, in Germany, kept silent; and all those who had so assiduously served him were prodigal in their favors toward the new authorities. Finally, Monsieur Albert Lebrun brought the melancholy ghost of the Third Republic into the general approbation. I shook his hand cordially and with compassion.

As head of the state, de Gaulle lacked two things: that he should be a leader, and that a state should exist.

Before such pride, even if tinged with anxiety, one can only bow. The General had decided to wipe out the four years of the history of Vichy France, and replace with his own image that

of Pétain, whom he had successively wanted to equal, excel, and
to destroy.

From this refusal to accept any amalgamation was born a
divided France, with leftist leanings which would *vacharder* for
twelve long years. (The word is De Gaulle's, coined from the
noun *"vacherie,"* a dirty trick.)

MOSCOW: DECEMBER, 1944

Although the provisional government of the French republic
was recognized by Washington, London, and Moscow on October 23, 1944, it was still not admitted to the conference table
of the Great Powers. De Gaulle invited Churchill to Paris. The
British prime minister, accompanied by Anthony Eden, the foreign secretary, arrived on November 10 and, next day, both
watched the victory parade with the General.

During the afternoon, de Gaulle and Bidault, Churchill and
Eden, discussed the possibilities of "Franco–British co-operation
to settle world affairs." The English were evasive. They did not
mention the Far East or Indochina, avoided discussing the Near
East, and pointed out that if France had the right to occupy
Germany, they had given way to the demands of Russia concerning the frontiers of the Soviet Union and Poland.

"Under the studied courtesy of their answers, one felt," said
de Gaulle, "that they were playing a game which we had not
been invited to join, and they were showing us a reserve which
had been imposed by others."

Hence, when M. Bogomolov, the Soviet ambassador, as soon
as the British had gone, transmitted an invitation to visit the
U.S.S.R., it was more than welcome. It meant making direct contact with Stalin and his ministers.[2]

Via Cairo and Teheran, de Gaulle, accompanied by Bidault,

Juin, and Palewski, reached Moscow on December 2, 1944. He had two objectives: to reduce the power of the communist movement in France, and to win a place at the conference table of the Great Powers.

The first was only mentioned obliquely during the fifteen hours of conversations that de Gaulle had with Stalin. The Soviet dictator said, smilingly:

"It must be very difficult to govern a country like France, where everyone is so turbulent."

"Yes," replied de Gaulle. "And I can't use you as an example, for you are inimitable."

Stalin then mentioned Maurice Thorez, who had been allowed by the French government to return to Paris. When the General said nothing, Stalin added:

"Don't be annoyed by my indiscretion. Allow me to say that I know Thorez, and in my opinion he is a good Frenchman. If I were you, I wouldn't put him in jail." And he added with a smile: "At least, not yet."

With regard to foreign policy, the debates were on surer ground.[3] It must be acknowledged that there was much good will on both sides. The U.S.S.R. had encouraged Free France long before the U.S.A.[4]

The English ambassador in Moscow, Sir Stafford Cripps, had even said to Molotov in the summer of 1941 that "it would be embarrassing for the British government if the Soviet government showed more good will toward the government of de Gaulle." Nonetheless, the Russians, through their ambassador in London, Maisky, as early as September 26, 1941, recognized de Gaulle as "head of all the Free French" and affirmed their desire to restore "the independence and grandeur of France."

On December 9, 1941, Ambassador Bogomolov had announced to de Gaulle that the Soviet Union would willingly receive three of de Gaulle's representatives in Moscow, a proposal which was immediately accepted. De Gaulle, therefore, offered a squadron to the Russians, the celebrated Normandy–Niemen group. On June 6, 1942, de Gaulle, at the peak of his quarrels with Churchill, had considered leaving London and installing his committee in Moscow.

Bogomolov wrote to Molotov:

"I have seen de Gaulle. According to his information, the Americans are preparing to occupy Dakar and the English are ready to install themselves in Niger without any participation of the Free French. If that happens, de Gaulle will break with the English. If this should happen, he asked me whether the Soviet government would be prepared to receive him and his forces within their territories." [5]

On December 2, 1944, in Moscow, the General told Stalin that France must in the future face Germany in a territorial situation that had been substantially reinforced. For the French, the ideal line, geographically as well as historically, was the Rhine. The river must be the definitive barrier in the east against Germany and the German menace. There might be other fortifications, but what was needed was a real geographical barrier.

Stalin thought that the French would probably want to include the Palatinate and the Rhineland in her territories. De Gaulle replied that it would be a good decision to detach the Rhineland from Germany and reunite it with France. As for the Ruhr, it could be placed under international control. Stalin wondered what the Allies would say to these proposals, and replied that nothing could be decided without consulting them. De Gaulle agreed, but pointed out that the English and Americans would not always be on the Rhine, whereas France and Russia would always remain where they were. It will be seen that Father Butin's pupil had not forgotten the lessons of his youth.

To get his views accepted, de Gaulle conceded that the Russians had the right to draw up the eastern frontiers of Germany

⚜

to suit themselves. He proposed the signature of a Franco–Soviet pact, but Stalin made it dependent on the recognition by France of the Polish government in Lublin. De Gaulle refused and prepared to leave Moscow.

After a comic-opera evening, punctuated by toasts drunk in vodka and propaganda films, the General asked Bidault whether the Russians were ready to sign the pact, yes or no. The minister confirmed that the Russians were waiting for the French declaration concerning Poland.

"In those conditions," said de Gaulle, "it is useless and it is becoming inconvenient to continue the negotiations. I shall end them."

The General took his leave of Stalin, and seeing that Bidault had not followed, sent for him.

The Russians continued the discussion with the French experts Dejean and Garreau, and agreement was reached on a compromise: the pact would be signed, and the French would exchange diplomatic agents with the Lublin government.

De Gaulle returned to the Kremlin, and in Molotov's office, at 4 o'clock in the morning of December 10, 1944, the Franco–Soviet pact was signed.

De Gaulle had maneuvered cleverly, but the pact was not very consistent: the two countries agreed not to negotiate or sign a separate peace with Germany and to collaborate over the peace terms. The treaty was to last for twenty years, but was denounced by the Russians on May 7, 1955 after the French ratification of the Paris agreements on the remilitarization of West Germany.

On December 10, 1944, Stalin wrote to Roosevelt:

"Together with General de Gaulle, we have concluded that the signature of a Franco–Soviet pact of mutual assistance would be useful both for Franco–Soviet relations and for the security of Europe in general. A Franco–Soviet pact was signed today. As for the frontiers of France after the war, the settlement of this question was deferred to a later date."

The announcement of the pact was well received in Paris, and the National Consultative Assembly approved it unanimously on December 30. But Stalin knew that de Gaulle did not share his views as to the future of Eastern Europe, and the General was afraid that the Russians would only give moderate support to French plans for the dismemberment of Germany.

Stalin used a significant phrase to de Gaulle:

"You stood firm. Well done. I like dealing with someone who knows what he wants, even if doesn't share my views."

De Gaulle's ambitions, a dismembered and parceled-out Germany, and a firm Franco–Russian Alliance which would settle the international relations of the countries of Europe, had neither sense nor future. Nevertheless, as soon as he returned to Paris, the General encouraged the agitators for self-rule in Bavaria and the Saar.[6]

YALTA: FEBRUARY, 1945

The meeting of the three Great Powers at Yalta finally put an end to de Gaulle's dreams. He had always been afraid that the peace terms would be discussed without him, and clarified his views publicly on February 5, the first day of the Yalta conference:

> As for the peace settlement, we have made it known to our Allies that France cannot be bound by any terms that she has not discussed and agreed to on the same footing as the others. . . . I appreciate that the presence of the French forces along the Rhine, the separation of the territories of the left bank of the river and the basin of the Ruhr from what will become Germany, the independence

❧

of the Polish, Czechoslovak, Austrian, and Balkan nations
are conditions that France would judge essential. . . .
We need not be concerned as to the possibility of our real-
izing some of them, since 100 million people, firmly established under the French flag, stand in close proximity to
what concerns us most directly.

The Yalta conference took place in the worst possible conditions from the point of view of France and of de Gaulle. The
three great men, Stalin, Roosevelt, and Churchill, were all elderly,
complacent in their victory and convinced that they were masters
of the world. To them, France mattered remarkably little. Stalin,
the "red Tsar," was not interested in de Gaulle's opinions, but
thought he could use him to prevent the creation of an anti-Soviet
"Western bloc." The meeting in Moscow had disillusioned him.
He realized that de Gaulle wanted to join the ranks of Great
Powers and obtain support for his plans for German reparations.
Afraid that de Gaulle might try to divide the Allies in order to
get his views accepted, Stalin preferred for the moment to side
with Churchill and Roosevelt, who seemed to be more favorable
to his plans. Why should he support someone who would be
much more difficult to handle?

In all the debates at Yalta and later in Potsdam, Stalin opposed
de Gaulle. In answer to the suggestion that France should control
one of the occupied zones in Germany, he said:

"I am in favor of allocating a zone of occupation to France,
but I cannot forget that France opened her gates to the enemy."

Stalin considered that Poland and Yugoslavia were entitled to
more consideration than France.

If France were to be given a zone of occupation and a place
on the Allied Control Council, while at the same time refusing
the same right to the countries who had done more fighting than
France, this would certainly give rise to difficulties. He pointed

out that if this were agreed, France would lose no time before insisting that de Gaulle should take part in the conferences of the Great Powers.

Churchill spoke vehemently in support of French representation on the Allied Control Council. He explained that in England no one would be able to understand why questions concerning France and her zone of occupation should be settled without her participation in the debates. He added that this would not imply that France would demand the presence of de Gaulle at the conferences of the Great Powers, as Stalin had suggested. In his usual manner, the British prime minister concluded by saying that the conference "appeared to be a very exclusive club, whose entrance fee represented at least 5 million soldiers or their equivalent."

Stalin still feared that such a claim might be voiced. He declared that General de Gaulle totally lacked "a sense of reality" and repeated that, although France had not taken much part in the fighting, the General had demanded equality of rights with the Russians, the British, and the Americans, who had borne the brunt of the fighting.

President Roosevelt did not discuss the question of de Gaulle with Stalin. He had a great admiration for France and its people, but he did not admire de Gaulle. On several occasions, he alluded to a conversation they had had in Casablanca, when de Gaulle had compared himself with Joan of Arc, as spiritual and political leader of France. Faced with Churchill's insistence, Roosevelt and Stalin agreed that France should be invited to participate in the future government of Germany. In point of fact, the Great Powers had established their positions well before Yalta and were not prepared to budge.

As early as September, 1943, Roosevelt considered that it would be necessary to divide the world: the Far East under Chinese control, the Pacific under American direction, Europe and

❧

Africa under Britain and Russia. According to him it was certain that the Communist régimes would co-operate very well. Stalin would undoubtedly want Finland, the Baltic States, Bessarabia and Eastern Poland. Germany, Austria, Hungary, and Croatia would come under Russian protection, as well as Czechoslovakia.

There was no possibility that Roosevelt could oppose any of these schemes, since Stalin had ample means to satisfy them all.[7]

Going further still, Roosevelt thought that plebiscites should be held in France, Italy, Holland, Belgium, Norway, and Greece. France could only escape communism if she were to choose a government *à la* Léon Blum, so progressive that the communists could accept it.[8]

The American president saw himself as a realist, and thought he could come to an understanding with the Soviet dictator on this basis, whereas Churchill was too idealistic. The solution lay in dividing up the world to halt Stalin on a certain line. Stalin must have known nothing of Roosevelt's thinking, for if he had, it is easy to guess that his ambitions at Yalta would have been much greater.

For his part, Churchill, more realistic than Roosevelt liked to think, had already made the necessary sacrifice to Stalin during a visit he had paid to Russia on October 9, 1944. They had divided up Rumania between them as to 90 per cent to the Russians: 90 per cent of Greece to the English, a 50–50 split over Yugoslavia and Hungary, and 75 per cent of Bulgaria to the Russians.

Roosevelt advocated the maintenance of German unity without dividing it into zones, but Stalin and Churchill overruled him, and the lines of demarcation were drawn.

De Gaulle's ideas were completely rejected. Stalin knew exactly what his objectives were, and Roosevelt, who had been re-elected for a fourth term of office, saw himself as God's representative charged with bringing a just and lasting peace to the world. When he left Yalta, Roosevelt invited several kings and heads of state of the Middle East on board the cruiser *Quincy*. At the same time, he telegraphed de Gaulle to inform him of his wish to meet him during his stay in Algiers.

On February 13, de Gaulle replied to the American ambassador in Paris that it was impossible for him to go to Algiers at that time without previous notice, and that, consequently, he could not, to his great regret, receive the American president: that the French government had invited Roosevelt to come to Paris in November, and much regretted that he had not been able to accept, but "we should be happy to receive him in the capital if he chose to come at no matter what date: that, if he wished, during his trip, to stop at Algiers, would he be good enough to inform us, so that we may send the governor-General of Algeria the necessary instructions to ensure that everything will be done according to his wishes."

This incident—in itself normal and obvious—(it is hard to imagine the French president on his way through Antwerp or Rotterdam, inviting the king of the Belgians or the queen of Holland to visit him), created violent reactions in public opinion in America as well as in Europe. Nevertheless, on his way to Yalta,[9] the American president's special envoy, Harry Hopkins, visited the General on January 27 to discuss Franco–American relations. De Gaulle described his interview with the American president's close adviser:

> Hopkins expressed his views with the greatest frankness. "There is," he said, "a certain uneasiness between Paris and Washington. Now the war is coming to an end. The future of the world will depend largely on the concerted actions of the United States and France. How best may we get their relationship out of the deadlock where they seem to be engaged?"

❧

I asked Hopkins what, according to the Americans, was the cause of this unfortunate state of affairs between the two countries. "The reason," he replied, "was above all the stupefying disappointment we suffered when we saw France, in 1940, first collapsing in disaster, then in surrender. The ideas we had always held of her value and energy were overthrown in a moment. Added to which, the political and military French leaders we trusted, in turn, because they seemed to symbolize France, did not show themselves—and it is the least that can be said—equal to our hopes. Do not seek elsewhere for the deep reasons for the attitude we have adopted concerning your country. Judging that France is no longer what she was, we cannot trust her to play a great part.

"It is true that you, General de Gaulle, appeared: that a French resistance was formed around you: that French troops returned to the fight: that today the whole of France acclaims you and recognizes your government. As we had no reason to believe in this prodigy in the beginning, though now you have become the living proof of our error, and as you have not treated us very well, we have not been well disposed toward you until now. But we acknowledge what you have done, and are happy to see France re-established. How can we, however, forget what we have lived through as a result of her actions? Knowing her gnawing political inconstancy, why should we believe that you will be able to rule her long? Are we not justified in exercising great circumspection regarding what we expect of her, before allowing her to share with us the burden of future peace?"

Listening to Harry Hopkins, I thought I was hearing again what President Roosevelt had said to me in Washington six months earlier. But at that time, the Liberation

had not taken place. I myself, and my government, were
in Algeria. There were still reasons why the Americans
could question the state of mind of Metropolitan France.
Now, everything had become clear. Everyone knew our
people wanted to take part in the victory. It was possible
to assess the value of its reborn army. I was installed in
Paris, in the midst of national rejoicing. But was the United
States any more convinced that France was capable of
becoming a great power again? Were they, in fact, prepared
to help her? Those were the questions which, from the
French point of view, would govern our present and future
relations. I said to the president's envoy: "You have told
me why you say our relations are strained. I will tell you
what, for our part, contributes to the same result. Let us
forget the episodic and secondary frictions which arose
from the abnormal conditions in which our alliance is
functioning. The most essential of the mortal perils which
we, the French people, have experienced since the beginning of the century is that the United States does not give
us the impression that they consider their destiny linked
to that of France, that they would like to see her strong
and powerful, that they are prepared to do what they can
to help her remain so, or become so. Perhaps, in fact, we
aren't worth the trouble. In that case, you are right. But
perhaps we will rehabilitate ourselves. In that case, you
would have been wrong. But your attitude tends to drive
us apart."

These incidents between the French and Americans appeared
to have been smoothed out, but they occurred over and over
again. Roosevelt was always just as virulent about de Gaulle. He
told Stalin he considered that France had only made a small con-

tribution to the war and refused to count her among the ranks of the victors.

In November, 1943, Roosevelt had written to Cordell Hull:

"De Gaulle speaks openly of setting up his government in France immediately after the Allied landings. I am more and more inclined to think that the occupation, when it does take place, should be entirely military." Roosevelt wanted to prevent de Gaulle from taking power, for he considered that once installed, he would never give up his position.[10]

On June 6, 1944, in Algiers, Murphy reaffirmed these same views. "Neither President Roosevelt, nor the State Department, will allow General de Gaulle to take office in Paris." [11]

Nevertheless, a month later, after the successful landings, on the British initiative, de Gaulle went to Washington on July 6, 1944, and was courteously received by Roosevelt, correctly by the army (seventeen salvos instead of the twenty-one reserved for heads of State) but triumphantly by the American crowds. The General had long conversations with the president, but the latter talked more than he listened, and what should have been a reconciliation was only a repetition of opposing points of view. Roosevelt would only accept a *de facto* recognition of the *Comité Français de Libération Nationale*. It was not until the liberation of Paris that Roosevelt finally agreed to recognize the authority of de Gaulle's provisional government. He did it without enthusiasm, and the gesture came too late to seal their reconciliation.

"It cost Roosevelt a good deal to recognize de Gaulle," noted Leahy.[12]

In Washington there was still talk of French decadence, of this de Gaulle who compared himself to Joan of Arc, Foch and Poincaré, but Hopkins had written in his papers: "The story was a pure invention. . . . The oftener the president told it, the more authentic it seemed, and everyone ended by believing it to be true." [13]

Twenty years later, de Gaulle's stubbornness and Roosevelt's dislike remain partly inexplicable. The General said: "I will never know whether Franklin Roosevelt thought that in matters concerning France, Charles de Gaulle was being selfish for France's sake or for his own." Franco–American tension continued to grow until Roosevelt's death on April 12, 1945.

Other incidents occurred during the military operations. In December, 1944, at the time of the German counteroffensive in the Ardennes, Strasbourg was threatened. Eisenhower had taken the decision to evacuate the town. De Gaulle ordered General de Lattre to defend Strasbourg in spite of Eisenhower's instructions, and had telegraphed Roosevelt to ask him "to authorize Eisenhower to take the national interests of France into consideration." Roosevelt categorically refused to act, declaring that it was a purely military matter,[14] and it was under Churchill's influence, who arrived specially from his own headquarters, that Eisenhower finally agreed to defend and save Strasbourg.

On March 29, 1945, de Lattre received orders from de Gaulle to cross the Rhine. "You must cross the Rhine, even if the Americans are not willing, even if you have to use boats. It is a question of the highest national importance." But the French general did not have to outstrip the Americans. He entered Stuttgart on May 20 and was appointed administrator of the conquered town by de Gaulle.

Eisenhower reported to Washington, and Truman, Roosevelt's successor, telegraphed to de Gaulle: "If you think the French army should now be considered as an instrument destined to serve the policy of a French government, a complete reorganization of its command will be necessary."

De Gaulle replied in the same tone: "To reply with the same frankness you have been kind enough to show me, I think I should express the hope that such unfortunate frictions should be avoided. It only needs for the allies of France to acknowledge that questions which touch her as nearly as the occupation of German territory should be discussed and decided with her. As you know, this has unfortunately not been the case until now, in spite of my repeated requests." [15]

Truman replied by suspending the supply of arms to the French. While the British had armed three French divisions, the Americans allowed the war to finish without equiping one. The only American material the French army had when it reached the Danube was what the Americans had given them in North Africa. At the time of the German surrender, on May 8, 1945, in Berlin, General de Lattre was allowed to initial the official document, but no French translation was made and the French flag was only hoisted at the last minute.

Immediately afterward, the coalition came to an end and fresh incidents broke out on the Franco–Italian frontier, where a division of Chasseurs Alpins had seized a few square miles of enemy territory. The French General Doyen refused to give up the area to General Alexander, and de Gaulle only agreed to retreat after receiving an angry telegram from Truman:

IT IS ALMOST INCREDIBLE THAT FRENCH SOLDIERS CAR-RYING AMERICAN ARMS SHOULD THREATEN TO ATTACK AMERICAN SOLDIERS AND THEIR ALLIES, WHOSE EFFORTS AND SACRIFICES HAVE SO RECENTLY AND EFFICIENTLY CON-TRIBUTED TO THE LIBERATION OF FRANCE. THE AMERICAN PEOPLE WOULD BE PROFOUNDLY SHOCKED IF THEY WERE TO LEARN OF THE MEASURES WHICH YOUR OFFICERS, PROBABLY WITH YOUR PERSONAL APPROVAL, HAVE THREATENED TO TAKE.

De Gaulle replied politely to Truman: "It has never been evident either in the intentions or orders of the French government, nor in those of General Doyen . . . to oppose by force of arms the presence of American troops in the small zones at present occupied by us." [16]

But at the same time as he gave orders to General Doyen to withdraw his troops, he instructed Bidault to open diplomatic negotiations with Italy. In August, 1946, this led to a bilateral Franco–Italian agreement, ceding La Brigue and Tende to France.[17]

All these incidents did not prevent Truman expressing the wish to meet de Gaulle. On August 22, 1945, they met, and in the following days, the two statesmen spent hours together at the White House.

De Gaulle described them afterward:

> The new president had given up his plans for world peace and admitted that henceforth the rivalry between the free world and the Soviet world would dominate everything. It was essential, therefore, to avoid quarrels between states and revolutionary upheavals, so that any territories which were not already communist should not be led to becoming so.
>
> As for the complicated problems of the Old World, they did not worry Truman, who viewed them from a simplified angle. In order to satisfy a nation, it was only necessary for it to follow the lines of democracy laid down by the New World. To put an end to the antagonisms separating neighboring countries—for instance, France and Germany—it was only necessary to institute a federation of these rivals, as had been done by the states of North America. To encourage the underdeveloped countries to turn to the West, there was one infallible recipe: independence, as America herself had proved, since once freed from her former overlords, she had become a pillar of civilization. Finally, in face of the communist threat, the free world could do no better, or indeed, could not do otherwise, than to adopt the "leadership" of Washington.

❧

The United States had just given the world an unequaled impression of power and organization. The atom bombs had just been dropped on Hiroshima and Nagasaki. In connection with the German problem, de Gaulle spoke of the guarantees essential for the safety of France: a decentralized Reich, autonomy of the left bank of the Rhine, the internationalization of the Ruhr. Speaking of colonial territories, de Gaulle summed up his own point of view:

> As for the countries of Asia and Africa, more or less "colonized," in my opinion, the new era will mark their achievement of independence, though the methods will inevitably be different and progressive. The West must understand and even desire this. But matters must be concluded with the West and not against it, otherwise the transformation of still backward people, and states without firm bases, will let loose xenophobia, misery and anarchy, and it is easy to see who will benefit.
>
> We have decided, I told the president, to work toward freedom of choice for the countries dependent on our own. For some, we can progress quickly, but perhaps not for others. France herself must be the only judge. But, in this domain, nothing would be as deplorable as rivalries between the Western powers.

De Gaulle's visit to the United States ended with a triumphal reception in New York, but it would seem that the meetings at the White House were no more productive than those at the Kremlin. Nothing seemed to show that the American government realized the importance to them of a rapid re-establishment of France. This is why it is thanks to de Gaulle and to him alone that the United States had not had to see a people's democracy established on the opposite side of the Atlantic.

⚜

THE GAULLIST CONCEPTION OF
THE WORLD

After his visits to Moscow and Washington, de Gaulle was convinced that a conflict between the United States and Russia was inevitable. He expected it would break out at the end of 1947. One of the reasons for his resignation in January, 1946, was that he felt ordained to take charge of France's destiny again on the outbreak of hostilities.

After a period of silence, de Gaulle launched the R.P.F., the *Rassemblement du Peuple Français*, on April 7, 1947, and detailed his views on foreign policy. Basing his conclusions on the assumption that an attack would be launched by Stalin, he endeavored to mobilized his countrymen on July 27: "Two thirds of the continent are dominated by Moscow. Things being as they are, in other words, very alarming."

On February 17, 1948, Malraux, addressing the militant elements of the R.P.F., gave the end of the month as the date for the Soviet attack. In Marseilles, on April 18, de Gaulle said: "We can feel the burning wind which we know so well, and which precedes the threatening storm."

The General's thinking was wrong, but he had every reason for alarm. 1947 saw the creation of the Cominform and the great show trials in the people's democracies. 1948 was the year of the bolshevization of the Eastern European countries, the blockade of Berlin, strained relations between the Allies and the U.S.S.R. in Germany, and the break between Tito and Stalin. The Iron Curtain came down between East and West. Stalin had military forces of exceptional size available (260 divisions), and in reply, the United States launched the Marshall Plan. Tension was at its height. It increased for five years and only ended with Stalin's eclipse on March 5, 1953.

Information that we now possess would seem to show that the

Red Tsar's intentions were indeed aggressive and that only circumstances, including the running sore of the Korean War (1950–1953) and the decision of the Soviet council to shake off Stalin's yoke, prevented the outbreak of World War III.

During this period of the Cold War, de Gaulle gave repeated warnings to the Americans: "The vital decision will be taken in Europe."

"The storm is approaching. The war in Korea is only a forerunner."

"Americans, defend Europe!"

To be fair, after the success of the R.P.F. at the municipal elections in October, 1947 (40 percent of the electorate), the political strategy of Washington altered toward de Gaulle. The father of the anticommunist crusade in the United States, William Bullitt, a former personal friend of Marshal Pétain, now military adviser to President Truman, along with Admiral Leahy—both violent opponents of de Gaulle—changed their tune: "De Gaulle is our man," they said, as they had said of Pétain. They saw the General as the champion of anticommunism in Western Europe and persuaded Truman to support him, though still considering him a dangerous man. A confidential report from George Kennan, at that time adviser to Secretary of State Marshall, is eloquent on the subject:

> In France, the powerful communist party is seeking every opportunity to reinforce its power. It in trying to scupper the plans for European reconstruction, because they hope this failure will diminish American prestige. France, the heart of Western Europe, stands at the crossroads.
>
> Charles de Gaulle has adopted an anticommunist attitude, but his openly totalitarian ideas have alienated the labor element, whether communist or not. As a result, his

only devoted followers are members of the discredited parties of the right, and his chances of returning to power will be slight as long as the present régime lasts.

By indirect means, including those of the C.I.A., the R.P.F. was supported in its anticommunist struggle until 1953, with a slight progression from 1948 to 1951, and a regression between 1951 and 1953. If he had been dependent only on Washington, de Gaulle as an anticommunist scarecrow would have been dropped at the end of 1953.

The Americans were afraid that the Gaullist foreign policy was entirely dominated by the resentment the General still felt toward Roosevelt and his collaborators Bullitt, Leahy, and Murphy, and their coolness to him during the war. This conclusion is right, but too narrow and too simplified. De Gaulle considered that France should be mistress of her own fate and the United States should not meddle in European politics. General Marshall himself, for the *Encyclopaedia Britannica,* drew up the losses suffered during World War II: 200,000 French, 280,-000 American. If civilian casualties are added to these figures, the balance is definitely heavier on the French side. What gave America the right to claim the domination of Europe? The General was extremely suspicious of American interference in the movement for European unification, particularly because their interventions were co-ordinated by the C.I.A. Between 1947 and 1953, $2,800,000 were paid to the European movement by the American Committee on United Europe (W. Donovan, Chairman).[19]

In 1948 the Congress of Europe was held at The Hague, which regrouped the supporters of European unification at the instigation of Churchill. This unification seemed possible in view of the communist danger and thanks to the support of the Marshall

❧

Plan. Its first move was the creation of the Federal German Republic on June 1, 1948.

It would seem that the "Europeanists" were not altogether aware of the United States' part in this policy of unification. Nonetheless, it is clear that the American objective was to reestablish Germany as a first line defense against the Red Army, and a strong and integrated power in the Western camp; secondly, to support the constitution of a European defense plan in which France would play the part allotted to her by Washington.

These plans being the exact opposite of de Gaulle's, he decided to oppose them. Two generals behind the scenes pulled the strings for and against the European Community of Defense: de Gaulle from Colombey, and Donovan from his office in Wall Street. Both paid regular visits to Paris to keep up the morale of their supporters.

Donovan was the first to score. The president of the French cabinet, René Pleven, a former companion of General de Gaulle, presented the project of a European Army to the French National Assembly on October 24, 1950. The "Europeanists" of all shades of political opinion supported him, but the General's most faithful supporters fought vigorously against the project. Foremost among them were General Billotte, who attacked it in the National Assembly on December 29, 1951,[20] and Gaston Palewski who, on the same day, presented a plan for European confederation, which he considered should precede any attempt to organize a common defense.[21]

In spite of these parliamentary skirmishes, the French government signed the treaty with five other countries, instituting a European Community of Defense of Western Europe.

The General threw the whole force of the R.P.F. into the struggle. He himself took sides against this "antipatriotic machinery . . . this hybrid creation . . . where France finds herself hurled in alongside a defeated Germany and Italy . . . this protocol of surrender." He emphasized that the C.E.D. would inevitably lead to a "special alliance between the United States and Germany" and to the "resurrection of the Germany Army without any guarantee for us." In fact, the Europe of this community was only a word; it was merely a question of creating a hybrid army under American command.

The next presidents of the council, René Mayer and Joseph Laniel, did not dare submit the treaty to the French parliament for ratification.

Monsieur Michel Debré headed the Gaullist opposition. This senator, dark and lively, outstandingly intelligent, was always ready to fling himself into the breach. He possessed the broad flat forehead of a Pole, as well as their fanaticism, French national passion, and sense of individuality. Enthusiastic and argumentative, by turns violent and pettifogging, he criticized the party system and fought for de Gaulle's return to power. He conspired too, with a keen sense of efficiency, promising the guillotine to any colleagues who hesitated, and total subjugation to America to his countrymen.

At the Palais Bourbon, Jacques Soustelle, secretary-general of the R.P.F., played the same rôle. His was a fine intelligence placed at the service of Machiavellian plans. De Gaulle has always been slightly suspicious of him. This dyed-in-the-wool Gaullist was no companion of the Liberation. Sure of his own strength, he is both powerful and secretive. Coming from the intellectuals of the left, he nourishes ambitious plans, which he barely conceals. He graduated at the top of the Ecole Normale Supérieure at seventeen, made first-class honors in philosophy at twenty, was vice-director of the Musée de l'homme at twenty-five. He is too much accustomed to playing a leading part not to join any movement that will carry him to the fore. In London,

❧

de Gaulle had entrusted him with the direction of the secret service (B.C.R.A.), but afterward seemed to lose confidence in him and gave him only minor offices in 1946: minister for information, minister for the colonies. Soustelle imitates the General in every way: speaking, walking, tone of voice, even his way of eating and behaving.[22]

Soustelle and Debré joined forces to combat the régime. Soustelle complained later that de Gaulle only tried to establish his place in history by refusing to accept any other French policy, but the General said of Debré: "We have no problems, for he has no ambitions." [18]

In 1952, the two Gaullist leaders were both forty, and at the height of their powers. They fought with contagious enthusiasm. Debré overthrew the governments of Mayer and Laniel, Soustelle brought down Bourges-Maunoury and Gaillard. The concerted efforts of the Gaullists brought the C.E.D. to an end on August 30, 1954, by 319 votes to 264.[23] All the same, de Gaulle felt it important to record that his opposition to the C.E.D. was not aimed at the principle of the unification of Europe.

In 1949, Michel Debré had elaborated a plan for European political union limiting the common domain of the union to defense, economic and social affairs, and justice. According to this plan, only the foreign policy of members would be co-ordinated. This was merely a preliminary sketch. On January 6, 1953, after consultations with de Gaulle, Debré presented a new proposal to the National Assembly. This time it was a suggestion for a confederation of states, whose workings could be summed up under a few main headings:

1. A policy council fixing the policy common to the majority.
2. A parliamentary assembly, a body for control and appeal.
3. A consultative council and a legal council.[24]

This plan had no success whatever, and together with the plan for a community policy adopted at The Hague by the Conference of Foreign Ministers on November 28, 1953, was duly buried.

THE UNITED STATES OF EUROPE

When he returned to power in 1958, as far as European politics were concerned, de Gaulle was faced with a clean slate. He divided up the responsibilities: "The assemblies debate, the ministers govern, the constitutional council thinks, the president of the republic decides."

The president of the National Assembly, J. Chaban-Delmas, added that there was a *"domaine reservé"* (private preserve) belonging to the president of the republic: Algeria, without forgetting the Sahara, the Franco-African community, foreign affairs, defense.

During his first seven years, with the help of the Debré government, de Gaulle directed the "private preserve" assisted by a handful of collaborators—the prime minister himself being one of them—together with Georges Pompidou, René Brouillet, Olivier Guichard, at different times.

In 1959, Jacques Foccart was in charge of African affairs, after having been the General's secretary at the Elysée during the last quarter of 1958. A business man working in exports, he had the reputation of being very secretive and operating behind the scenes. All secret-service reports passed through his hands before they reached the General. He was succeeded at the Elysée by Geoffroy de Courcel, who in turn was succeeded by Etienne Burin des Roziers.

As for the men who provided the link with the army, a special place was kept for Admiral Cabanier who, in June, 1940, had brought the Free French naval forces their first submarine and

❧

had been created director of the Ecole Navale by de Gaulle in 1945. In 1958, he was appointed head of the National Defense. Bernard Tricot was the technical adviser for Algerian affairs, and his good sense, as much as his enormous capacity for work, meant that he found himself responsible for all questions concerning the army, its disaffected elements, its rebels, and its hostile adversaries. Appointed later to the secretariat-general of the Ministry of Defense, he returned to the Elysée in 1967 to succeed Burin des Roziers.

Among the General's advisers, Maurice Couve de Murville holds an important position. When he is mentioned, his friends refer to Talleyrand, his enemies evoke Ribbentrop. In a word, he is the ideal counsellor-diplomat of his chosen master. With Talleyrand, he has a sense of continuity: he has been minister for foreign affairs in all the governments of the Fifth Republic. It is true that he has few accounts to render to the prime minister, since he works directly with the president of the republic. This brilliant inspector of finances, slow and even-tempered, has always known how to shift gears at the right moment. In 1942 he married the daughter of one of Ernest Mercier's friends and was able to protect himself at Vichy. Director of the Ministry of Finance, he was able to safeguard French interests at the Armistice Commission at Wiesbaden, then left Vichy in time, in March, 1943, provided with genuine authorizations. Via Spain, he reached Algiers, where he became secretary-general of High Commissioner Giraud. At the height of the de Gaulle–Giraud dispute, he chose to align himself with de Gaulle, and helped to tip the balance in his favor.[25] Appointed ambassador to Rome in 1945, he remained outside the quarrels of the Liberation, but was exiled by the Fourth Republic from 1950 to 1954 as ambassador to Cairo. Having served as ambassador at Washington (1955), then at Bonn (1956), he spent the next ten years reorganizing the Quai d'Orsay, like Talleyrand.

Unlike his illustrious predecessor, he has neither cunning nor the capacity to enjoy life. Couve de Murville is a melancholy man, and a teetotaler, but he prefers to follow his famous leader rather than to formulate France's foreign policy himself. In that respect he resembles Ribbentrop, whose great quality was to have the same ideas as his master a few moments before. Through his agents, he increases the pressure, or applies the brake, in matters of European union. Through the diplomatic advisers at the Elysée, he reminds the General of the necessary instructions to be telegraphed to the ambassadors. It must not be concluded from all this that M. Couve de Murville is merely "his master's voice," as Nora Beloff has said.[26] The minister behaves toward the General as Rommel did to Hitler: an over-all brief, an objective to be achieved by his own chosen means, a final report. In the European negotiations in Brussels, it was clear that M. Couve de Murville had a wider lattitude for discussion, acceptance, or refusal than his foreign colleagues.

In this to say that the General only clarifies his feelings in matters of diplomacy according to the reports of his minister for foreign affairs? Certainly not. De Gaulle asks his special advisers to give him their advice on special points. Alain Peyrefitte[27] was one of these before becoming a minister himself, as were Christain de la Malene, and Maurice-Schumann, former spokesman for the BBC, who has sometimes served as the General's special envoy, notably to President Johnson.

This direct control established by the General over the diplomatic corps is explained by his distrust of the personnel of the Quai d'Orsay ever since 1945: "The personnel of our diplomatic corps only faintly conformed to my own attitude. For many of the men who were in charge of foreign relations, agreement with Great Britain was a kind of principle. . . . Between the impetus I wanted to give, and the behavior of these men who exchanged notes, established contacts, inspired communiqués, the gap was

❦

too wide for our partners to ignore, which diminished the effect of my own firmness."

De Gaulle prefers to see Couve de Murville at the Elysée each week, receiving him with a joke: "Come along, no long faces— you're not at the office now." Together, they plan the foreign policy which the minister will then implement.

The General's list of signed agreements include the Treaty of Paris in 1951, the creation of the European Community of Coal and Steel and the Treaties of Rome in 1957, which set up a European Economic Community and a European Community of Atomic Energy. His first move was to explode the myth of communist thinking: supranationality is a meaningless word. It is an end without defining the means: integration is a completely unacceptable dissolution of nations.

Confusion reigned supreme on all levels of these first European constructions. There was no question of Europe, but of six countries; no real Common Market, merely a customs union; no executive body, but a reunion of experts; no European parliament, but a collection of parliaments devoid of power.[28]

These somewhat obscure pronouncements show a muddled and confused conception, and during his first seven-year term of office, de Gaulle made a remarkable effort at clarification.

Let us emphasize immediately that, since 1941, de Gaulle has favored the setting up of a European union. Detailed examination and comparison of the General's writings, covering the years from 1906 to the end of 1965, show it without any doubt.[28] All the same, this European union cannot be an end in itself. Europe must constitute a third force between the U.S.S.R. and the U.S.A., and according to their comparative strength, she will ally herself with the weaker side.

France cannot abdicate her own sovereignty, therefore there cannot be a federal Europe, supranational or integrated, any more than there can be an Atlantic Europe or a Vaticanate

Europe. Europe should be a confederation of sovereign states, co-operating on a technical level without renouncing their rights to diplomatic initiative.[28] As a result of these clear ideas, several decisions and projects were put in hand.

Because of de Gaulle, since December, 1959, the high authority of the European Community of Coal and Steel can no longer resolve crises on its own authority; since November, 1960, the European Economic Community is only recognized by France as an "international legal personality": since December, 1961, Euratom knows that France will always be opposed to an integration of the French atomic effort in a European program: since January, 1966, majority rule no longer maintains between the member states of the communities.[28] So much for the negative side.

Conversely, France has definitely opted for the acceleration of the reduction of customs tariffs between member states. On several occasions, France has taken the lead in such measures as well as in matters of the common agricultural policy. Finally, on April 8, 1965, the "fusion of executives" was agreed to, thanks to the decisive action taken by the French representatives.

It must also be noted that it was the Fifth Republic's stabilization plans which enable France to carry out the terms of the Treaty of Rome. The Fourth Republic would not have been in a position to do so. Among the projects launched by de Gaulle, we must also include the Fouchet proposals and the Franco–German treaty.

Between 1959 and February, 1962, General de Gaulle and Chancellor Adenauer met on nine occasions. Their talks at Rambouillet on July 29 and 30, 1960, were particularly important. The cordiality of the relations between the two men facilitated the discussions, although it seems that the chancellor must have listened more than he actually spoke. More phlegmatic and slower, but more objective than his interlocutor, Adenauer admired de Gaulle, who had several lively exchanges with him: *"Monsieur*

✤

le Chancelier," said de Gaulle, "America is a long way away. France and Germany are neighbors."

"Oh! *Monsieur le Président,* how can one mention distances in the jet age?"

"More than the distance between states, what counts is the difference in civilization."

"So many Germans have emigrated to America that one can almost declare that American civilization is essentially Germanic."

"Ah, *le voilà bien, Monsiuer le Chancelier,* the famous German imperialism."

To his colleagues, the General confides: "The chancellor is the only man in the world who has succeeded in combining political skill with the intellectual honesty!" [18]

During the Rambouillet meetings, de Gaulle presented a plan for the political organization of Europe. It envisaged a confederation, whose heads of state would meet every three months to make major decisions. The key ministers of foreign affairs, finance, economy, and national defense would meet once a month. The decisions taken would be implemented by permanent commissions. During a secondary stage, a European parliament of two houses would be formed, consisting of a lower house, elected by universal suffrage, and a senate, elected by the national parliaments. The entire project would be submitted to the people of Europe by referendum. Existing communities would be reformed to enter into the framework of this confederal plan.

At first Adenauer was enthusiastic, but as soon as he returned to Bonn, he came up against those who were not prepared to run the risk of a reform of communities, or of NATO: this was a first barrier of suspicion and bureaucracy.

During a holiday in Italy, the chancellor consulted with the directors in Rome. MM. Debré and Couve de Murville went to Bonn on October 7, 1960, to reassure Dr. Adenauer as to the French intentions. On February 10, 1961, a summit conference in Paris brought together the heads of state or of government of six countries with a view to encouraging a political union of Europe. A study commission was set up, under the presidency of M. Christian Fouchet, French ambassador to Denmark.

This diplomat is a faithful supporter of the General. Built like a drum major, but subtle and friendly in manner, he is a born follower. In 1940, at twenty-nine, he left a diplomatic career to join de Gaulle in London. He carried out various confidential missions to Colonel Leclerc in Fezzan, to General Juin in Italy, to the Lublin Committee, before resuming his career at the Quai d'Orsay. In 1947, he resigned to join the R.P.F., and headed its Paris office. Elected deputy in 1951, he was a minister in Mendès-France's government before joining in the plot of May 13, 1958, which took him back to his diplomatic career. De Gaulle considers he is a grumbler who sulks occasionally, but remains unswervingly faithful. Nevertheless, he sees that he is kept in his place.

"Fouchet tells everyone he spends his entire time with me: they must think de Gaulle has nothing to do!" [18]

A new summit conference was held at Bad Godesberg on July 18, 1961, and set up a study commission, again headed by Ambassador Fouchet, to prepare proposals for a political union.[29] Smoothing out angles, they dropped the referendum idea, and the meetings of defense ministers, so as not to get involved with NATO, or with a reform of the existing communities.

This commission met on September 5 and ended its discussions on November 3. It put forward a project suggesting a permanent political commission sitting in Paris, with responsibility to prepare common ministerial decisions on matters of external policies, defense, and culture. The heads of states or governments would meet periodically, and a single European parliamentary assembly would debate the work of the political commission and the three existing communities. All decisions would require a unanimous vote, but the dissension of a single state need not prevent its application in the remaining five.

De Gaulle considered these proposals a long way behind his own. On January 18, 1962, the French delegation, on his instructions, put forward counterproposals which were more "confederal": all matters of defense and economy would be under the jurisdiction of the political commission, which would subtract from the real (or potential) powers of NATO and the European Economic Community.

The General would not admit defeat. He wooed Dr. Adenauer again at Baden-Baden on February 14. On April 4, he lobbied the Italian president, Signor Fanfani, in Turin, and he, in turn, conferred with the German chancellor on the 7th at Cadenabbia. The Italians offered a compromise: there would be no mention of NATO or the existing communities. On April 17, 1962, the ministers for foreign affairs met again in Paris at the Quai d'Orsay. In the course of that debate, the plans for a political union were finally buried—at least for a generation. The Italians were not even able to put forward their compromise plan.

M. Luns, the Dutch foreign minister, was particularly un-cooperative: he insisted on express reference being made to NATO, and that Britain should be admitted as a member state. M. Spaak, his Belgian colleague, declared on July 10, 1959: "A Europe made up of countries[30] is a narrow, outdated idea. . . . Europe must be supranational, or it ceases to exist." He still held this position on April 17, 1962. The two ministers stated clearly that "a European political union has no meaning unless it anticipates its own evolution into a political federation of Europe. If the French will not accept this, better to wait for Britain's entry into the Common Market."

M. Couve de Murville endeavored to save the project by

proposing that the plan for political union should also be submitted to Great Britain, but MM. Spaak and Luns rejected this
suggestion categorically.

The two positions were, therefore, very clear: MM. Spaak and
Luns did not want a European confederation, but would welcome
the entry of Great Britain into the Common Market. De Gaulle
didn't want a European federation, but didn't want Great Britain
as a conditional member of the Common Market.

M. Couve de Murville's suggestion was a good one, for he was
certain that Britain would be against the federal idea: like de
Gaulle, the British would never agree to a confederation. But MM.
Spaak's and Luns' position was so contradictory that it can only
be concluded that neither of them was really in favor of a European union but were merely against General de Gaulle and his
policy. They were afraid the General might become head of the
European political union, and would make use of this to foster
French interests with America.

What is surprising is the lack of long-term views of these two
Benelux ministers. The issue was clouded by the General's strong
personality, but he isn't immortal, and it is possible to imagine
that after he has left the scene his successor might be persuaded
to take a step toward the European federation proposed by the
ministers. By then, the dominating personality in Europe might
even be a Belgian or Dutch statesman.

Less limited in his views than M. Luns, M. Spaak, dominating
his personal dislike of the General, endeavored to reopen negotiations. On July 17 and 18, he called a secret meeting of a small
group of European personalities, including, notably, the opponents
of the General's policy, and endeavored to work out a compromise which he submitted to M. Luns on the 24th. The latter
opposed it categorically. On the 25th, he sounded out M. Couve
de Murville, and on the 26th, Dr. Adenauer. He then wrote to
de Gaulle to ask for a reopening of negotiations without the

preliminary provisos of the entry of Great Britain into the Common Market and the political federation. He made no mention of M. Luns' opposition. De Gaulle replied courteously, but without taking further action.

In fact, the Dutch had definitely turned their backs on the European construction, considering that there should be no confederal step on the road to a European federation. This unilateral decision blocked French and Britain participation in the political construction of Europe for an indefinite time.

At the end of 1964, M. Spaak tried to soften M. Luns' opposition. As a new approach, Chancellor Erhard suggested a consultative committee, and the Italian government invited its partners to form a political commission to prepare new suggestions, but none of these vague plans came to anything. The "Europeanists" who opposed General de Gaulle's proposals had no other concrete proposition to make.

Since the setback of April 17, 1962, the General has been totally disillusioned, and has speeded up the signing of a Franco–German treaty requested by Germany. This was concluded on January 22, 1963, and set out the means of closer co-operation between the two countries, very close to those de Gaulle had suggested for the European confederation.[31]

But Erhard isn't Adenauer. He travels much too frequently to Washington, which the General does not approve. He said as much to the new chancellor during one of his visits to Paris.

"Come and see us often, we will always be glad to see a friend of Dr. Adenauer," adding, aside: "He'd have his feet dyed green if Washington asked him." [18]

The Franco–German treaty of co-operation was both a substitute for the European political union and a framework which could be extended to include the European confederation initially envisaged. Its operation has so far not achieved any outstanding results, but it can only be judged on a long-term basis.

THE DECOLONIZATION

De Gaulle's first task, even before he could tackle the main international question, was to put an end to the Algerian war. But just as he used the Treaties of Paris and Rome in constructing his European policy, he wished to include the pacification of Algeria in an over-all plan. He had had no experience of the colonies, apart from a brief spell in the Near East, and his African service had been entirely limited to World War II. His ideas are well known. He had stated them in October, 1944: "French policy consists of bringing each of the colonial peoples to a state of development where they can administer themselves, and later, become self-governing."

But in August, 1945, he said to Truman: "We have decided to advocate the free self-government for countries that are dependent on us. With some, we can go ahead quickly, with others no: the decision rests with France."

At the time of the R.P.F., the General made long trips to the French colonies of Central Africa (1953), the Antilles and Oceania (1956), and North Africa (1957). He returned with the conviction that the process of decolonizing must be speeded up, both because the United States and the Soviet Union were trying to make everything into an international problem, and because the governments of the Fourth Republic had allowed the French position to deteriorate to an untenable degree.

On July 20, 1954, Pierre Mendès-France ended the war in Indochina by signing the Geneva agreements. On June 3, 1955, he granted self-government to Tunisia, and on March 2, 1956, France recognized the independence of Morocco. All three stages were approved by General de Gaulle: Christian Fouchet and Marshal Juin even accompanied Mendès-France to Tunis and the former was, in fact, representing the General.

On October 13, 1954, de Gaulle saw Mendès-France at the

✣

Hotel Lapérouse. The talks lasted for an hour and were on a very high level. Both men have a total grasp of affairs, devoid of all pettiness, all demagogy. They know themselves to be eleventh-hour men, for they stand head and shoulders above their colleagues. But Mendès-France always holds back slightly. The day he took office, on June 18, 1954, while de Gaulle was making his annual visit to Mont Valérien alone, Mendès-France sent the following telegram to Colombey:

ON THIS ANNIVERSARY, WHICH IS ALSO THE DAY I ASSUME SUCH HEAVY RESPONSIBILITIES, I REMEMBER THE GREAT LESSONS OF PATRIOTISM AND DEVOTION TO THE PUBLIC WHICH, THROUGH YOUR CONFIDENCE IN ME, I HAVE RECEIVED FROM YOU.

The night before their meeting, he told Michelet, the General's envoy: "I never forget I was a soldier under his orders. It's for me to go to him."

De Gaulle and Mendès-France exchanged confidences which have not been published, but as the General was saying good-bye to his visitor, he was heard to say to Mendès-France: "You'll see, they won't let you go on to the end. The executive is not sufficiently separated from the legislative. Personally, you stand outside the rule of the Assembly, but men change, and if, after you, the institutions remain. . . ."[32] Did the General think Mendès-France would be in favor of his return? Did the prime minister think he could save the assembly system by his personal authority? The sequence of events showed that both men cherished illusions, but both were too proud, too self-contained to discuss these matters. Their intentions were straightforward, disinterested, and they could afford to disregard critics.

If the conversation has not been reported, the General must have been thinking: the Constitution first; and the prime minister must have thought: economic and social programs first. But the French will never know what a Mendès-France government would have been like under a de Gaulle presidency: a combination of the two most brillitant postwar French statesmen.

Once again, de Gaulle's foresight proved correct: "They won't let you go on to the end." A European trap was laid in Brussels on August 19 by Spaak, who attacked Mendès-France, and in Paris, on February 5, 1955, a parliamentary trick overthrew his government.

To return to 1958 and General de Gaulle's grand tour of Africa from August 20 to 27: he offered to all the African countries of the French union the choice between joining the French community and secession. His intention was to create a framework for a confederation within which each country, including Algeria, would be able to become self-governing. The right to total independence was reserved, and each country could leave the community whenever it wished, but a transition period would give everyone a chance to become accustomed to this new independence. The offer was clear, and very well received, every country choosing the community solution with the exception of Guinea. This came about through a misunderstanding, Sekou Touré not being correctly informed of the General's proposals.[33]

Application was more difficult. France had proposed, in fact, a federal solution, for she wished to remain mistress of her own fate, and offered the other countries of the community a language, a flag, a foreign policy and a diplomatic service, an army and a common defense force. The nationalist leaders reacted unpredictably, and it became difficult to delay the anticipated independence. After various modifications, de Gaulle preferred to scrap the community formula and sign agreements with each of the fifteen states concerned, recognizing their independence and offering French co-operation.

Between September 28, 1958 and October 18, 1960, fifteen states became independent, thus ending the French African empire south of the Sahara. The method was empiric, but the results have been encouraging. The wars of independence in Kenya, the Belgian Congo, and Algeria were avoided, and peace has been maintained in all these territories.

In Algeria conditions were very different.

On May 13, 1958, France was in a difficult situation. Algerian affairs[34] had assumed international importance, since the United States had openly taken a hand in French North Africa; it was no longer possible to offer special status to Algeria and to grant French citizenship progressively to the Moslem population, following the example of the Roman laws in the matter of civil rights. An attempt by Guy Mollet's government to destroy the main supply sources of the Algerian revolution in the United Arab Republic had been stopped short by John Foster Dulles during the Suez war. From then on, the decolonization process became irreversible.

General de Gaulle was ready to grant independence to Algeria as early as 1958, but his action was checked by two French groups: the European population of Algeria, which expected a kind of revival, and the French Army, which believed in a hypothetical victory over the rebellion and turned against the government in Paris when its actions were prevented.

By the referendum of September 28, 1958, 80 per cent of the French population had said yes to de Gaulle. But the yes was by no means clear. Just as the majority of Americans who voted for Eisenhower in 1952 did so hoping to win a victory in Korea and speed up the return of "our boys back home," France trusted de Gaulle in 1958 to maintain Algeria as part of France and grant the Moslems the independence they wanted.[35] This twofold wish was a contradiction, and the miracle-working General was expected to provide the answer.

On October 23, 1958, de Gaulle offered the rebels "the peace of the brave," but the provisional government of the Algerian Revolution (G.P.R.A.), set up in Cairo, demanded a settlement on neutral territory. De Gaulle considered that the conditions for successful talks had not been met and broke off negotiations for two years.

The so-called "Constantine Plan," launched by the General, envisaged a program of modernization in Algeria. After a year of efforts, he thought himself strong enough by September 16, 1959, to make a fresh offer of peace based on "self-determination." The G.P.R.A. accepted the proposal but asked that France should hold the discussions with the nationalist leaders she was holding in her prisons, Ben Bella and his companions. In the meantime, on January 24, 1960, a group of extremists, supported by a group of colonels in the French Army, staged a rising in Algiers to stop the negotiations.

De Gaulle was surprised and disconcerted. Robert Buron, one of his ministers, noted: "At the councils of Monday and Wednesday, I thought he looked upset, profoundly disturbed. He had not expected this to happen, it was totally unexpected. He had been confident, if not in the army, at least in his authority over it; it took him several days to recover his usual control and his normal attitude." [36]

The rising was crushed, and marked the first defeat of the extremists, but it also put an end to the Constantine Plan. Soundings continued; secretly at the Elysée on June 10, 1960, with an Algerian military delegation, and on June 25 at Melun with representatives of the G.P.R.A., but no progress was made.

The General decided to take another step forward: to recognize internal autonomy, and on January 8, 1961, he submitted this policy for the approval of the French people. Of his compatriots, 75 percent agreed with him, but a terrorist organization was created by the extremists, the O.A.S. (*Organisation Armée Secrète*), to block the decolonization. Between December, 1960, and May 25, 1965, this organization made ten attempts on the

⚜

General's life, but only the attack at Petit-Clamart (August 22, 1962) came anywhere near succeeding.[37]

The way to peace was opened by secret negotiations in Switzerland in January and February, 1961. On March 15, official negotiations were opened in a joint communiqué issued by the French Government and the G.P.R.A., but a group of generals seized power in Algiers on April 21 and tried to stop the talks. Through a touching appeal to the nation, de Gaulle succeeded in mastering the rebellion.

The Evian conferences (May, 1961 to February, 1962) finally paved the way for peace, approved on April 8, 1962 by 90 percent of the French. On March 19, 1962, the cease fire was everywhere proclaimed, and Algeria became independent. With the ending of the protectorates in Tunis and Morocco, France had given freedom to eighteen African nations.

It had taken four years to end the war in Algeria. The General's opponents can imply that "it should have been possible to deal with the matter more quickly, in better terms, and take better care of the transition and the future, that 'boldness' (perhaps) was lacking in the conception, and vigor in the execution." [38] But in fact, General de Gaulle's policy of decolonization managed to avoid serious conflict. In Algeria there was more fluctuation, but the General found himself involved in an open conflict between two ethnic groups, and managed to free himself by avoiding civil war in France, which had been threatened by a group of extremists, supported by a section of the army.[39] The French population of Algeria and Black Africa has borne the cost of this policy, but there again, de Gaulle, by allowing time to do its work, has managed to wipe out the worst of the crying injustices. To his ministers who spoke of the urgency of the problem of resettling the French from Algeria in France, de Gaulle replied: "It is like a good stew—you must leave it to simmer." [18]

And indeed, after three years of patient efforts, and some moving episodes, two million repatriates from overseas possessions have been assimilated and reintegrated socially and economically into metropolitan France. This favorable balance must undoubtedly be credited to the government of General de Gaulle.

NATO OR THE AMERICAN ALLIANCE

When General de Gaulle drew his own conclusions from the history of the Algerian war in 1962, it is certain that he received a clear impression that the terms of the North Atlantic Treaty had not, could not, and would never operate, except on a one-way basis, *i.e.*, to the benefit of the United States. At no stage in the process of settling the North African problems, or during the Suez crisis, was there any question of France being supported, rightly or wrongly, by her allies.

"In Algeria, we are defending the West," said Michel Debré in October, 1960. "By fighting in Algeria we are faithful to the spirit of NATO, and the other Atlantic powers should, accordingly, give us their support."

In de Gaulle's view, NATO should be binding on all its signatories, and the treaty, which he did not approve in the first instance, was signed by the Fourth Republic on April 4, 1949. According to Article 3, its members "separately and jointly, by means of continuous and effective self-help and mutual aid, will maintain and develop their individual and collective capacity to resist armed attack." Article 4 states: "The parties will consult together whenever, in the opinion of any of them, the territorial integrity, political independence or security of any of the parties is threatened." Article 6 specifies that the territory shall be "in Europe or North America, the Algerian departments of France," and the treaty was to be binding until 1969.

❧

In 1958, when he was sorting out the commitments and obligations undertaken by France, General de Gaulle took particular interest in NATO. He noted that, during the Suez crisis, not only did the United States not come out in support of France and the United Kingdom, but they joined with the Soviet Union in a majority vote at the U.N. condemning their allies.

Without denigrating the first results achieved by NATO in 1949—the raising of the blockade of Berlin and the consequent transfer of communist forces to Korea—he considered that any new moves in Western defense policy should be made within a global strategy defined by the Great Powers, and that ten years after its signature, the conditions of NATO were largely out of date.

In 1958, the armed forces of NATO had more than doubled, while its total cost had quadrupled. Against the 6 millions of the Soviet Union and other Socialist countries, the West could muster a defensive force of 8 million men. The share of the cost to the European members represented one quarter of the amounts contributed by Canada and the United States. The percentage per head of population in relation to the national productivity was higher for Europe, especially for France. General de Gaulle tabled his views on the Atlantic Alliance during talks he had with Harold Macmillan in Paris on June 29 and 30, 1958, and with John Foster Dulles on July 4 and 5 of the same year. He advocated the reform of NATO, unadapted, according to him, to the situation created by the latest events, among which the overthrow of the Iraqian monarchy and the struggle for Quemoy illustrated the lack of global strategic thinking. He also demanded the right to have France's views considered at the highest strategic level.[40]

On September 24, 1958, he handed a weighty memorandum, together with personal letters, to Eisenhower and Macmillan, summing up these ideas.[41] This unpublished document shows that instead of integrating its forces within NATO, France proposed a formula for co-operation with the two Great Powers. This is of great importance, since it expresses the General's thinking on the eve of his election for his first seven-year term of office (with 80 percent of the votes), whereas Eisenhower was due to retire in two years' time and, in 1963, Macmillan had to resign because of ill health. The General's ideas were as follows:

1. The World Powers should co-ordinate their policies on a global scale.

2. The use of the nuclear deterrent should be subject to common decision.

3. The zone not covered by NATO should be divided into distinct theaters of operation, clearly defined and apportioned.

France would not lend her support on a wider scale unless these three propositions were accepted.

Mr. Foster Dulles having hinted that Bonn and Rome might not be in agreement, de Gaulle sent M. Couve de Murville to visit the two capitals. He had himself taken care to invite Chancellor Adenauer to Colombey to explain his intentions, and it seems that de Gaulle did not meet with the objections in that quarter foreseen by the American secretary of state. The only discordant note was struck by the secretary general of NATO, M. Spaak, on July 10, 1959: "The creation of a three-handed directorate would seriously displease the less important countries, and strengthen the neutralist current, always present in Europe."

It is possible that M. Spaak was expressing the Washington point of view, but his advice was traditional: it referred to the rights of equality of the Small Powers, the same which had caused the breakdown of the League of Nations and which the Great Powers, since Yalta, had been careful to reject. It is true that the Belgian politician had far-reaching personal ambitions, notably in the direction of the European union.[42] But he, too, went out of office on January 25, 1961, and de Gaulle took no notice of his advice. He said to his ministers: "I shall sit him out." [18]

On September 20, 1958, Eisenhower had sent an evasive answer to the General's personal letter which accompanied the memorandum of September 24, 1958. (The tenor of this evasive answer was published in an *aide-mémoire* to Dean Rusk in August, 1966.) Dulles was sent to Paris on November 15, 1958, to meet de Gaulle. The American secretary of state announced the creation of a committee of three charged to examine (without applying) de Gaulle's proposals; among them was an old opponent of the General, Robert Murphy. Considering this a provocative move, the General on February 7, 1959, withdrew his Mediterranean fleet from NATO control and wrote secretly to Eisenhower to advise him to stand firm in Berlin. At the end of March, 1959, Eisenhower replied: "Co-operation, but within the framework of NATO." Faced with this disguised but repeated rejection of his proposals, de Gaulle reacted publicly on March 25, 1959, by announcing that France had recognized the Oder-Neisser frontier. The seesaw policy began. This maneuver was cut short in August when Moscow and Washington announced that Khrushchev of the Soviet Union and Eisenhower of the United States would exchange visits in the near future. This announcement was received very badly in the Western countries, and Eisenhower had to come to Europe to reassure London, Paris, Bonn, and Rome as to his intentions: there would be no new Yalta.

His first visit was to de Gaulle, at Rambouillet, on September 2 and 3, 1959. The talks were cordial, the relations between the two men having always been very friendly. Both were activated by the same motives and shared a military viewpoint. Eisenhower was essentially conciliatory, and de Gaulle knew that he had softened many difficulties between himself, Roosevelt, and Truman. Ever since Eisenhower's return to power, the two men had

exchanged an important confidential correspondence, maintaining
the friendly tone of "wartime comrades." The two men liked
each other very much. During the war, Eisenhower had been
able to deal with de Gaulle's difficult character, and had made
no capital out of the rivalries between the supporters of the two
generals, de Gaulle and Giraud.

Eisenhower complained of the difficulties of government in
modern times. De Gaulle replied jokingly: "Ah, you play golf.
. . . Do as I do . . . use a prime minister!" [43]

But in spite of these friendly discussions, in spite of the General's worldwide perspectives, Eisenhower would not agree to a
three-handed directory.

In 1956, Ike had said to Dulles: "Listen, Foster, our own hope
in Europe is the return of de Gaulle. He's the only man capable
of saving his country."

Dulles had replied: "Yes, I agree with you, Mr. President, but
don't forget, if we do bring him back, it's you who'll have to deal
with him."

Eisenhower told de Gaulle: "Listen, I'll do anything else you
want. I will consult you as you ask. I promise not to move, and
nor will the English, until we have agreed together what we should
do, but we must not publicly proclaim our agreement under the
form of a directorate of the three powers."

The talks took place without witnesses, except for an interpreter.[44] A few days later, General de Gaulle handed over to his
publishers the final corrected proof of volume III of his *Mémoires*.
The manuscript had been typed by his daughter, Elizabeth, and
she had given him the typescript on the airdrome of Oran at the
time of his first visit to Algiers on June 6, 1958, which meant he
had waited a full year before giving the green light to Orengo,
his editor.

Volume III came off the presses on September 25, 1959, three
weeks after Eisenhower's departure. The following phrases of

❧

Chapter V, which sum up the General's thinking, would be hard
to miss:

> It seems that the new era may allow me to set in motion
> the execution of the vast plan I have formed for my coun-
> try. To guarantee the security of Western Europe by en-
> suring that a new Reich can never again threaten her. To
> collaborate with the West and the East, by contracting the
> necessary alliances with one side or the other, without
> ever accepting *any form of dependence*.[45]

The plan would group the Western European countries and
"make this organization one of the three planetary powers and, if
necessary, become the arbiter between the Soviet and Anglo-
Saxon blocks." [45]

These phrases are too full of meaning not to be considered
decisive. Various expressions should be noted: "the new era"
(after September, 1959), no "form of dependence," "the three
planetary powers," "the arbiter." The ambition is great, the design grandiose. It would mean putting an end to France's integration in the Atlantic Alliance. In addition, de Gaulle (or France)
would like to reshape Europe, becoming the arbiter. Great Britain
was included in the Anglo-Saxon camp.

However often Eisenhower insisted that Great Britain was not
tied to the United States (*cf:* Suez), de Gaulle considered that
the Atlantic Alliance, in fact, meant both countries making common cause on a global level.

Once the American president had gone, de Gaulle prepared
fresh attempts to get his plan accepted. On November 2, he
announced to the pupils of the Ecole Militaire that France would
create an independent atomic weapon. On November 10, he told
the press that France would give favorable consideration to
Soviet plans for a summit meeting, and that Khrushchev had
accepted his invitation to come to France on March 15, 1960.[46]

The first French atom bomb was exploded in the Sahara on February 13, 1960. Between March 23 and April 3, Khrushchev was a guest in France, after which de Gaulle paid courtesy visits to Macmillan in London (April 5 to 8) and to Eisenhower in Washington (April 18 to May 3).

On his return to France, June 10, the General resumed his private correspondence with Eisenhower, who left the White House at the end of the year. He repeated his belief in a co-ordinated policy and the opportunities arising from decision taken in common. The American president objected that the proposals for a tripartite committee had been put forward a year earlier. De Gaulle replied by return, proposing the setting up of a three-handed committee in order to set up the plans for global strategy and a proposal for the reform of NATO. Ike wrote a final private letter to de Gaulle, asking him to put forward these proposals in the form of a memorandum. He added that no discussions could take place before that, and afterward a meeting might be useful.[47]

On November 8, 1960, John F. Kennedy was elected president of the United States. During the interim period, from summer 1960 to spring 1961, American policy became incomprehensible. The state department was more or less favorable to the French plans for a settlement in Algeria: the decolonization must proceed, for the policy of keeping Algeria French would throw the Algerian nationalists into the arms of Moscow, which would create a grave danger for NATO. The American army, at least that part of it concerned with the direction of NATO in Paris, sympathized with the anti-Gaullist French generals, who were more "Atlantic" than de Gaulle, but at the same time, in favor of French Algeria. The C.I.A., which pursued its own policy, had links with the French extremists in Algeria. Out of this contradictory policy, which Kennedy brought to a close a year later, grew the generals' coup, which exploded in Algiers on April 22, 1961.

❧

De Gaulle had even more reason to complain of the lack of solidarity in NATO, but Kennedy reacted very quickly, and no sooner was the coup announced than he telegraphed to de Gaulle offering his help. Later, at the time of the events in Bizerte, Kennedy announced: "Everyone forgets the uncertainty of de Gaulle's position. We have no wish to see the extremists take power in France. Despite all his mistakes, the General represents the sole hope of a solution in Algeria." [48]

De Gaulle and Kennedy only met once, from May 31 to June 2, 1961, in Paris. The seduction was complete, mutual and lasting, as between the youngest and oldest heads of state in the West.

Kennedy, despite his youth (only forty-four), was entirely at ease with the seventy-one-year-old General. Even the disaster of the Bay of Pigs on April 17, 1961, had not upset his equanimity. The only question which worried him a little was to know if the General knew of a speech he had made in 1957 in the senate attacking French policy in Algeria, but he added: "I am happy I made that speech before de Gaulle's return to power." [49]

The American president admired the General personally, and told him as much, even reciting passages from his *Mémoires* by heart. He asked about Churchill and Roosevelt. "I always quarreled violently with Churchill," said the General, "but we always understood each other very well. I never quarreled with Roosevelt, but we never understood each other at all." [50]

When the discussions turned to current affairs, the exchange of views was frank and cordial. It was clear that Kennedy did not share the prejudices of his predecessors: he created his own policy himself, and de Gaulle could not hold him responsible for the mistakes made (as far as he and France were concerned) by the American leaders of the last two decades. But while Kennedy admitted that a reform of NATO was desirable, he would not accept the idea of a three-handed directory, any more than had Eisenhower. Kennedy reported his conversations: "as impossible to be more cordial. I couldn't trust any man more than de Gaulle. He has shown himself to be an excellent counsellor, and he would much rather we stated our differences frankly than pretended we were in complete agreement." [50]

In contrast, the American Ambassador Gavin said: "I was surprised by the coldness with which de Gaulle declared that the United States should not meddle with the affairs of Europe."

Nevertheless, President Kennedy did not reveal his own grand design to the man he called "the Captain of the West." He had been laying the foundations during his first term of office: North America and Western Europe, having reached unequaled economic prosperity, should together and by common agreement continue their expansion and maintain their defense.

Rereading with de Gaulle his private correspondence with Eisenhower, Kennedy took a step in the direction desired by the General: the points of tension were Berlin and Laos, therefore, why not establish a three-part military directorate with a view to formulating common plans of action on these two issues? De Gaulle was delighted, but made no move to follow up the suggestions. What he wanted was "public recognition of France's standing as a Great Power within an organization of the three governments." [49]

Conversations were, however, fruitful on the various points under discussion. With regard to Berlin, the General considered that the West could never win a military victory, and Khrushchev must be "dissuaded" from an attack by persuading him that such an act of aggression would inevitably lead to war. With regard to Laos and Southeast Asia, de Gaulle believed in the necessity for neutrality. Speaking of Central Africa, the General stated his firm opposition to the United Nations' actions in the Congo, and the threat to the peace of Europe that would result from the support of a revolutionary government in Angola. Regarding Britain's entry into the Common Market, the General considered she should choose between the preferential tariffs of the Commonwealth and the Common Market, but in either case, she should adhere completely or not at all. On Latin America, the General declared that it should be cosidered as coming within the United States' zone, but that France had cultural links with these countries, which the American president endorsed, adding that he hoped France would play her part in the development of the Latin American continent.[51]

Returning to NATO, de Gaulle stressed that they were discussing an alliance and an organization: an essential alliance, but an out-of-date organization. The Kennedys were acclaimed by the French people, Malraux conducted Jackie round the Jeu de Paume and Malmaison, and the talks ended on a cordial note.

A close and private liaison was kept up between de Gaulle and Kennedy. Several letters were exchanged at moments of crisis: in August, 1961, over Berlin; in 1962, on a three-part action to be taken toward the *Tiers Monde*. Then, on June 19 and December 12, 1962, Kennedy sent Dean Rusk with personal messages for de Gaulle. Unfortunately, de Gaulle took a personal dislike to the secretary of state: "A boxer's mug where you can't tell the smile from the grimace." (*Tr.'s Note: An untranslatable pun: "grimacer un sourire" means to grin. De Gaulle said you couldn't tell the "sourire" from the "grimace."*)

The new United States ambassador, Charles ("Chip") Bohlen, a distinguished Soviet scholar, had no more luck. De Gaulle avoided him systematically, finally inviting him with several other ambassadors to a presidential hunt at Rambouillet. Bearing down on him, he said: "How have you been, my dear ambassador? We haven't seen anything of you lately." [18]

Later, the ambassador was welcomed at the Elysée: "Well, *Monsieur l'Ambassadeur*, how's America?"

⚜

"Fine, *Monsieur le Président*, but we miss you very much."

"As much as that? Well, tell America that General de Gaulle will come to see her as soon as possible."

"Everyone misses you, *Monsieur le Président*."

"What a pity! Tell America to come and see me, I'm always delighted to receive her." [18]

Following these sibylline reports from his representatives, Kennedy decided to install a direct telephone line between the Elysée and the White House, a proposal which de Gaulle greeted joyfully. The two presidents telephoned each other several times, using a single interpreter, William Tyler, assistant secretary of state.

On October 22, 1962, at the time of the Cuban missile crisis, Kennedy sent Dean Acheson to Paris to show the General the photographs taken by a U-2. De Gaulle, hurrying back from Colombey where he was on holiday, received Acheson in his private apartments at the Elysée. He examined the documents with a practiced eye and exclaimed: *"C'est formidable, c'est formidable,"* [18] then he reassured Acheson and through him, President Kennedy: "France is 100 percent behind you." [18]

Apparently this surprised the American president, all the more because at the same time, Bonn and Rome were counseling prudence, which prevented the forces of NATO being put in a state of immediate alert.

After this spectacular *rapprochement*, the positions diverged again. De Gaulle, without wanting to insist on his three-handed directory, spoke of national defense and co-operation, instead of common defense and integration. Kennedy mentioned an Atlantic association, with a leading role for Great Britain.

The break came over Nassau. For several months, Kennedy had been having doubts about de Gaulle. The man he considered, rightly, as one of the greatest military experts of the West, a "strategic visionary," was making moves he considered meaningless and contradictory: the negotiations in Brussels for Britain's entry into the Common Market were dragging (January 29, 1963); the French Atlantic fleet had been withdrawn from NATO (June 21); France refused to sign the Treaty of Moscow on the suspension of nuclear tests (July 29); de Gaulle was advocating the neutrality of Indochina (August 29). Certainly, Kennedy did not see NATO as an end in itself, but he considered it necessary and realized that it was inevitable relationships between states should be difficult.[50]

De Gaulle appreciated the situation. At the time of the Moscow agreements, he received a letter from Kennedy informing him of the *fait accompli*. To his colleagues who asked how he had replied, he said:

"I told Mr. Kennedy that France had always loved America, before and after Christopher Columbus." [18]

When the American president paid a series of friendly visits to Western Europe without going through France, de Gaulle did not give it much importance: Adenauer was about to retire, Macmillan had resigned, Pope John XXIII had just died, Fanfani was about to hand in his resignation.

"It's a journey through a land of shadows," said the General, and when Kennedy, in the course of a speech made in Germany, added various unkind remarks about France, de Gaulle commented briefly: "Nothing but hot air." [18]

In contrast, he followed the president's fight for civil rights with great interest:

"He is the nineteenth president since Lincoln who has tried to end the War of Secession." [18]

In fact, as David Schoenbrun, a keen and well-informed CBS observer noted, there was "a battle of grand designs." The other members of NATO, apart from France, developed the idea of a multilateral nuclear force (M.L.F.), which the Americans supported when they had to give up the manufacture of the Skybolt rockets, ordered by Great Britain.

Harold Macmillan met John F. Kennedy on December 17, 1962, at Nassau to examine the proposal. Both were in agreement that they should not extend the distribution of atomic weapons to all the member countries of NATO. But, in order not to restrict the benefits of this weapon to the two Great Powers, Kennedy and Macmillan agreed to place Polaris rockets at the disposal of NATO, allowing France to use them "if her supreme national interests" were threatened. In addition, the M.L.F. would include units under French command.

When Kennedy returned to Washington, Secretary of Defense McNamara and military circles considered that the president had made too many concessions. On the other hand, de Gaulle felt that the compromise was useless from a military point of view and that it did not end the American monopoly of atomic weapons. He refused the Nassau offer, in the same way as he had refused the suspension of the French Army's nuclear experiments after the signature of the Moscow agreement.

Three French atomic bombs were exploded in the Sahara in 1960: on February 13, April 1, and December 27. Two French rockets were launched from Mammaguir on March 8, 1965, and on November 26, 1965.

General de Gaulle and his French military strategists considered that, at the basis of any strategy, there is a political decision, a kind of gamble which only one man or a restricted group of specialists can make.[52] If the French experts were divided on the decision as to whether there should or should not be a wider distribution of nuclear weapons, all agreed that the Americans should not hold a monopoly either of weapons or the decision to use them. They felt it desirable that Europe, like the United

States, should possess its own nuclear defenses, but in the present state of affairs, and in expectation of the realization of this hope, France must be allowed to participate in such decisions and to make her own nuclear armaments, which she would co-ordinate or not with the Allies.

Not being invited to make decisions on this level, de Gaulle increased his withdrawal, not from the Atlantic Alliance, but from NATO. These decisions became more marked under Kennedy's successor, Lyndon Johnson—the departure from NATO (March 10, 1966) and the ending of the single command.

From mid-1963 onward, President Kennedy had anticipated the crisis. He had eliminated his weaker opponents: notably the Canadian Prime Minister Diefenbaker, in favor of the opposition leader Lester Pearson, and increased his cordial relations with the leader of the opposition in Great Britain, Hugh Gaitskill, and also, elsewhere, with Willy Brandt, the socialist mayor of Berlin. But he reserved his attitude toward France. To Ambassador Gavin he said, at the end of October, 1963:

"Fine. I'll see the General again in a few months, and I hope we'll manage to do something together." [51]

To all advisers who urged him to act, if necessary by economic reprisals against France, Kennedy replied that it would be better "to let things build up," adding:

"Besides, if I take so much trouble over the Russians, I can at least spend a little time on de Gaulle." [51]

To Spaak, during his visit to Brussels, he had said in May:

"The whole question of a European atomic force makes no real sense, for Berlin isn't involved, and Europe as a whole is very well protected. For the moment, what matters, is the rest of the world." [51]

Kennedy and de Gaulle never saw each other again. On November 22, 1963, the tragedy at Dallas took place. The General watched television every night. The pictures of the assassination completely shattered him. He watched the program with painful attention, then rose and said to his companions:

"A Greek tragedy in modern dress." [18]

VIETNAM

On his return to power in 1958, General de Gaulle had found the Geneva agreement of 1954 among his Southeast Asia papers, together with a report on the current situation.

Vietnam was ruled by a dictatorial government whose creation was supported by the Americans. French troops had left Indochina in 1955, and France intended to continue only her rights to cultural and technical co-operation in the country. De Gaulle loudly proclaimed these rights and regretted that the Diem government, violating the Geneva agreements, had provoked the break between North and South Vietnam.[53] He appreciated the desires of the American government to defend the free world against communist subversion, but he did not think that the strong-arm methods hitherto employed by France, from 1946 to 1954, were right, particularly if they were running against the current of history. Our era being one of national independence, as the Americans have repeated so often since 1941, de Gaulle detected a grave contradiction in their action in Vietnam: what good can force of arms do against a nationalist idea which, rightly or wrongly, must triumph in the end?

The General advocated the neutrality of Vietnam: the laying down of arms and the withdrawal of American and Chinese troops. But the Diem régime remained deaf to these appeals to reason, creating in South Vietnam a National Liberation Front which resisted American pressure with increasing efficiency.

✤

At first, de Gaulle actively worked for neutrality. He had supported Prince Norodom Sihanouk, head of state of Cambodia from the beginning of 1963; and before the fall of the Diem régime, he sent a special envoy to Pnom Penh, M. Edgar Faure, who also paid a visit to Peking, saw Mao Tse-Tung, and on his return to Pnom Penh, proposed neutrality to Ho Chi Minh in Hanoi and to Diem in Saigon. This offer was made at the end of October, 1963. Ho Chi Minh accepted, and it must be assumed Mao knew of his agreement, but no answer came from Saigon.

Admittedly, Diem was confronted with an insoluble dilemma: the American ambassador Henry Cabot Lodge insisted on the ending of persecutions against the priests: an unfavorable answer to the Faure proposals would make Diem give way to the American ambassador, who meanwhile had suspended American aid to South Vietnam and insisted that Washington should recall the head of the C.I.A. If, on the other hand, he accepted the Faure proposal, American aid would be completely withdrawn and his rule by force would be brought to an end.

Diem had no time to reply, for on November 1 he was assassinated by . . . unknown persons. General de Gaulle's first attempt at mediation had failed lamentably.

From 16,000 men in 1963, the American forces increased to more than 370,000 by the end of 1966. France remained outside the struggle, contending herself by supporting attempts at mediation when her help was requested. On May 20, 1965, M. Mai Van-bo, representing North Vietnam in Paris, approached M. Couve de Murville and told him:

"We would like to make peace, but the principle of unconditional withdrawal of American forces must be agreed before any negotiations take place. This does not mean that the departure must take place before negotiations begin." [18]

The minister informed Washington, but these subtle nuances

escaped President Johnson. On January 24, 1966, de Gaulle received a letter from Ho Chi Minh clarifying his position. De Gaulle replied on February 8, summing up French opinion:

"A return to the terms of the Geneva agreements, the independence of Vietnam guaranteed by the nonintervention of all foreign powers under whatever form, and a policy of strict neutrality on the part of the Vietnamese authorities. These are the methods by which we are convinced the problems of Vietnam must be solved. We also think that no other successful method exists. In other words, we exclude all military solution and cannot accept that hostilities should be prolonged, *a fortiori*, under pretext of obtaining it." [18]

In fact, de Gaulle seemed to forget that the Geneva agreements had been outdated by virtue of the fact that they carried no mention of sanctions in case of violation. He appeared to ignore the difficulties facing the adversaries before they could retire to their respective camps.

The General sent a new special envoy to Hanoi, Jean Sainteny, and followed the Rumanian attempts at reconciliation in 1966 with great interest.[54] Then, on September 1, 1966, he went to Pnom Penh, where he declared that France did not propose to act as mediator. He said, however, that there was no solution except by negotiation, and before beginning talks, the United States should undertake to "repatriate their forces within a reasonable and agreed delay." He added that the United States would lose no prestige by giving up this far-flung enterprise.

Neither Hanoi nor Washington replied to this speech. It was clear that the belligerents wished to treat between themselves without intermediaries. When the Rumanians made a fresh attempt at mediation in 1967, de Gaulle followed the operation sympathetically and skeptically.

Since the United States and the Hanoi government are in agree-

⚜

ment on the necessity of reunifying and neutralizing Vietnam and that no military solution is envisaged, or even possible, it only remains to wait for a political move, and new Geneva agreements after the American presidential elections.

The General's adversaries consider that his actions in Vietnam have had an entirely negative effect. His supporters think that by preventing France and Western Europe from coming in on the American side, he has avoided the unleashing of World War III.

BRITAIN AND THE COMMON MARKET

Why has France separated herself from her traditional ally, Great Britain?

Contrary to many of his compatriots, de Gaulle was well disposed toward Britain. He was well placed to judge the British in 1940. He saw them at work before the French armistice, during the Battle of France, during the Battle of Britain, then on most of the various fronts.

His disputes with Churchill—the better to assure the independence of his movement—did not prevent him from acknowledging that the B.E.F. and the R.A.F. had fought bravely on French soil. He knew Churchill was right to save the best part of his men and machines from the French collapse, and that that handful of soldiers would become the kernel of the armies of liberation.

Because he was a soldier, more than any other head of a refugee Allied government in England in 1940, he appreciated the political strategy of Churchill and Alanbrooke's military genius. While the other political leaders, such as M. Spaak, arrived in London after the Battle of Britain, de Gaulle followed it day by day, hour by hour—the battle which decided the fate of a civilization. The British officers who worked with him remember the strategic and tactical notes he slipped occasionally to the various experts at Allied Headquarters. Several of them were acted on, and left their mark even on the plans for the Normandy landings.[18]

In 1944–1945, de Gaulle knew that Churchill and Eden fought "like lions" for France. He never forgot the quarrels of the Near East, but he remained attached to the theory of Franco–British co-operation "from instinct and by reason." He said as much in London on April 7, 1960.

In his grand European plan, he knew the British position which Churchill had often expressed: Europe must unite and co-operate with Great Britain, though she is not part of Europe.[55] On February 5, 1962, he spoke of a Europe organized "the full length of the Rhine, the Alps, even perhaps the Channel." On June 17, 1962, he said that Europe will recover "with, perhaps, one day, England." He expressed his confidence in "ancient and dependable Britain."

One of his first political gestures after his return to power was to decorate Churchill with the Cross of the Liberation on June 18, 1958. When Churchill died, in January, 1965, de Gaulle publicly and privately expressed feelings of grief, which were certainly deep and sincere.[56]

The General would like the two countries to co-ordinate their political, economic, and military plans in order to counterbalance American power. On July 31, 1961, Harold Macmillan announced to the House of Commons his intention of opening negotiations in connection with Britain's entry into the Common Market, and the request was presented in Brussels on October 10.

Macmillan and de Gaulle knew each other well, and if there was a certain restraint in their friendship, there was a certain understanding. But the London–Paris talks began badly. On August 2, 1961, Macmillan stated:

"What General de Gaulle has called *Europe des patries* seems to us more adapted to the national traditions of the European countries and particularly to ours. It is a conception to which we can subscribe with good will and complete agreement."

This was a complete misunderstanding. The General had never spoken of Europe *"des patries."* His European plan was confederal, and it is important to note that the yes to confederation was a no to the European federation advocated by the "Europeanists." As a result, any possible political agreement with France would be made on a level where the country was not in agreement with several of its partners.

De Gaulle saw Macmillan several times (June 29, 1958, March 9, 1959, March 12, 1960), then went to see him in London (April 5, 1960) and talked to him again at Rambouillet (January 28, 1961). Macmillan considered de Gaulle:

"A strange figure, attractive, but impossible . . . passionately devoted to France, pitiless every time French interests are at stake, insular, half-revolutionary, half-reactionary."

The General sketched plans for co-operation, above all in nuclear or military matters, but the prime minister did not follow them up. The Brussels negotiations dragged on, lasting eventually for sixteen months.

Macmillan returned to see de Gaulle at the Château de Champs on June 2, 1962.

"In Great Britain," he said, "they say you are personally hostile to my country's entry into the Common Market. Is this true?"

The General smiled:

"You know it's not. I was the first to advocate your adherence. Unconditionally, of course." [18]

In Brussels, the British negotiators were very demanding. They wanted a long period of adaptation and protection for British agriculture, until 1970, and exceptions for economic relations as between Great Britain and the Commonwealth. According to an English observer, Nora Beloff, who is not very sympathetic to de Gaulle:

"It is possible that, without these objections, the General would never have had occasion to use his veto." [57] At no time did the British offer to join the Common Market unconditionally.

On the other hand, the multiple discussions of experts, including the representatives of industry, the trades unions, and French farm workers provoked a violent reaction in France. United for once, all these forces usually so divided combined to bring pressure on de Gaulle to oppose Great Britain's entry. On January 14, 1963, the British request was rejected at the suggestion of France.[58]

It is true that, in the meantime, a new element had arisen with which de Gaulle was infinitely more concerned than the negotiations in Brussels.

On December 15 and 16, 1962, Macmillan came to see him at Rambouillet to talk about nuclear arms and the Atlantic Alliance. He had constantly been in touch with President Kennedy on these matters, and as usual, France was not invited to this summit conference. Macmillan brought de Gaulle the unwelcome news that Kennedy, as Eisenhower had done, was not in agreement with the idea of admitting France to a tripartite directory of Atlantic nuclear weapons. The General concluded that Britain would continue to play the part of a brilliant second to America and would always do so in Europe, particularly in the Common Market. He was acutely disappointed and told his ministers:

"At the worst moments of the Battle of Britain, when all seemed lost, Churchill and the English, even to save themselves from German invasion, would never have agreed to become the fifty-first American state!"

The Nassau conference, held from December 17 to 21, 1962, between Kennedy and Macmillan was "one of the most badly prepared and badly conducted in modern history," remarks E. Jouve.[56]

The final communiqué was outstandingly clumsy. It stated that

⚜

Macmillan had informed Kennedy of the state of negotiations in Brussels and that the American president had reaffirmed the interest Washington took in finding "a quick and favorable solution." There could be no better way of dictating their conduct to the Europeans and to General de Gaulle.

In Brussels, France said no. And de Gaulle let it be known that the Nassau conference would lead to the enslavement of London by Washington. He said jokingly:

"Of course, the English will be allowed to keep their traditions for the benefit of American tourists: the judges' wigs, the Horse Guards, and the cat o' nine tails." [18]

But his spokesman, M. Peyrefitte, said later, after this period of bad temper and bitterness: if the conditions which prevented Britain's entry into the Common Market could be modified, France would receive the new development sympathetically.[59]

FRANCE'S WORLD POLICY

At this time, the end of 1967, the General had had two serious failures: his plan for a three-handed directory and his attempts to form a European confederation. He had had two great successes: a peaceful settlement in North Africa and co-operation with French Africa. Several important lines had been developed, which marked French foreign policy: the anti-American reaction, a revision of European policy, a new orientation of her policy toward the *Tiers Monde* (the noncommitted countries).

The anti-American reaction was certainly influenced by the General's bitter feelings toward Roosevelt and his anti-French policy, the remembrance of his successive setbacks with Truman, Eisenhower, and Kennedy, but it stems above all from an analysis of the world political situation. American hegemony is a menace to the free world. As a Gaullist of the left, Emmanuel d'Astier, has said:

"How can one accept as a guide a country that doesn't know where it's going?"

And de Gaulle has said:

"Since the death of President Kennedy, America worries me . . . she is losing her grip; she has no real policy; one has the unpleasant feeling that she doesn't even believe in herself." [18]

The General thinks that any too-powerful state threatens world peace, and that a balance of strength must be maintained; "a balance of fear," as it has been called. This is why he toyed for a while with the idea of countering the Washington–Moscow polarization by the creation of a Paris–Peking combination, but it was impossible to establish diplomatic and political relations with a country that was still in process of revolution. De Gaulle had to change his tactics and resign himself to belonging to the "Western dogs." After this disappointment, he could only support the weaker partner of the two Great Powers as often as possible, that is to say, the U.S.S.R., in world political strategy. Hence the moves initiated in Vietnam, Latin America, in Quebec, and within the framework of NATO.

Thus it is possible to sum up Charles de Gaulle's new European plan. Here again, the experience and prejudices of the septuagenarian must be taken into account. In 1934 he wrote:

"Our country has no ambitions of aggrandizement and has no ambitions except to keep what she has. Contrary to appearances, this conception of its destiny involves certain dangers. We should know, in fact, if some grand national dream is not necessary for a people to maintain its authority and preserve its cohesion." [60]

Country by country, the General's thinking is as follows:
BELGIUM: the country de Gaulle knows best through having lived there for several years is "a very important element in the reorganization of Europe." He envisages a "Western grouping with

the Rhine, the Channel, and the Mediterranean as arteries." [61]
But his plan for European confederation was coldly received by
the minister for foreign affairs, M. Wigny (1960), and a visit
by the king of the Belgians to Paris (May 24, 1961) changed
nothing.

HOLLAND: remains an enigma to the General. He explained his
plans for confederation to the Netherlands government, including
M. Luns, before presenting it to the Belgians (1960). He welcomed Queen Juliana and Prince Bernhard to Paris (1961) and
returned their visit (1963). In vain. The General found his way
blocked by Holland.

LUXEMBOURG: is very friendly to the General, who has a special
admiration for the grand duchess. She paid him a state visit in
1963, and with her, he opened the Moselle canal in 1964.

The attitude of the Benelux countries in seeking the traditional
and historic support of Great Britain in the Common Market
having resulted in the failure of the General's plan for a European
confederation, he must widen his perspective.

SPAIN: after the war, the General was extremely reticent towards
it. But from 1948 onward, in view of the exigencies of Western
defense, he has considered that Spain is essential to European
strategy. After 1958, he noted the necessity for Franco–Spanish
co-operation in Latin America and his hopes of seeing the entry
of Spain into the European context. [62]

PORTUGAL: it is for defense reasons that the General has developed relations with it. A French missile station has been installed
in the Azores, but de Gaulle has also helped Portugal's cause with
President Kennedy: a revolutionary force in Angola, as in Portugal, would threaten the peace of Europe.

SCANDINAVIA: the links with the Scandinavians, privileged clients
of Great Britain, are more tenuous, but the General has tried to
strengthen them, particularly on the economic level, and notably
with Denmark, which has so often been the ally of France. Hence

the visits paid by the kings of Norway (1962), Sweden (1964), and Denmark (1965) to Paris. The president of the Finnish republic has also been a guest at the Elysée (1962).

ITALY: together with France, "two daughters of the same family." The General accords Italy a special place, and if he has no fears on the economic or military level, he pays particular attention to her participation in the defense of Europe and the European economic institutions. He has been to Italy four times since 1958 (1959, 1962, 1965, 1967) with a view to harmonizing the European policy of the two countries. He has also received the Italian leaders in Paris (1958, 1960, 1961, 1964) and, together with President Saragat, opened the Mont Blanc road tunnel. The attempts made by de Gaulle and Adenauer during the summer of 1962 to create a triple entente France–Germany–Italy (FRALIT) as the basis for a united Europe failed owing to the lack of enthusiasm shown by the Italians.

GERMANY: the European country that preoccupies de Gaulle most. The General who, in 1944, could not get his ideas for the dismemberment of Germany accepted, realizes that, in spite of Churchill's wishes, the heavy industry of the Ruhr has been rebuilt, thanks notably to the political ineffectiveness of the coal–steel community. He considers that the reunification of Germany is inevitable, sooner or later.

"It is no more reasonable to maintain the division of Berlin than to try and split Paris by installing iron barriers in the Place de la Concorde." [18]

Bearing in mind the extraordinary power which a reunified Germany would represent on an economic and military level, particularly if she should benefit from the unconditional support of America or Russia, de Gaulle desires to attach Germany firmly to Europe and control its future development within a solid European construction. Hence the many meetings with Dr. Adenauer and the Franco–German treaty.

❧

EASTERN EUROPE: after the failure of his European confederal plan, de Gaulle conceived a new project, which could be called "Revision of the Yalta agreement." According to him, the liberalization of the Soviet Union after Stalin's death requires a revision of the problems of relations with the socialist countries. Under the General's direction, a relaxing of tensions between France and the socialist countries was followed by visits to Paris of the leaders of Yugoslavia, Rumania, and Czechoslovakia (1964), Hungary, Bulgaria, and Poland (1965).

On June 20, 1966, de Gaulle said in Moscow:

"France would like the evil spell to be broken, and, at least as far as she is concerned, that the European states called Eastern should instigate new relations aimed at relaxation, understanding and co-operation."

This was the moment when M. Couve de Murville visited successfully Bucharest, Sofia, Warsaw, Prague, and Belgrade, so as to place diplomatic relations on a new footing. As a result of this tour, de Gaulle declared on October 28, 1966:

"Everyone must know that we are renewing our relations with Poland, Rumania, Yugoslavia, Czechoslovakia, Bulgaria, and Hungary. Between all these peoples and our own, today, a cold war seems laughable, while a growing and friendly co-operation is afoot."

This action was not directed against the U.S.S.R. nor the United States. It aims at ending the division of Europe settled at Yalta, without France, and to bring together around the same table the Europeans of East and West to create a peace treaty with Germany which would permit German reunification. This presupposes that the Soviet Union, by means of its economic and military alliances, notably those of COMECON (Common Market of the East) and the Warsaw Pact, would not oppose this more or less independent action of the socialist countries, or that the United States, through its economic and military alliances—

notably those of the Common Market (and the Kennedy Round and the European Association of Free Exchange) and NATO— do not excite opposition in certain countries, such as the Benelux union. If de Gaulle's plan succeeded, it would lead to the simultaneous dissolution of NATO and the Warsaw Pact, and the fusion of COMECON and the Common Market.

This was the meaning behind General de Gaulle's declarations at Gdansk on September 10, 1967:

"France can offer no advice to Poland, but she has enough friendship for her, enough respect, to congratulate her on her new vocation. I hope you can now see a little further, and on a wider scale, than you have been obliged to do until now. The obstacles that today seem insurmountable, you will undoubtedly overcome. You know what I mean." [62 bis]

Mr. Gomulka replied clearly:

"Poland has drawn all possible conclusions from its historical experiences. . . . The Alliance with the U.S.S.R., together with the treaties of friendship, co-operation and mutual assistance concluded with the socialist states, as well as the R.D.A., is a cornerstone of the policy of the People's Republic of Poland."

We must have no illusions, however, on the obstructions offered to his plan by the Russian communist party and its brothers in the East and by the American C.I.A. in the West.

M. Couve de Murville was right when he spoke of the necessity for "ideological disarmament." Nevertheless, when I was in Bucharest, I noticed that this speech, which was warmly applauded, only appeared in the Rumanian press very much censored and shorn of its essential terms. We consider that this plan of de Gaulle's, which has our entire support, cannot overcome all these obstacles at once.

It remains for Germany to fight her own battle for reunification, even if it means recourse to arms. We know that its leaders have attempted this already on several occasions.[63] The failure of the de Gaulle plan has given them the green light, and will un-doubtedly give Russia (who alone can offer Bonn East Germany) every opportunity of bringing Germany around to her side. After that, the prospect of owing America debts of money and gratitude is not likely to protect the West from Soviet blandishments.

On a world level, de Gaulle has also given a new direction to French policy toward the *Tiers Monde*. He considered this should be based on co-operation, and has met with violent opposition in France. A well-known journalist, Raymond Cartier, headed an attack on this policy. De Gaulle did not seem to mind. He sees this policy as an ensemble: independence plus co-operation. This is particularly true of French Africa, and perfectly demonstrated in certain cases. For instance, on July 15, 1961, M. Debré wrote to the president of Gabon, Léon m'Ba:

"I should be glad if you would confirm that, as soon as inde-pendence has been proclaimed, the government of the Gabon Re-public will sign agreements for co-operation."

This attitude of the French republic has been very marked. Direct investments and loans, in millions of American dollars, reached 2,688 for the countries of O.C.D.E. in 1958, and 2,329 in 1964, *i.e.*, a slight decrease. Of this total, France contributed 432 in 1958 and 364 in 1964, while the United States paid out 1,321 in 1958 and 1,242 in 1964. Great Britain's share was 389 in 1958 and 271 in 1964, while the Federal Republic of Ger-many's support was 120 in 1958 and 146 in 1964.

The United States is the main exporting country of capital to O.C.D.E. (36 per cent average 1962–1964), France follows next (17 per cent), then the United Kingdom (11 per cent), Germany and Italy (9 per cent each). The United States is also the main direct investor (44 per cent), followed by France (20 per cent) and the United Kingdom (9 per cent).

The program of public aid by France to the developing coun-tries is second in total value, and the only one which has always represented more than 1 per cent of her national revenue. France is the leading provider of technical personnel (43,500 in 1965) and is among the countries offering the highest number of students' grants and exchanges (12,429 in 1965).

This public aid of more than $700 million a year is valid for more than 90 per cent of the countries of the franc area, and the "technical aids" sent by France consist largely of teachers (29,000 in 1965) and civil servants (10,000). The countries outside the franc zone which benefit from French aid are Brazil, Chile, Cambodia, Laos, and Vietnam.

Is this policy of co-operation paying off? A debatable point. De Gaulle sees it from his global angle. The *Tiers Monde* now constitutes a majority in the UN, and the French representatives in New York have been instructed to establish good relations with its delegates. In the year 2000, Asia and Africa will represent 4.3 billion inhabitants out of the 6.3 billion of the world's population. Of these 4 billion, 3 will have memories of Western oppression. There can be no question of disinterest, particularly at a time when the leaders of world policy since 1945 have shown themselves incapable of resolving economic problems, beginning with alimentary problems in countries such as India or Brazil.

In 2000, the experts anticipate that the U.S.S.R. will have 420 million inhabitants, North America 410, and Europe 590. It is important to reckon on the potential power of Europe in relation to the two current Great Powers, and not to mortgage the future by tying it to one or other of the two blocs. At all costs it is vital to avoid World War III between whites, which would result in a further tipping of the balance in favor of the *Tiers Monde*. This explains why, in the conflicts in the Near East, France has not sided with Israel or Egypt. Too many long-term interests were at stake for France to become involved with either side. The ties with the Arab countries, their effect on the affairs of North Africa,

including the petrol interests, the importance of Israeli co-operation, made any other course impossible.[64]

On June 21, 1967, de Gaulle stated to his *Conseil des Ministres*:

> France has taken a stand against the war in the Middle
> East. She recognizes that each country concerned—nota-
> bly Israel—has a right to live. She condemns the threat
> to destroy her uttered by her neighbors, and she accepts
> her position with regard to the movement of ships in the
> Gulf of Aqaba. But she condemns the opening of hostilities
> by Israel.
>
> In an endeavor to avoid open conflict, the French gov-
> ernment proposed that the four Great Powers should join
> together in common opposition to the use of arms. At the
> same time, it had informed each of the parties that it
> would be held to be in the wrong whichever should first
> open hostilities. She cannot rcognize any of the territorial
> changes achieved through military action. But if the war
> is extended to the Middle East, France considers that there
> is no chance of reaching a peaceful settlement in the
> world situation, unless a new element should be intro-
> duced. This element should and could be the ending of
> the war in Vietnam, by limits imposed on foreign inter-
> vention.

De Gaulle has also said:

"Government is a painful, difficult, delicate business. War, war,
you see is horrible, but peace, we have to admit, peace is a deadly
bore." [65]

A blind adorer of the General, François Mauriac, has said:

"What would de Gaulle's policy have been if he had had
greater means, such as those of Soviet Russia or the United
States? I dare not think." [66]

A belligerent policy? Nothing is less sure, for de Gaulle's temperament, even when he is crossed, is deeply pacific, even if he is not resigned to playing the part which the introvert, Mauriac, assigns to him:

"To maintain France in her historic place, now that she has become a second-class nation, and cannot enter into competition with the really great ones." [66]

At the end of this brief survey of de Gaulle's world policy, one name springs to mind: Bismarck, the Iron Chancellor. Apart from secondary likenesses: the height, the enormous appetite and prodigious vitality, the cutting remarks, the personal ambition and disdain of men, the distrust of parliaments and journalists, it is easy to make comparisons: the princess von Bismarck was self-effacing and devoted. A tender, platonic, very romantic attachment linked the chancellor to Princess Orloff: through Bleichroeder, he kept up excellent and useful relations with the Rothschilds.

But three facts are striking: de Gaulle and Bismarck both came to power late, in their full maturity: Bismarck at forty-seven, de Gaulle at fifty-four. They both followed a policy of grandeur summed up in *l'État* (Reich) which they created with their own hands—at fifty-six for Bismarck, at sixty-eight for de Gaulle. Identifying themselves with their respective states, they followed a policy of balance of power, never hesitating by treaties of insurance and counterinsurance to overthrow alliances, making and breaking them according to strictly personal rules. This policy, compounded of duplicity and provocation aimed at reinforcing the state, they had created and contributed to the maintenance of world peace. Their final objective would be: —to consolidate French (or German) unity and prevent the French (or Germans) from taking their revenge.

De Gaulle admits a certain admiration for this illustrious model, replying to Michel Debré, who said:

❧

"Bismarck is one of the very great statesmen of history."

"He, at least, knew when to go."

But if he divides his friends and adversaries in order to rule, we shall know his methods when his secret diplomacy is published, fifty years after his death. It will be remembered that Bismarck's departure left Germany for a quarter of a century in a difficult situation, politically and diplomatically, his weak successor showing himself incapable, as he said himself, "to juggle five balls and always keep two of them in the air."

To assure the success of their policy, de Gaulle and Bismarck have both been forced to deal, sometimes with one, sometimes with another, without ever taking part in an existing system (in de Gaulle's case, UN, NATO, or the socialist countries). They adapted their diplomacy to the needs of a policy conceived, pursued, and known to them alone. Their departure can only create the diplomatic isolation of their countries.

History will say of de Gaulle, as it is beginning to say of Bismarck, that by a clever policy of supporting the weak and opposing the strong, he made a considerable contribution to the maintenance of peace in the sixth decade of our century.

The Administration Will Follow

In asking Eisenhower on August 21, 1944 not to forget to liberate Paris, de Gaulle was thinking, naturally, of the prestige to be won for France, as well as his government, which needed it badly. He was also thinking of the necessity of seizing the capital before the communists.

He knew that the risks of insurrection were great. On August 23, 1944, at the Château de Rambouillet, he received Alexandre de Saint-Phalle, who arrived in Paris with two safe-conducts, one signed by General von Choltitz, the German commandant of Paris, the other by Alexandre Parodi, General de Gaulle's delegate in France.

The General was extremely suspicious. He knew that Parodi and certain of the Resistance leaders were not expecting the Allies to reach Paris for some time and had signed a truce with the German command, which had been broken almost at once by the

⚜

Resistance. He knew that the National Council of the Resistance (C.N.R.) was directed by a small group (Saillant, Villon, Copeau, Bidault, Blocq-Mascart), the first three supporting the communist point of view, while Bidault, the president, secretly belonged to the *Front National*. He also know that his military delegation in France, headed by Jacques Chaban-Delmas, had not yet brought together the threads of the secret army, whose leaders, General Delestraint and Colonels Marchal and de Jussieu, had been successively arrested. He was aware of the frantic activity of the *Comité d'Action Militaire* of the C.N.R. (COMAC), which was not prepared to obey the orders of General Koenig, nominated by de Gaulle to command the *Forces Françaises de l'Intérieur*. COMAC was led by the communists, and on August 17, 1944, they had prized out of de Gaulle the authorization to continue their activities autonomously "as delegated by General Koenig," whose orders they were prepared to execute on a priority basis.

At the time of the liberation of Paris, de Gaulle was obsessed by the necessity to maintain order and to overcome any popular rising. At the Gare Saint-Lazare, where General Leclerc received General von Choltitz's surrender, he was surprised that the commandant of the Second Armored Division had allowed Colonel Rol-Tanguy, the communist military leader, to sign the official document as well.

On August 27, two days after the Liberation, de Gaulle received the C.N.R. and informed them that the F.F.I. would henceforth form part of the army, and that COMAC and the patriotic militia would be disbanded. He brought two communists into his reshaped government, Charles Tillon, as minister of aviation, and François Billoux, as minister for health. But as de Gaulle said: "The communist party tried to exploit the disturbances in order to seize power in the provinces as it had endeavored to do in Paris."

The situation had worried the Allies, and on August 5, in

Naples, Colonel Zeller consulted with the American General Patch
as to the means of avoiding a popular rising in Lyons. By September, the communist party controlled a large part of France.
The southwest had been liberated by the Resistance, without the
help of the Allied armies. Several larger cities were in the hands
of the communists: Bordeaux, Limoges, Montpellier, Toulouse,
and Lyons, which was on the verge of riot.

On September 27, the communists took control of the most
important of the trades unions, the C.G.T., and a large number
of newspapers fell into their hands. In Paris, the communist press
had more than a million readers. The industrialists, the bourgeois,
the engineers, who were afraid of the purge, belonged to communist or para-communist organizations. The administration, the
ministers, and big business were honeycombed by communist-
party cells.

General Eisenhower could not give de Gaulle the military
means necessary to re-establish order. The head of the provisional
government, therefore, personally had to face the storm, which
he did with authority. De Gaulle related:

> In Lyons, on September 15, I reviewed the Forces of the
> Interior. Colonel Descour, who had distinguished himself
> with the *Maquis*, and more recently, at the recapture of
> Lyons, and was now the military regional commander,
> marched past me the troops who were as moved as mov-
> ing. It was touching to see them in spite of their different
> appearances, trying to assume a certain uniformity. Mili-
> tary tradition was strong in this force that had created
> itself. I left Lyons convinced that the government, pro-
> vided it did govern, would overcome all obstacles, and left
> behind in the city the feeling that order would be restored
> since authority had reappeared at the head of the nation.
> . . . In Marseilles, the Forces of the Interior had bravely

helped de Monsabert's troops to recover the city. I congratulated them and inspected them. It was easy to see
which units—the greater number—wanted to join the
fighting in Alsace, and how a few, obeying some hidden
command, wanted to stay at home. I ordered General
Chadebec de Lavalade . . . to give the earliest satisfaction to the former and to disband the latter, and asked the
minister for war to send a regiment from Algeria to Marseilles immediately to facilitate matters. . . .

September 16 in Toulouse, the communists were well
placed and well organized, and stirred up trouble in an
endeavor to take over. They had partly succeeded. I found
the commissioner of the republic in process of being
trampled upon by certain of the fighting leaders. Pierre
Bertaux, who directed a large unit in the Resistance, had
expected to be given the job when the holder, Jean Cas-
sou, had been seriously wounded in the fighting at the time
of the German flight. Bertaux was trying to hold the reins
of power, but Colonel Asher, alias Ravanel, the *Maquis*
leader from the Haute-Garonne, had taken command of
the military region and exercised a control that was as
widespread as ill-defined. Around Ravanel were grouped
armed units almost like a Soviet.

On the 17th, in the morning, with calculated solemnity,
I reviewed all these elements. By making direct contact
with the *Maquis*, I hoped to arouse in each of them the
soldier he wanted to be. As I went down the lines, a certain trembling showed me I had been understood. Colonel
Ravanel then arranged a march past. The procession was
picturesque. At its head, with fixed bayonets, was a Russian battalion, made up of men from the "Vlassov army,"
conscripted originally by the Germans, but who had deserted in time to join our Resistance. Then followed the

Spaniards, led by the generals, after which, the French
Forces of the Interior. The sight of their improvised flags
and banners, the care they had taken to organize themselves into sections, companies and battalions, the effort
they had made to give their clothes a military appearance,
above all, their attitude, their looks, the tears of the men
marching past me showed how efficacious and strong is
military rule. But also, as far as I was concerned, the same
universal popularity appeared which had everywhere been
shown. I was perfectly certain that this devotion would
substitute for everything that was lacking to assure order.
At the very least I could be sure that it would prevent
dictatorship by a few, or even general anarchy.

At Bordeaux, on the 17th, it was the same. In the courtyard of the administration, I inspected those Forces of the
Interior who were still there. Nearly all presented a very
smart appearance on which I complimented them. A few
leaders showed signs of discontent—I offered them the
immediate choice between submitting to the orders of the
colonel commanding the district or going to prison. They
all chose the former. As I left Bordeaux, I felt the ground
was firm again.[67]

De Gaulle had avoided the most disturbed towns, Limoges and
Montpellier. At the end of September, he summoned to Paris all
the commissioners of the republic and ordered them to re-establish
order and the authority of the state.

But the trial of strength was not yet over. On October 8 and 9,
the states-general of the Resistance met in Avignon. Four presidents directed them: André Philip, Louis Saillant, Emmanuel
d'Astier, and Pierre Villon. The first was a socialist, the other
three had communist leanings. Emmanuel d'Astier, who refused
the embassy in Washington which de Gaulle offered him, spoke

for the fusion of all the Resistance movements, the objective of the communist party.

The states-general consisted of the representatives of the departmental committees of liberation from forty departments. They were still trying to reunite all the Resistance fighters with a view to taking power, but no action was decided upon.

De Gaulle brought into play every means of political strategy. He decided to dissolve the militiamen on October 28, 1944. The C.N.R. reacted very quickly, and the political communist bureau stated that "once again the president of the government has taken the responsibility of treating the French Resistance as a negligible quantity." [68] On November 4, the communists organized a grand protest meeting at the *Vélodrome d'Hiver*, but did nothing more.

On November 6, de Gaulle announced that Maurice Thorez, secretary-general of the communist party, who had deserted in 1939 and taken refuge in Moscow, where he lived with Khrushchev, would be granted a full pardon. He told his staff: "We should not reproach Thorez—who is a brave man—as a soldier, for obeying the orders of his government. I like him very much. He is a good middle-class Frenchman. He probably had a Russian conception of the national interest, but we can trust him to direct certain affairs of state for the best: he has the outlook of a bourgeois family father. Obviously, we can't expect him to have revolutionary ideas." [69]

De Gaulle judged correctly. To Colonel Groussard, he expressed his basic thinking: "I brought Thorez back so as to disarm the militia."

As soon as he returned to Paris, on November 30, Thorez addressed a meeting at the Vélodrome d'Hiver. The tenor of his speech was clear: fight the war, create a powerful French army, rebuild the factories, unite all the Resistance fighters, and form an eternal alliance with the Soviet Union.[68]

All the communist leaders followed this line, and on January

23, 1945, Thorez said at Ivry, in the presence of the central committee of the party: "The civic guards and all the irregular army groups should no longer be maintained."

The state was saved, thanks to General de Gaulle's political skill.

We have seen that Roosevelt considered that France, like the majority of European countries, should be handed over to communism. We know, too, that Churchill did not share this point of view. After his discussions with Stalin, he wanted to save Europe from Stalinistic imperialism and worked vigorously to this end, notably in Belgium and Greece. In France, de Gaulle reacted in the same way and saved his country from the disasters Roosevelt had predicted, which would unfailingly have occurred if the administration of the liberated country had been left to the Americans, as the president wished. It is easy to understand that the Americans do not appreciate the behavior of this general, who proved their president a liar.

Another point: why, with all the trumps they held, did the communists not seize power? Georgette Elgey put the question to Thorez; Thorez replied:

> We could have seized power, but such an action would have started a civil war, which we would have lost. With the Americans in France, revolution would have been wiped out. France would have suffered the fate of Greece on an even larger scale. At the time, the greater proportion of the French were not thinking of a socialist revolution. When Lenin summoned the workers and soldiers to revolution in 1917, he knew he would be followed. In 1944–1945, if we had mobilized them for a socialist revolution, some of our sympathizers would not have understood.
>
> We must remember the responsibility of French communism in relation to the international situation. To start a

⚜

revolution would have been to ignore that reality, it would have been a total lack of the sense of our responsibilities.[70]

There were, therefore, three reasons: 1) the presence of the American troops; 2) the mass of the people would not have followed; 3) the revolution was not opportune.

It is certain that in Paris, the communist leaders were waiting for orders from Moscow, which did not come.[71] Or rather, Thorez counseled patience and the maintenance of order. He was the communist leader closest to Stalin, and certainly his faithful interpreter.

The truth is that the Soviet Union, terribly weakened by the war, was still fighting very hard battles. In Teheran and Yalta, Stalin had acquired the right to control about ten states of Eastern Europe, with about 113 million inhabitants, a quarter of Europe which he had to convert to Soviet rule. Why drop the substance for the shadow? Stalin would respect treaties. The role of the French communists was, therefore, laid down: to support the Soviet Union with a powerful French Army, to avoid the creation of a Western anti-Soviet bloc, and to prevent an overthrow of alliances which would lead the Western Allies to a reconciliation with Germany, aimed at the Soviet Union.

It was fortunate for France that Stalin was unaware of Roosevelt's pessimistic views.

NO TO MENDÈS-FRANCE

The majority of the governments who had taken refuge in London had studied the problems of the aftermath of war. The *Comité Français de Libération* had done the same. The finance minister, Pierre Mendès-France,[72] had made a detailed study of the financial policy to be applied to the liberated country.

This lawyer, the youngest to qualify in France and the youngest deputy, representing the Eure from 1932 to 1940, attempted to reach North Africa in 1940. Arrested by the Vichy police, he managed to escape and reached London in 1942, where he served in the French Air Force. Nominated commissioner for finance, he was appointed minister of national economy in September, 1944.

At twenty-one, he had studied the financial achievements of the Poincaré government (1928), and at thirty-one was undersecretary of state at the treasury in Léon Blum's government (1938). The youngest minister in the entire history of the Third Republic, Mendès-France is a man of thought coupled with a man of action, a radical who came to grips with financial problems at an early age. Of superior intelligence, with nothing but disdain for demagogy, he is highly strung, extremely shrewd, but perhaps a little lacking in a capacity for carrying out long-term enterprises.

The plan he had prepared was austere. It involved blocking accounts and deposits immediately after the Liberation, followed by an exchange of bank notes to strangle inflation. The unblocking of accounts would be progressive and parallel to the restarting of production. This plan would hamstring the black market, establish price control, and contribute to financial stability.

Mendès-France explained his over-all views to General de Gaulle, who appreciated their strength and liked their breadth. He tried them out at the time of the liberation of Tunis, then more intensively in Corsica in the presence of Belgian and Dutch observers. As soon as he arrived in Paris, Mendès-France met de Gaulle: "So, *mon général*, so now you are the head of the *Front Populaire*." [73]

Conditions for the application of the plan were ideal. The government's authority was respected and popular enough for the imposition of severe measures. But an unforeseen difficulty arose.

The minister for finance in the provisional government, René Pleven, was against the Mendès-France plan.

The economic and financial position of France was catastrophic: 1 million families were homeless, 75 billion francs (by 1967 values) of war damage were due, the levels of production had dropped from 100 per cent in 1938 to 33 per cent in industry, and 60 per cent for agriculture, whereas prices had gone up as much as 250 to 300 per cent. The circulation of paper money had quintupled. The national debt was four times what it had been before the war; 390 billion francs in expenditure was faced with a revenue of 176 billion francs. By the end of 1944, production was less than half the 1938 figure, and there was no trade at all with other countries.

The provisional government did not want to do anything in a hurry. Against the policy of austerity advocated by Mendès-France, two suggestions were put forward, though independently and not as a joint action.

M. Monick, governor of the Bank of France, advocated the floating of a large loan which would produce the essential liquidity. This was a move toward a liberal solution, and it won the support of the bank's representatives and the financial experts.[74] The General hesitated to make a decision, but he appreciated that the loan would not prevent the blocking of accounts at a later date, and accepted the Monick proposals.

The loan was floated on November 5, 1944; the results were good (encouraging, said the liberals): 164 billion francs. Not enough, said Mendès-France, who had registered a result of only 127 billion francs.

The liberals wanted to raise the price of wheat again. Mendès-France, almost alone, reacted immediately and offered his resignation, which de Gaulle refused: he had not yet chosen either of the proposals. Mendès-France maintained that financial austerity alone would permit the practice of a really socially progressive policy. Pleven and his supporters, without offering an over-all plan, considered that the economy was being crushed by penury, that higher prices would stimulate production, and higher salaries would encourage the workers.

In January, Mendès-France repeated his arguments in a letter which he handed to General de Gaulle, pointing out that the administration was obstructing his plans. De Gaulle called Mendès-France and Pleven to his home on the last Sunday in March, 1945. The two men explained their theories, which were again presented to the *Conseil des Ministres*. Mendès-France demanded a vote. The socialist postmaster, Augustin Laurent, was his only supporter. All the other ministers, notably the socialists and communists, agreed with Pleven. His course was clear. Mendès-France resigned and refused any other ministerial position; he left office, without a word of condemnation, on April 5, 1945. Said de Gaulle:

> After debating at length with them and with myself, I chose the progressive method and rejected the blocking of accounts. Not that I was convinced by theoretical arguments. In economics, as in politics or strategy, in my opinion, there is no absolute truth, but there are circumstances. My own conception governs my decision. The country was sick and hurt. I considered it preferable at that moment not to upset its subsistence and activities, all the more that the coming months must, by force of events, improve her condition. If there had been no other means of saving her than to stake everything on one throw, I would certainly not have hesitated. But why throw it into dangerous convulsions, when it would recover its health. . . .
>
> As was natural, Pierre Mendès-France left the government, at his own request, in April. He did so with dignity. I have continued to esteem this colleague's exceptional

worth. Though I did not adopt the policy he advised, it does not in the least mean I may not one day make it mine, if circumstances change. But if Mendès-France was not able to apply it at the time, he had to remain faithful to his doctrine. It is in this sense that a minister's departure may sometimes be a service rendered to the state. I combined the two ministries of finance and economy and put Pleven in charge.

Such was the General's description written ten years after the event. It is certain that his was the deciding choice: by submitting Mendès-France's plan to a hostile circle, he was condemning it utterly. De Gaulle was attempting to explain his attitude, but his decision seems to rest on three foundations:

1. His ignorance of social and economic spheres. He had had no experience of business and could only choose between theories. His own instinct was to reject compromise.

2. His desire not to upset the people. "When he made his triumphal entry into liberated Paris, de Gaulle underestimated his popularity," said Parodi, who was with him.

In London, on June 4, he had seen the newsreel pictures of the tumultuous welcome the Parisians had given Marshal Pétain on April 25, 1944. When he arrived in Paris himself, he could not judge the relative importance of the clandestine press which praised him and the censored press which daily insulted him. This explains his desire to delay the introduction of an economic austerity which would inevitably be unpopular. During his tours of France, his fears were strengthened. In Marseilles, Toulouse, Bordeaux, and above all, in Lille, he was struck by what he saw:

The moment I arrived, I was struck by the pressing and dramatic urgency of the problem of sustenance in the district. The working people during the Occupation had been forced to accept wages which enemy orders had maintained at the lowest level. Many workers found themselves out of work in the face of factories without coal and plants without machine tools. In addition, food rationing had fallen below subsistence level. I visited my native town, where the citizens received me joyfully, and saw too many faces where the smiles could not hide the pallor nor the emaciation.[75]

3. His intention to rally the people by some spectacular gesture. This was the easy way out. It was decided to raise wages, and they continued to rise until 1958. De Gaulle spoke of it lightly enough:

In June, we proceeded to the exchange of banknotes, expecting a bonus for the state with regard to those of older issues which were not presented. But the operation went through franc for franc. Naturally, between January and December, adjustments had to be made to prices and salaries, but the government remained in control, and in all, the increases did not rise above 50 per cent. At the same time, production continued to rise, particularly following agreements made in February and March with Belgium, Switzerland, Great Britain and the United States: imports were resumed. By the end of 1945, the economy was double what it had been at the time of the Liberation, and the circulation of paper currency was no higher than at the time of my arrival in Paris. At a time and manner where it is impossible for everyone to be satisfied, I do not expect this result to arouse enthusiasm. I was satisfied myself, since after having trembled on the edge of the abyss, by the end of the year the country had been set on the road to a new prosperity.[76]

In fact, the Pleven plan was not really a plan, but a series of isolated measures, leading to the inflation which Mendès-France had feared. In 1946 the budget showed 311 billion francs in revenue and 487 billion francs in expenditure. The number of civil servants, which had almost doubled since 1939, continued to increase. The parallel race between wages and prices continued until 1958. Between April, 1944 and October, 1945, the over-all rise in salaries was an average 133 per cent for the workers and 127 per cent for unskilled labor. The devaluation of the franc in December, 1945, badly handled, had no lasting effect.

Little by little the door was opened to foreign aid, necessary, certainly, in a period of reconstruction, but which went to the point of madness, so that on October 6, 1952, the *président du Conseil*, Antoine Pinay, was obliged to refuse a bill from the United States, which, had it been met, would have constituted a virtual interference in French internal affairs. The American Ambassador, Mr. James Dunn, apologized and withdrew the bill. Washington explained that it had been presented by mistake.

THE PLAN

With Mendès-France, de Gaulle operated a policy; with Pleven he merely countersigned improvised decisions. To Mendès-France he would often say: "Well, what about our structural reforms? Nothing's ready."

"*Mon général*, you have often opposed me, and you know, we wouldn't have to envisage such reforms if we were the directors of our affairs. But I have prepared a dossier and I shall be ready to show it to you in time."

To Colonel Passy, the General said in confidence: "I know perfectly well what we ought to do. Unfortunately, Marshal Pétain did it first."

Despite opposition from Pleven and the Liberals, de Gaulle signed the laws for nationalizing the airlines (June 26, 1945) and the leading banks (December 2, 1945). These decisions had been prepared by Mendès-France, but it was only after his departure that coal mines were nationalized (March 17, 1946), then gas and electricity (March 29, 1946) and then insurance companies (April 25, 1946).[77]

On October 4, 1945, the provisional government created Social Security.

On December 13, 1945, de Gaulle received from the head of the French economic mission to Washington, Jean Monnet, a memorandum insisting on the necessity of putting in hand "a plan of modernization of the French economy" so as to "break the spiral of rising prices and wages."

Jean Monnet is not a technician like Mendès-France. His book learning has been sketchy, but his experience of affairs is very great.[78] He is passionately interested in economics, thrives on obstacles, never bothers about details, and entrusts analyses and application to his assistants.

The General was immediately captivated. Jean Monnet told him: "France can only be great when the French nation is great. Today, it is very weak. We must give it means to produce, and to modernize those means." [79]

De Gaulle spoke at the *Conseil des Ministres* on December 21 and obtained approval for the creation of a plan for economic development and a *commissariat général*. The decree was published on January 3, 1946, at the same time as another naming Jean Monnet commissioner-general for the plan.

Monnet is a man of decision. He maintains that "half a good idea is no idea."

c'est bien dit

"Why compromise with what you know is right? I don't know what these wise compromises are that everyone talks about. I only know bad ones, which always reduce problems to the lowest common denominator. . . . When you feel you're going in the right direction, don't keep asking all the time what other people think!" [80]

He obtained permission for his commissariat to be directly attached to the *président du conseil*, which gave him an interministerial authority. A dynamic team, as unconventional as their leader, created a first plan of modernization within a year.

"The commissariat will direct and persuade," says Jean Monnet; "it will not administer, it has no life: it will help, but stands in for nobody." [81]

Monnet amazed his colleagues.

"He only knows five or six production figures."

"I never learned a sentence by heart while I was at school, or since," he says.

He waits on the technicians and is cautious in evoking the imagination of intellectuals. He lives in the country, at Montfort l'Amaury, and takes his exercise in the forest of Bazoches every morning in hunting clothes. It is here that the *"motards"* come from Paris to collect "big sheets of yellow paper or little pink slips torn from a notepad, where the commissioner-general has scribbled a few instructions." [82]

These methods bring results. The first plan was ready on November 23, 1946, 198 foolscap sheets in a blue cover, approved by the *Conseil du Plan* and adopted by the government on January 14, 1947. It attained 87 per cent to 115 per cent of its industrial objectives, 70 per cent to 88 per cent of its agricultural aims. Exceptional results, quite extraordinary for a first attempt at planning, carried out voluntarily; for Monnet and his team achieved the impossible by obtaining the co-operation of all the trade-union organizations, both employers and employees.

But despite the stability of the commissariat (three commission-
ers-general in twenty years under thirty governments), the carrying out of the first three plans came up against the permanent
obstacle of inflation. Jean Monnet had forgotten that any large-
scale economic undertaking stems from a political decision. When
General de Gaulle resigned on January 20, 1946 "the train was,
so to speak, on the rails, but there was no engineer." It was not
surprising, therefore, to see the first plan bogged down in dead
ends. "Steel production" had been chosen as its basic motto:
i.e., cars, but housing had been neglected, a problem which be-
devils every government. It favored technical achievements but
forgot to give technical training and techniques the essential en-
couragement and development. It increased communications but
allowed the economy to center on the capital, thus creating *"le
désert français."* [83]

Economic planning, like stability, cannot be fully realized except
in a state, and in 1946, there was no state. As de Gaulle said:
"The trouble with this country is that the right is against the
nation and the left is against the state!"

THE STATE

When he returned to power in 1958, de Gaulle set himself
above all else to the building of a state.

"I love my country more than my soul. I can say that with
sixty years behind me. We have never been in a more critical
situation than we are now, where peace is necessary, but where
war cannot be avoided, and where the prince's choice can be for
peace or war." [84]

It was not de Gaulle who wrote that, but Machiavelli in 1527.
It must, however, have been the General's attitude in 1958, and
in any event, he followed the Florentine philosopher's thinking:

❧

"Whoever obtains the government of a city or a state, above all, when his power is based on weak foundations . . . has no surer method of maintaining himself on the throne than to renew, at the very outset of his reign, all the institutions of the state . . . in a word, there should be no rank, order, employment, nor riches which is not known to stem from him alone."

In five months, from May 29 to September 28, 1958, de Gaulle gave France a constitution. As he was going to Paris for a final visit to President Coty before taking parliamentary office, de Gaulle met Raymond Janot's car at Bar sur Aube: this friend of Georges Pompidou, a supporter of the General and secretary-general of the *Conseil d'Etat*, had been asked to go to Colombey as quickly as possible to help de Gaulle create "his Constitution." The General stopped his car and took Janot aboard. In the black D. S. Citroen, between Bar and Paris, de Gaulle dictated to the forty-one-year-old lawyer the basic ideas he had been preparing for ten years.

1. The sovereign is the nation, from which all power stems.

2. The executive, legislative, and judicial bodies should be separate.

3. France and her colonies should form a single community.

There remained the problem of the responsibility of the government and the head of state: if the government is responsible to parliament, the head of state is only a supreme arbiter. On the other hand, if the head of state is, at the same time, head of the government and is responsible only to the nation, the régime is presidential and, say the General's opponents, a dictatorship, which is a simplification and is to judge the American Constitution very harshly.

But de Gaulle, despite the zeal of certain of his partisans, including M. Jacques Soustelle, chose a parliamentary rather than a presidential régime. He would be head of state, but there would also be a head of the government responsible to parliament.

The Constitution was created on this scheme. Raymond Janot collated all the opinions of the constituents in his function as technical adviser to the cabinet of Charles de Gaulle, *président du Conseil*. Michel Debré, *garde des Sceaux*, presided over the meetings of an inner committee, which were held every evening from August 1 to 14, 1958, at 22 hours.[85]

The discussions were particularly lively between MM. Mollet and Debré. The former wished to make the president of the republic a figurehead, and the latter was pegging away in an endeavor to reinforce the executive.

Guy Mollet only wished to give the General plenary powers for two years, the time to make peace in Algeria, and then send him back to Colombey, but the other socialist leaders, including MM. Auriol and Troquer, had been advised to give the General six months "to make a Constitution" [86] before returning to his retreat, and they had won this point, despite opposition from the socialist party. In any event, Mollet wished to restrict the powers of the president of the republic and make the prime minister responsible to parliament. Michel Debré made the prime minister the collaborator of the president.

Debré was right: the president of the republic became a kind of republican monarch, able under certain conditions to appoint and dismiss ministers, consult the nation by referendum, dissolve parliament, and even assume supreme powers in "dangerous circumstances." Sixty-eight per cent of the French approved the new Constitution (80 per cent affirmative out of an 85 per cent poll).

The only voices raised in dissent were those of the communists, the extremists, and a small group of socialists, plus a few personalities, including MM. Mitterrand, Mendès-France, and Poujade.

The General was elected president of the republic on the following December 21. He is indeed the legitimate ruler of the

⚜

French state. This question of legality has obsessed him since his childhood, when his father "a monarchist in spite of himself" as he put it, was faithful to his king, the Comte de Chambord.

Charles de Gaulle also regrets the monarchy. He said in 1945: "What this country needs is a king. A special being we can bring out now and again in difficult moments. But that has all been destroyed, and you can't put it together again." [87]

De Gaulle has had to fight the battle for legality, in spite of himself, throughout World War II, in the teeth of the Allies, to get recognition, in the teeth of France, to oppose Vichy. With René Cassin's help, he queried the legality of the Vichy government, but his arguments hardly stand up to examination.[88] He had to invent the thesis of the armistice—treason canceling the legitimacy of the government of anti-France. This thesis is impossible to maintain.

Throughout 1945, the provisional government had remained under discussion, and de Gaulle left before he could acquire the Constitution which would give him sovereign power. In 1958, the Constitution became the state, and de Gaulle could be at peace with his conscience.

THE MONETARY REFORM

After a few months in power, de Gaulle stated, disillusioned: "There are two ministries in perfect working order: the interior and finance. The others prevent them from functioning properly." [69]

M. Foccart kept one eye on the police, the watchful eye of a Florentine related to the clergy, the cunning hand in the velvet glove. M. Pinay was the great monetary authority. He is a small industrialist from the Stephanoise district who addressed the communists in round terms at the time of the *Front Populaire* in 1936, served in Pétain's administration and distinguished himself under the Fourth Republic by his offensives against the communists and his defensive actions toward the employers. When the Americans dropped the R.P.F., it was to him and his Independent party that the dollars were diverted, originally earmarked for the "good elections."

In 1958, Pinay was among the first to make the pilgrimage to Colombey to bring back Charles de Gaulle to power. With the help of his two lieutenants, Bertrand Motte, a stolid and loyal northerner, and Valéry Giscard d'Estaing, a Parisian Auvergnat, he rallied the conservatives.

His first task was to find some ready cash. He achieved this, on July 12, 1958, by a loan which was oversubscribed beyond all hope, 320 billion francs, of which 290 billion were in cash. In other words, a fact unique in the history of the Bank of France: the French people had brought their leader a treasure of 140 tons of gold: a genuine plebiscite. Fifty billion in new taxes imposed at the end of July reinforced the margin of maneuver placed at de Gaulle's disposal. He then explained his plan: a monetary and fiscal reform in depth.

On September 30, a committee of experts was set up with the object of suggesting to the government the broad lines of this reform. It was led by M. Jacques Rueff, a liberal economist, and included Pompidou, director-general of the Rothschild Bank, on leave for six months, and *directeur du cabinet* for the General.

The committee was called upon to fill a deficit of 600 billion francs and to enable France to back up her signature of the Common Market, which she could not do in 1958, since she had become "the sick man of Europe."

The medicine proposed by the government was violent, but radical. It can be summed up thus:

1. 300 billion in new taxes and 390 billion saved on expenditure.

2. Devaluation of the franc by 17.55 per cent.

3. A 30 per cent growth of industrial production in four years.

4. Reduction of expenditure by means of discount and credit taxes.

The Rueff plan was accepted by the government in spite of criticism by the parties and the press,[89] and General de Gaulle imposed it on the nation on December 27, 1958.

The fears of the plan's adversaries proved to be unfounded. The prestige of the General and his government, the skill of his technicians, resulted in almost total success, all the more remarkable because the country was still carrying on a war in Algeria.

The objectives reached were:

1. The freeing of exchanges at 90 per cent.

2. A 30 per cent increase in industrial production in four years.

3. A return to the convertibility of the franc.

4. A 10 per cent lowering of customs dues in the Common Market.

5. A reversal of the balance of payments in the export market, which rose from $275 million to more than $600 million in one year.

From May, 1958, to the end of 1960, gold reserves and bills rose by $19 million to $2 billion.

The reform had been one of the finest successes of financial technique in the twentieth century.

Nevertheless, with the years, inflation began again, and a brake had to be applied on September 12, 1963, by the stabilization plan, of which M. Giscard d'Estaing, M. Pinay's successor, was the architect. It was designed to last for thirty-six months, and endeavored to tie rising wages to production increases.

General de Gaulle, trusting his technicians, was seduced by the over-all conception of the reforms undertaken. He was all the more attracted by the fact that their results re-established the independence of France in regard to the Moscow–Washington axis.

Economic stability enabled France to repay a good proportion of her debts to the United States and to accumulate gold stocks and shares which, by the end of 1966, had risen to $6 billion, of which 83 per cent were in gold.

Fortified by this reacquired power, General de Gaulle, perhaps ill-advised by M. Giscard d'Estaing, thought he could teach the United States a lesson. On February 4, 1965, he proclaimed France's desire to return to the gold standard. This bold move resulted in such countries as Spain, the Netherlands, and Federal Germany insisting, like France, on the conversion of their dollar holding into gold, and causing the export by the United States of $1.6 billion in gold in one year. The strength of a country no longer rests on its gold reserves but on its industrial production. France, fortunately, abandoned this unfriendly maneuver on August 26, 1967.

The checking of American investments in France was also decided within the framework of the policy of French independence, and when the General visited the *Salon de l'Auto*, he greeted the president of the Simca company, recently taken over by Chrysler, with a gay: "How do you do?" (*sic*) which says a great deal for the feelings which animate his struggle against American domination in France.

The policy was the General's own. If he accepted the critical advice of M. Pinay, if the latter was mounted on his high horse, he was impatient of the attitude of M. Giscard d'Estaing.

"One day," he says, "he gets himself filmed in a bathing suit, next day he goes on show in a second-class underground compartment. All he needs is to appear at the head of a procession of strikers, crying: 'Charlot, give us a penny!' " [69]

⚜

The Minister of Finance reverted to M. Debré, a man devoid of ambition, and remained more closely under the government's policy.

The criticisms which have been leveled at the government are directed above all at its basic economic policy, much too favorable to the banks, the big companies, the higher-echelon salaries, its lack of social perspectives, and its caution in over-all views and investments.

But the General's supporters reply by quoting the celebrated names which have carried the news of French success and its recovery to the four corners of the world: Caravelle, Mirage, Le France, Berliet T 100, the BB motor carriages, Renault, Orly, Lacq, etc.

CONCERTED ECONOMY

If the General has been personally able to direct over-all French policy, he owes it to Georges Pompidou. In effect, after the latter became head of the government, there was no more *"domaine réservé."* [90]

This son of a professor from the Auvergne was born in 1911 in a small village of Cantal, Montboueif. His original ambition was the teaching profession. He achieved top of the Ecole Normale Supérieure in 1934, became professor at the Marseilles Lycée in 1935, was drawn into politics by the Resistance. After serving in the General's cabinet, he remained fascinated by the personality of Charles de Gaulle. Overflowing with energy, simultaneously he was *chef de cabinet* of the R.P.F., *maître des requêtes* at the Council of States, *conseiller au tourisme,* and lecturer at the School of Political Sciences.

In 1953 it was he who advised de Gaulle to give up the R.P.F., which was beginning to lose direction. At the same time, after supporting the election to the senate of René Fillon, *fondé de pouvoirs* of the Rothschild Bank, he succeeded him in the famous establishment. He left this appointment in 1958, after having been the General's enlightened adviser, the one who never suggested a false move; he was absent for only six months and went back to the Rothschilds until 1962.

Michel Debré had been torn to pieces by the war in Algeria. A sentimentalist and a fervent Gaullist, he hesitated to abandon French Algeria, which many of his friends, and he himself, had hoped to keep for France.

On several occasions he had been tortured by doubts and had offered to resign, but the General had too high an opinion of his intelligence and fidelity, and had always persuaded him to continue in his chosen task: to stop the war without breaking France.

"You want to leave me, Debré, but do you realize this would be tantamount to deserting at the height of a battle?" [69]

After the cease fire and the 1962 referendum, Debré's resignation was accepted, and Pompidou appointed prime minister. The General (who had said to the leaders of the R.P.F. in 1949: "Pompidou isn't a name you can take seriously. In Auvergne, perhaps, but in Paris it sounds as though it's laughing at everyone. Believe me, Pompidou, you'll never amount to anything if you insist on keeping that name!") [69] had allowed himself to be convinced by the outstanding qualities of the professor-banker who, twenty years his junior, showed himself to be calm and full of good sense at the height of the storm. This adviser of the extreme center was his ideal critical mirror.

Whereas everything divided the characters of the General and Michel Debré, with Pompidou the team was harmonious and perfectly integrated, probably because great men have to be understood by similar characters, but younger, therefore more flexible, obedient, therefore more discreet.

With Pompidou, master and disciple work at the same task. In addition, this clever man has succeeded in becoming leader of the majority. He is at once the man chosen from above and the man put in office from below: prime minister and leader of the Gaullist party.

"Serving with the General is both difficult and easy," said Pompidou. "He listens. He short circuits neither his premier nor his ministers. But on important subjects, one must agree with him."

"Working with him," he continued, "personalities disappear and only functions remain."

There is an enormous difference between the relations which existed in 1958 between de Gaulle and Debré and the relations existing today between de Gaulle and Pompidou.

> The General placed great confidence in Michel Debré: the latter had no existence, so to speak, but became an instrument . . . the General knew he would not commit him where he did not wish to go.
>
> Pompidou, on the contrary, is a politician who has his own entity, a personal position to maintain. He is someone different. De Gaulle has a great respect for office, including his own, for which he insists on the maximum authority, but also for that of others. His confidence in his premier is less complete according to the degree in which he allows him more independence. He pays the greatest attention to the prime minister's actions.
>
> For the system to work well according to de Gaulle's conceptions, the prime minister must share the views of the head of state on the main lines of general policy, for the machine could not turn over without grindings and shakings, if these views were divergent on essential points.
>
> Parliament must also have a majority in agreement with the president of the republic. One of the essential functions of the prime minister is to establish and maintain this par-

liamentary majority. General de Gaulle considers he has
no direct constitutional relations with the Assemblies: he
cannot be dismissed. The one who can be dismissed, is the
leader of the government who, therefore, constitutes a link
with parliament, and to whom, in this area, the General
allows great freedom.[90]

There is something strange in this de Gaulle–Pompidou com-
bine, a modern Don Quixote and Sancho Panza. Inseparable,
friends and accomplices, they are both united by a great realism.
This anti-Marxist couple is totally unlike another famous pair,
Marx–Engels. They are neither doctrinaires nor Messiahs. They
apply various classic rules to the creation of a state, this state
which Marx described as a cold monster from which every ill
derived. It is true that the socialist countries who consider themselves faithful to the spirit of Marx have also had to reinforce the
authority of the state.

Pompidou translates into simple language the General's global
views; he regulates the irruptions from the Elysée and cooks the
mixture with an Auvergnat's avarice and skill. He is the senior
executant, the faithful interpreter, and so it is said, the secretly
designated successor.

"L'intendance suivra"
THE ADMINISTRATION WILL FOLLOW

"This expression has been attributed to me, though I have never
used it, for the good reason that I have never thought it," said
General de Gaulle to Michel Droit on December 13, 1965.

We can interpret his ideas, but the facts would give him the
lie. The General has never concerned himself with details. For
more than thirty years, the economic and administrative centrali-

zation of France has been accelerated. An author has been able to speak of "Paris and the French desert."

Trains, roads, airlines, all converge on the capital and every responsible Frenchman, social or economic, administrator or politician, spends a certain number of hours each week in "the Paris train," which has become a national institution.

This sterilization of living forces in an arbitrarily dead-end capital has attracted the attention of experts. If the Third Republic had to admit itself powerless to avoid the danger, the government of Marshal Pétain decided to take the necessary measures. A splitting up into twenty provinces had been included in the plan for the constitution the marshal wanted to submit to the country. Among them was a Paris region which would have included the departments of Seine, Seine-et-Oise, and Seine-et-Marne. The creation of satellite cities and the organization of main routes into the capital had already been envisaged.[91]

We know that these plans remained dead letters. Worse, considered as being fostered by a power suspected of fascism, they were condemned by the Fourth Republic and put off till a later date. Far-seeing leaders of the Resistance, including Michel Debré, wished to revive them. In vain. But in 1959, a great administrative reform was put in hand, and the prime minister advocated the idea of dividing the country into twenty-one regions, directed by a regional prefect assisted by a regional Commission of Economic Development (CODER), which is the heir of the Provincial Council outlined by Pétain.[91] The plan was only put in hand in 1964, and the responsibility for its launching was passed to Baron Olivier Guichard. In addition, the district of Paris was created in 1961, and four "urban communities" were established in 1966. "Critical zones" were brought to the attention of the authorities, and an effort was made, by subsidies, to encourage the creation of employment in those regions (Nord Pas-de-Calais, Brittany, Massif Central). The government also improved communications between Paris and these regions, but the great decentralization so much to be desired has hardly been started. Above all, the network of auto routes under construction is again centered on Paris, instead of creating fast aerial links between the regional capitals. Everything leads to a Paris of 1980 where 25 million Frenchmen will spend at least three days in every week.

The capital itself, equipped with new amenities (underground expresses, fast through roads) is still unable to cope with its provincial visitors or its European clients.[92] Several important problems remain unresolved, not having been included in the over-all solution: housing (the gap has not been filled), schooling, scientific researches. It is true that the opposition has not put forward any large-scale counterproposals.

Nevertheless, the General, more than any of his immediate predecessors, possesses to a great degree the nation's confidence, and has made himself the sponsor of several important decisions. He has little interest for these subjects, no technical competence, and is hesitant to break new ground. He said: "No one can reproach de Gaulle for not having done everything to equip France with stable institutions. The drama of our country is to be divided, split up, detailed to an extreme degree. We have gone from absolute to individual monarchy. We do not think as a coherent and harmonious whole but purely for personal interests and political minorities."[93]

The formation of a great liberal party has not been put in hand, the definition of a Gaullist doctrine has not been promulgated, and the great decisions of internal policies have been repeatedly delayed and put off.

As the General himself has said: "In affairs of state, indulgence is to be condemned, intransigence is essential, indifference is the easy way out."[93]

A good example of this timid policy is shown by the law giving the workers a share in the profits of their businesses.

⚜

This is an old anti-Marxist idea, dating from the Polytechnicians' circle of 1930 (Louis Vallon, G. Boris, R. Lacoste), renewed by the national revolution at Vichy, then by the R.P.F., and finally by the Pompidou government (1967). But under the grand demagogic phrases of the Gaullist leaders, there is only a vague conception and the General's own confused ideas (Strasbourg, April 7, 1947) : "The noble and fruitful association of those who pool within the same enterprise their labor, their technique, or their capital, and who participate, openly and as honest shareholders, both in profits and in risks."

(Saint-Etienne, January 4, 1948) : "To create within professions a psychology other than that of the exploitation of one group by another, that is, the class struggle."

(Paris, December 14, 1948) : "Since a large part of the workers' profit would depend on the collective production of enterprises, the trade unions would be responsible, within that profession, for everything that would increase productivity."

(Paris, December 31, 1960) : "The object is to finish with the outdated aftermath of the old class warfare, to involve directly in the development of the country all those who contribute toward it, and to speed up progress by this general engagement."

(Paris, October 28, 1966) : "This reform must be carried out without pulling down the other pillars which . . . are the investment of capital for the equiping of enterprises and . . . the initiative and authority of those who have to direct it."

But all this vague phraseology ends only in a derisory application, favoring the workers in the big industries. Let us take note that it was insisted upon by the General in spite of the opposition of his ministers, civil servants, and the employers. It would seem that the General has based his entire domestic policy on two main principles: stability and planning. Stability has been achieved, but it is not an end in itself, and the opening of the Common Market in 1969, will be the moment of truth which will demonstrate if the French economy can "hold," confronted by a German economy heavily injected with dollars.

Planning is more theoretical than authoritarian.

"The French solution to the economic problem, which faces us in this second half of the century," said the General, "lies in collective individualism." [93]

The end of the "colonial epoch" has permitted the attainment of the highest standard of living ever known. A new semiliberal economy has been born of the quarrels between liberals and directors, which today are forgotten. It has been tested in relation to countries which refused economic programs (Belgium, for instance) and those which remained prisoners of rigid formulae of directed economy (socialist countries).

But the third plan conceived by the Fourth Republic did not achieve its objectives. The fourth put in hand by the Fifth Republic has not succeeded either. The fifth, which took into account the failures and previous experiences, set out with fine ambitions, but is already behind schedule.[92] The balance sheet will be drawn up in 1970, the year of the next legislative elections.

"*L'intendance a suivi* (the administration has followed)," said François Mauriac, awarding himself a certificate of self-satisfaction. He is alone in the belief.

Vive le Québec Libre!

The words "French Imperialism" have been used several times following speeches made by de Gaulle, notably during his visit to Canada in the summer of 1967.

Today, the imperialism of the Great Powers appears in multiple forms. The Russian aim is to preserve the Soviet communist party's rights of seniority over its brother parties. The United States is assuming the responsibility for the destiny of the free world. Red China's aim is to liberate the *Tiers Monde* from colonialism and capitalism. Germany's ambition is economic. But with France it is cultural.

Rightly or wrongly, the French are convinced of the quality and superiority of their language. This, as they think, gives them the right to interfere in the affairs of others, just as the Americans "in defense of the free world," consider they should drop bombs on North Vietnam, and the Soviet Union intervened in Budapest in 1956.

Why did de Gaulle choose to interfere in French Canada; for everything would seem to show that this move had been long in preparation? Probably because Canada, a territory greater than China, has 6 million inhabitants of French descent out of 21 million. The country has more Frenchmen than any other outside of France. Montreal is the second largest French city in the world, and the Montreal Expo '67 had won worldwide acclaim. Quebec, three times larger than France, cannot impose its views on Ottawa, counterbalanced as it is by the pressure of the immense American hinterland. Without outside help to allow it to achieve an *"ausgleich,"* a compromise on the Austro-Hungarian model, at least in cultural affairs, the inhabitants of Quebec can only expect a gradual stifling of their ambitions.

With a sharp sense of ideological strategy, and after many moves and urgent appeals from the Quebec citizens, de Gaulle decided to help the French Canadians, to establish their strength. Did he want to encourage secession? Anti-Americanism? It would seem not. But his front-line intervention in a fanatical, almost religious atmosphere—which neither the Canadian authorities nor the General could restrain—provoked a strong awareness of its strength by the Canadian minority, and to a certain degree, confirmed the independence of Canada. Only 56 per cent of the French disapproved of the Canadian maneuver, and the leaders of the opposition approved it, while not agreeing with its form.

In Canada, the majority, 69 per cent of the French Canadians, pronounced themselves satisfied with the General's statement, without mistaking his deeper meaning, in spite of the provocative expression: *"Vive le Québec libre!"*

After a violent preliminary reaction, the Ottawa government has shown itself most receptive to the Quebec claims. This is the Budapest policy. It required reaction to Russian tanks to liberalize Hungary. The American policy of force in Vietnam is a preliminary to pacific liberation.

In Belgium, home of the second largest French minority, an independent author, Marcel Grégoire, wrote: "We must profit from the respite which the present affords to settle our domestic problems, before others not only take the initiative, but help to find the solution. . . . The interest of the Belgians lies in working out a reasonable compromise themselves, worthy of the spirit of tolerance which, traditionally, characterizes our entire population." [94]

Unfortunately, this declaration will be filed with other prophecies of Cassandra, and will be quoted in the anthology of warnings that should have been heeded.

Does General de Gaulle's "imperialist cultural policy" go beyond these statements of principle; will the tanks follow the infantry? It would seem not.

In all corners of the world where French presence is felt, in Pnom Penh, in Tunis, Dakar, Kinshasa, cries ring out for the creation of a French cultural commonwealth, but French cultural expansion is far from following. Certainly French teachers and technical advisers make their contribution, but everywhere they come up against their American colleagues. This perfectly useless competition among the white races will be severely criticized by history.

One example of the hesitant policy of French bureaucracy is publication. Whereas books are exempt from tax in the United

⚜

States, Great Britain, the Netherlands, and Switzerland, and are taxed at a 4 per cent rate in Italy and 5 per cent in Germany, French readers are penalized by a 13 per cent tax in France. In foreign markets, French editions have to compete with French-language titles from Belgium, Switzerland, Canada, Tunis, etc.

On the other hand, the success won by France in color-television sales in the European market should serve as an example. This was due to one of the General's closest advisers, M. Alain Peyrefitte, who has been entrusted with cultural affairs in Quebec.

A well-thought-out policy, embarked upon with a keen sense of strategy, has been sabotaged by the administration. The General, isolated on his mountain peak, doesn't care.

After his great days in Quebec, he struck a new high note:

> The fact that France, without in any way denying the friendship she bears for the Anglo-Saxon nations, but breaking away from the absurd and narrow conventions of self-effacement, takes a purely French stand . . . stupefies and enrages the apostles of decay. . . . Rejecting all doubt, this demon of decadence, let us continue on our way! It is that of a France who believes in herself and through that belief opens her way to the future!

And, as the press said: "he left Paris and returned to Colombey les deux Eglises."

Post-Gaullism

At the (provisional) end of this long period of greatness, one may ask: what is Gaullism?

Let us begin with happy definitions. For Malraux: "It's the Metro, you meet everyone." For de Gaulle: "It is sometimes a thousand faithful, sometimes the entire country. Everyone has been, is, or will be Gaullist."

An expert and severe critic, Pierre Viansson-Ponté, has said that it is an experience in three parts: Free France and the Resistance, the R.P.F., the Gaullien Republic. Gaullism is the companionship of those who have taken an active part in one of these three episodes.[95] No doctrine, no political thinking. A leader and his "companions," either pushed out into the cold or set up on a pedestal. It is Mussolini and his hierarchy without the fascism.

To the "companions," all is allowed, all is forgiven. They know they can always ask for indulgence. This system of government—

❧

for Gaullism is a system of conquering power and a direction of the government—brings two results: the law of the leader and the mandarinate.

The leader is infallible and allows no argument. De Gaulle speaks in monologues, avoids journalists who might ask questions and try and engage him in conversation: "To see a great many journalists is a pleasure. A few, a bore. Just one—torture." [69]

Madame de Gaulle, vying with him, replies to all questions: "Why? He owes you everything!" [69]

The General pays no attention to the opinions of the written press, which is almost unanimously anti-Gaullist. He uses the ideal mid-twentieth-century weapon, television, to mesmerize the crowd.

"I believe in television," he has said, showing himself to be a marvellous actor, faithful to his elocution master,[96] rehearsing his part carefully and methodically in front of a mirror and a tape recorder. Through television, and his "companions," the Gaullist truth is disseminated. The *Conseil des Ministres* is only an obligatory relay, which is often useless. The ministers do not often have a sense of responsibility.

"When a minister asks to speak," says the General, "it is because he has done something that needs to be forgiven. When a minister says nothing, he is afraid he may have to tell the truth. When a minister offers excuses, it is because there is a decision to make." [69]

He spoils them, reads them lectures: "In a minister, naïveté is a proof of stupidity, ignorance, or corruption."

The régime has reshaped the state as the General and the nation wished, but it has only created mandarinates instead of training a governing class. A Gaullist thinker, Jacques Bloch-Morhange, who was the youngest *chef de bataillon* of the Free French Forces, has said: "No leader has survived unless he has created, not a crown prince, but a ruling class." [97]

Instead of realistic and competent ministers, in too many cases there are only chatterboxes and doctrinarists. Instead of officials, "companions" who do not always deserve to be indulged.

One minister "follows the ox," instead of reforming the means of distribution; another will zealously censor plays and considers equipping the Venus de Milo with a modesty vest. Another is described as being the first minister for industry in more than twenty years who never seems quite certain which industry his visitors represent.[98]

> Why not create an indispensable ruling class? The General is not interested. Of his followers, he says:
>
> "Of course they call themselves Gaullists, but are there more Gaullists at the U.N.R. than in the M.R.P., at the S.F.I.O., or elsewhere? There are Gaullists of the right who follow Debré; they are idealists by interest. There are Gaullists of the left; they are disappointed idealists. Finally, there are the Pompidouists, who are realists! But in all that, it is very hard to find a real Gaullist, sharing my convictions, my ideas, and my philosophy." [69]
>
> And in a melancholy hour, de Gaulle continued: "The U.N.R. is a party that chose de Gaulle as others have chosen Garap." [69]

Nevertheless, Bloch-Morhange isn't resigned. He wants the *Conseil des Ministres* to become a college of experts, that the higher echelons of the nation should take over from the aristocracy of old, and he addresses this immediate call to the General: "Do not leave fate to settle this task which devolves on you!" [97]

There are, however, many young people who believe in the future of Gaullism; 350,000 of them, of which 42 per cent were students, belong to a Union of Youth for Progress (U.J.P.). They consider that a Gaullist movement will continue after 1972. They place it alongside the traditional political forces of order and progress, of right and left. But will the U.J.P. bring out a program and a doctrine in time? Nothing is less sure.[99]

THE ANTI-GAULLISTS

General de Gaulle has numerous opponents in France. We can begin by separating those who look to the past from those who look to the future.

MM. Lecanuet, Mollet, and Tixier-Vignancour are turned to the past. These gentlemen speak with nostalgia of the Fourth Republic or the Vichy government, and their audience is limited, particularly among the young. M. Guy Mollet, the socialist leader, like M. Tixier-Vignancour, a leader of the extremists, are both advocates of a reform of the Constitution in a retrograde sense. They want to see a splintering of parties, which runs counter to the preoccupation with efficiency of the younger generation.

M. Lecanuet, the Catholic leader, groups around him a certain opposition of the right under the label of "centrist," which shows his desire to assemble certain sections of the conservative parties. He profited for a while from American support. His program is more precise than that of MM. Mollet and Tixier-Vignancour, and aims at a strengthening of the Atlantic Alliance. The programs of these three anti-Gaullist groups are vague and their points of view are expressed more by negative criticism than by concrete counterproposals: "The disgraceful policy of de Gaulle is alone responsible for the immense peril which threatens French economy." (Tixier-Vignancour, July 12, 1967.)

"By questioning the value of all alliances, by bringing no enthusiasm to a European construction, which alone can guarantee real independence, by rejecting Great Britain's membership of the Common Market, by fixing narrow limits to international cooperation in economic and technical fields, the head of state is pursuing a policy of isolation. The social progress he speaks of, always announced for tomorrow, can be translated into economic stagnation, a crisis of unemployment and a marked insufficiency of investments. The inroads made on Social Security will not be balanced by the ultimate participation of certain workers in the profits of enterprises." (Lecanuet, August 10, 1967.)

"Foreign policy: the affirmation of an outmoded nationalism which, whatever he may say, has isolated France. . . .

"Internal policy: not a single valid word on serious problems, Common Market, Social Security." (Mollet, August 10, 1967.)

Among the General's opponents we can differentiate between those who belong to the majority and those who resist it. These two political forces, the traditional French parties of order and progress, divide France. They are situated geographically north and south of the Loire.

The voices of progress are predominantly in the territory which formed Unoccupied France during World War II. The voices of order come from the rest of the metropolitan territory: they are definitely in the ascendant in Alsace, Lorraine, and Brittany.

These two forces are roughly equal: eight to ten million voters for the progressive party: ten to twelve million for the party of order, based on the results of the legislative elections of 1958, 1962, 1967, and 1968, and the presidential elections of 1965.

The proportion was reversed in the legislative elections of 1945–1946, 1951–1956 (under the Fourth Republic), when the personality of the General attracted the floating voter. Many voters of the left supported de Gaulle, but reverted later to their usual political loyalties.

On which side will the two million "don't know" electors vote in the post-Gaullist period? Political observers think that this figure will increase until it becomes a center of an apolitical and technocratic government. We do not think so. The *"force de frappe"* of television tends to emphasize a man rather than an

✤

idea, but it is certain that the electorate, particularly the young, who are mainly uninterested in the petty war of labels, will pay more attention to plans presented for their approval, and so prove Pierre Mendès-France right when he repeats: "A program first."

The leaders of the anti-Gaullist groups are: on the majority side, M. Giscard d'Estaing; on the opposition side, MM. Mitterrand and Waldeck Rochet. Their main criticisms are leveled against the political future of France, internal and foreign affairs.

As for the political future of France, their opinions differ considerably in matters of the parties, the Constitution, and the separation of powers.

Two or several parties? According to Giscard, the structure of political life should be simplified, leaving only two main nonextremist formations, as in all the great modern democracies (U.S.A., United Kingdom, Federal Germany).

François Mitterrand, leader of the Federation of the Left, certainly represents a tendency to a renewal of social democracy. After the failure of the socialist party under the Fourth Republic, and the impotence it showed either to carry out the decolonization successfully or to unite the forces of progress, party recruiting has been reduced in favor of concentrating on schoolmasters and post-office employees. The result has been a great effort toward a renaissance of French political thinking, particularly among the young intellectuals, which has been manifested in the organization of 100-odd clubs throughout France.[100] There is no doubt that these political clubs have been behind the constitution of the Federation of the Left, of which M. Mitterrand is at present the leader. It would be unjust not to say that Mendès-France, on the level of ideas,[101] and M. Defferre, the mayor of Marseilles, by his personal energy,[102] have contributed a good deal toward bringing the left out of the Byzantine divisions in which it was floundering. The union of the left is still in the planning stage. Within the Federation, certain socialists have remained attached to the system of splitting up the parties. Mitterrand has opted for regrouping, but he remains lucid and knows that the left has no chance of governing except with the participation of the communists, or by forming an alliance with the moderates: the Gaullists of the left, the Radicals, and other parties of the center not being in themselves powerful enough to create a majority government. In other words, the choice facing the left lies between a coalition formed of the Federation plus the communists, or the Federation plus a section of the Gaullists. Mitterrand is at present making overtures to the left.

Waldeck Rochet, the communist leader, has come out in favor of a union of the left, but with sharp mental reservations. Everyone knows that the communist party eventually wants to rule alone. In this expectation, its tactics are to practice the policy of the *Front Populaire*, in other words, to open up recruiting to its right wing to create a maximum number of members, then indoctrinate them, eventually separating officers and members to form a strong party, and so on. This very clever method is extremely successful, and the communist party has continued to consolidate and extend its position in France: 1.5 million voters in 1936, 5 million in 1945, 5.5 million in 1956, 3.8 million in 1958, 4 million in 1962, 5 million in 1967, and provisionally estimated in 1968 at 4.5 million.

It is clear that the communists will never agree to join a union of the left which they do not lead.[103] To achieve this, it is in their interest to divide the parties and return to the previous régime. The only unifying element of the left is de Gaulle, the common enemy. The General's departure will probably set off the splintering effect. For the moment, the communists are offering their support to the left without giving it fully. Said Rochet in September, 1967: "The noncommunist parties of the left must definitely reject any prospect of alliance with the right, even if this is camouflaged under a centrist label, so as to achieve a solid and lasting

✧

agreement with the communist party on the basis of a program that has been jointly discussed."

The present Constitution or a return to the Constitution of the Fourth Republic?

Giscard, Mitterrand, and Rochet would reply in chorus: no more personal power. Says Giscard:

> Our great concern, is the fear that the individual exercise of power, should it become the rule, would not prepare France for the opening up of ideas and the permanent direction of her future.
>
> Among our aspirations is that of seeing our country finally capable of experiencing an organized political régime, where each man would bring his talent and capacities, but which would constantly be reaching toward a future beyond the means of the individual.
>
> To put this régime into operation, there is no question in our minds of jeopardizing the authority of the president of the republic, but it is indispensable for that authority not to be used except after the necessary deliberations. Governmental debate if it is a question for the executive, parliamentary deliberation if it involves the legislature. Consultation does not weaken authority. It can illumine its functions and assure a true national cohesion.
>
> For us, the preparation of the political future of France must include the following elements:
>
> The exercise of the indispensable authority, in conditions which respect and seek preliminary deliberations.
>
> Unequivocal acceptance by the majority and opposition of the existing constitutional cadre.
>
> The establishing between the majority and opposition of reasonable and modern communication, causing the disap-

appearance of the civil war between simplified judgments and extreme opinions. Two different categories of Frenchmen do not exist: the good and the bad. There are two groups who, on the exact problems of economic and social organization or international co-operation, have different solutions to offer.

The installation within the majority and opposition of organized democratic debate will allow an evolution toward a régime based on two truly representative tendencies.

With a framework thus clarified, the presentation by statesmen, not of their own skill or their tactical arrangements, but their essential proposals on the problems of the future.

Mitterrand is distinctly and unreservedly opposed to individual power: "Frenchmen question themselves anxiously on the conditions under which power is exercised and where the enterprise is leading." The constitution by the Federation of the Left of a countergovernment has not brought the expected results. "The Left should win its right to govern."

To tell the truth, Mitterrand is taking the leadership of the federation, and the "I" is becoming more and more noticeable in his utterances. Clear thinking and preparing himself for a takeover, he seems in a certain measure to approve of the existing Constitution: "Twenty-two years after World War II, after a régime of Assembly which was able to reconstruct, but did not know how to assume the continuity of its executive power, after a régime of personal rule which is drawing to a close, the duty of the left is to prepare the way for a strong democracy, just and brotherly, which will be a socialist democracy."

Waldeck Rochet and the political bureau of the communist party are frankly in favor of the reform of the Constitution, which must no longer permit the exercise of individual power, nor the

❧

choice of a *"domaine réservé."* The communists question each other, however, with regard to "the political gambits of the Fourth Republic, which seemed to inspire a real repulsion in a notable portion of the electorate." [104]

Said Rochet in September, 1967: "We do not make the abolition of the existing Constitution a condition of our agreement with the other parties of the left, even though we are against it. We merely ask for the immediate abrogation of the articles which have instituted individual power," a position which was confirmed at the time of the elections in 1968.

Separation or confusion of powers? Giscard considers that the future should bring about "a search for a new balance between the executive and the legislature. The power should be represented in triangular form: at the apex, the president of the republic, at the base, the government and the assemblies."

Mitterrand and Rochet wish to restore its legislative powers to parliament, but the communists ask for a return to proportional representation which would insure their majority in the Federation of the Left. It is, therefore, very unlikely that the Federal leaders will do much to speed up this angle. During the 1968 elections, they left this problem in abeyance.

In brief, a map of probabilities shows that, as far as the political future of France is concerned, the "post-Gaullists" are divided as follows:

1. For the two-party system: more than 10 per cent of the electorate.

2. For the multiparty system: more than 25 per cent.

3. For the maintenance of the Constitution: more than 50 per cent.

4. Against personal powers and for a reinforcing of the powers of the Assembly: more than 50 per cent, as the first round of the 1968 elections confirmed.

In domestic policy, the situation is clearer. Giscard d'Estaing has noted two new elements: the rapid rise in the level of teaching and education in France, and in the standard of living. He thinks that the majority of economic and social problems could find a regional rather than a national solution. In other words, he believes in the future of regional development.

Mitterrand is more vigorous, but equally vague. He protests against slum dwellings, the nondemocratization of teaching, insecurity of employment, the injustice of the scale of salaries. But he puts forward no over-all plan and does not say, like Mendès-France, that "a policy of the left in financial matters will show itself tougher than a policy of the right because the left wants to be generous."

Waldeck Rochet is even more vehement and not less vague: "The parties of the left cannot and should not take power to create a policy of monopolies by sacrificing the standard of living of the workers, as the Gaullist powers have done."

The poverty of the economic and social ideas of the left is striking: prejudices, ancient clichés, but nothing constructive. No views on the future. The leftists have not understood that in economic matters the guiding plans of France after 1945 have been proved right, while the broader-based Soviet plans have failed in the socialist countries. They can only make social claims. This demagogic attitude will probably pay off in times of crisis.

As for foreign policy, the differences of the anti-Gaullists are minimal. On the subject of Europe and NATO, there seems to be a kind of unanimity. Gaullists and anti-Gaullists have chosen independence.

Giscard thinks that the major problems should, in the future, be treated on a European scale rather than within a French framework, whether economic, diplomatic, or defensive.

Mitterrand believes in the future of Europe, like de Gaulle, and his attitude would probably be tougher toward the existing

❦

communities, which he considers as a "Europe of technocrats and cartels." On the other hand, he supports the entry of Great Britain into the Common Market, without citing his conditions. He demands the "simultaneous dissolution of the military Atlantic and Warsaw Pacts."

Waldeck Rochet shares the point of view of foreign communist parties on the majority of international questions:

1. That of the Soviet communist party on the Middle East (for the Arabs, against Israel) and on Vietnam (for North Vietnam, against the Chinese of Peking)

2. That of the Canadian communist party on the Quebec affairs, etc.

He expresses his hostility toward "the installation of a supranational government on the scale of the little Europe of the Six" and calls for the dissolution of the NATO and Warsaw Pacts.

In short, the map of probabilities is established as follows for domestic and foreign policies:

1. For a social relaxation (wages, social housing): nearly 50 per cent of the electorate.

2. For a total disengagement from NATO: more than 50 per cent.

3. For a stiffening in European affairs: nearly 50 per cent.

From this brief examination of the anti-Gaullist positions, it may be concluded that no political attitude is really cut and dried. According to the problems, the chances of reform rise from 1 to 5 out of 10, except perhaps on the diplomatic level, where de Gaulle expresses the policy of 76 per cent of the French. The anti-Gaullists would like to change the means of diplomatic expression, but this would be to use softer means to make the positions stronger.[105] If an analysis of the parties about to disappear

were made, French political forces could be regrouped under four
main headings:

Programs:	Conservatives	Liberal (progressive right)	Left National (noncom- munist)	Communist
policy:	order	progress	order	progress
economics:	order	order	progress	progress
leaders:	V. Giscard	E. Faure	F. Mitterrand	W. Rochet
	J. Duhamel	E. Pisani	G. Defferre	R. Leroy
	M. Debré	M. Schumann	P. Mendès-	
	G. Pompidou	M. Faure	France	
			C. Hernu	

A certain number of Socialists and Radicals (Gaillard, Lacoste,
Lejeune) must join up with the Liberals. Several popular Demo-
crats must move over to the National Left. In the post-Gaullist
period, certain Gaullists (D'Astier, Vallon) must rejoin the National Left.

When the regrouping is finished, three majorities might be
formed: Conservatives plus Liberals, or Liberals plus National
Left, or National Left plus Communists. The electorate will decide. Since 1958, de Gaulle has steadily won the votes of the
National Left.

Political observers can ask if the regrouping will be finished by
1972 or 1973. The Parliamentary majority of 74 per cent which
resulted from the 1968 elections deceived nobody since it only
represented 47.79 per cent of the voters. The opposition continues
to represent the majority of the French electoral body, and its
internal divisions alone bar its way to power.

It was the two million floating voters that secured the Gaullist
majority. It is obvious that on the second round the electors did
not follow their instructions to vote for the candidates of the left

❧

supported by the Communists. The National Left has lost considerable ground at the time of this writing.

What must we think of the development of the left-wing Gaullists? Will their deputies join the 57 Federal deputies in the post-Gaullist period?

If the current regrouping is completed by 1972, while Charles de Gaulle is still president of the republic, he will probably be obliged to form a government based on the coalition Liberals plus National Left, or to resign. If he continues to rely on a Conservative plus Liberal coalition, in spite of the contrary verdict of the electorate, he will certainly insure for the next legislature a crushing victory of a coalition Left National plus Communists, that is to say, a *Front Populaire*, which will not be able to take office or build a Leftist program without the active participation of the Communists.

The premature disappearance or the resignation of General de Gaulle will probably result in a division of the parties of the left, whose unity has been developed essentially through anti-Gaullism.

The decision and the choices will be made in accordance with the bills presented and the events of the moment. The bills are as follows:

1. 1968—complete Common Market, with recession accelerated in certain sectors.

2. 1969—end of, and reform or dissolution of, NATO.

3. 1971—French H Bomb.

4. 1972—legislative elections (considerable proportion of the electorate, either new or young).

5. 1972—economic crisis predicted by the experts.

6. 1973—January 8, presidential elections.

At this time, the dynamism of youth, the economic and military strength of France, will not have diminished French pretensions to the role of a Great Power. On the other hand, social problems will have multiplied. The left and the Progressive party will be well placed to offer the solutions expected by the electorate.

But will the left be united? In other terms, will the Communist party make the necessary concessions to hold the federation of the left against an alliance with the moderate right?

If he is still alive, will General de Gaulle want to retire? That is to say, resign a year after Churchill, three years before Gladstone, five years before Adenauer?

He will not be able to continue if his government has not solved the social problems that are seen to be developing toward a crisis in 1972. Unless a sudden acceleration develops: the continuation in power of a government based on the right, conservatives and liberals, the absence of solution to the economic and social problems could become the cause, and precipitate the departure of the General and the coming to power of a divided Left.

FRENCH YOUTH AND THE LEADERS
OF ITS THOUGHT

What do the young think? On the political level, various soundings enable the tastes and aspirations of French youth to be established.

One out of five, between the ages of sixteen and twenty-four, cite reading as their favorite occupation.[106] But they read periodicals and illustrated papers. Two thirds of these young readers prefer newspapers and magazines to books. Among the book readers, less than 25 per cent read the classics or great modern works.[106] It's not much.

The paperback attracts 75 per cent of the young readers. The authors with the greatest influence over the young are: Saint-

⚜

Exupéry, Cesbron, and Fournier, followed by Jean-Paul Sartre, Albert Camus, and André Malraux. It is true that these three latter authors are less popular and drier to read.[107] Together with Françoise Sagan, they are read much more by adults, by the élite who see in their works (wrongly, it seems) a certain image of youth. We think that these authors transpose into literature the feelings that youth would like to express and, under that heading, they indirectly exercise an influence over the young by translating into intelligible concepts what is often only incoherent or suppressed aspirations.

Sartre and Camus are representatives of this new literature, Camus probably more than Sartre. And their political choices are significant, for the *"presse d'opinion"* has disappeared in France. The young are not interested in politics: with the exception of the university undergraduates who follow the life of the city, as opposed to the young people in the country, who only pay a very limited attention. Among themselves, young citizens are only moderately preoccupied with public affairs.

Surveys say that 53 per cent of the young show a certain interest in politics, with only 3 per cent evincing a great interest.[106] It will be noted that only three out of ten young people can quote the names of three ministers in office; seven out of ten are opposed to lowering the right-to-vote age to eighteen; five out of ten never have any political discussions with their friends and families. The most unpolitical are always the agriculturists, the "professionaless" and the workers.

On the level of international relations, five out of ten do not know if the great problems of our time could be better resolved in a national or international framework, and only two out of ten are very favorable to the Common Market.[106] It is true that seven out of ten are more attracted by the United States and Canada, or by England and the countries of the Common Market. Four out of ten consider that in twenty-five years' time, communism will have more power in the world than it has today, which does not mean they are communists or favorable to the movement, for eight out of ten are convinced that life is better in the West.

At the time of this survey (1961), the young Frenchmen were mostly preoccupied with the war in Algeria, which they considered as the main political problem of the country. The dissatisfaction of the young with the parties certainly played a leading part in the rising of May 13, 1958, which caused the end of the Fourth Republic.

The young who voted for the first time (plus or minus 750,-000) who had taken part in, or were about to take part in, the Algerian war, helped to put an end to the régime which promised victory and peace but was not able to bring about the one or assure the other.

The political maneuvers which put an end, in fairly lamentable conditions, to the experience of the only French postwar statesman, Pierre Mendès-France, have certainly enlightened the young. It should be noted that he was very popular with youth, probably for his courageous stand in the decision taken to end the war in Indochina and, on the domestic front, for fighting the ultracolonialists as well as the defenders of alcoholism. A surprising fact, which the young people noticed: Mendès-France had acquired, among the political parties, an unpopularity as widespread as his influence over the young.[69]

In short, in 1958 it can be said the young Frenchmen were indifferent to politics. They were reacting to all the propaganda with which the war had stuffed their parents and with which the Cold War, every day, was trying to intoxicate them. In consequence, they were favorable to any change of régime which might solve the problems in the face of which the Fourth Republic had shown itself impotent.

The war in Algeria, which swallowed up the lives of 500,000

❦

young people, was behind the attitude of youth. What did their masters say?

Jean-Paul Sartre is a philosopher of genius. His thinking, recondite and verbose, is expressed under different forms with a certain deliberate touch of scandal. He advises his disciples to free themselves from social, political, or religious constraints. This search for the profound freedom of the individual is pursued through his literary work and by various positions, numerous and frequent (weekly, say those who do not like him), for this philosopher of freedom is a committed politician.

This son of the upper middle class likes to say no—to God, to the state, to the family, to love, to friendship, to anarchy. He said no to the Nobel Prize, to America and capitalism, but yes to Castro; no to Communism, yes to Russia; no to democracy and no to Trotskyism. It is bewildering. Or rather, surprising, for his manifestos, or those he inspires, are systematically Left: for Ben Bella, against de Gaulle, for Israel against Nasser, for Vietnam, against NATO. Why in 1948 did he not raise his voice against the labor camps of the Stalin régime in the U.S.S.R.? In favor of the Arab refugees? It remains the secret of M. Sartre, whose political thinking is tinged with ballyhoo and often has no value except as publicity.

During the war in Algeria, on September 6, 1960, Sartre signed a "declaration of 121 intellectuals on the right to revolt." Has this text, which he largely inspired, had any influence? It would seem not, at least not on the call up. It may have hastened the process of decolonization undertaken by de Gaulle, who, on November 4, 1960, spoke of his opposition to two packs: that of "sterile immobility" and that of "vulgar desertion." De Gaulle said to his ministers:

"Hang on to the mast, she's going to pitch!" [69]

Later, in March, 1967, at the time of the tribunal organized by

⚜

Lord Russell which was to have been set up in Paris to condemn "American aggression in Vietnam," de Gaulle wrote to Sartre:

"Mon cher maître, you won't teach me that justice belongs only to the state."

The fictitious "tribunal' was set up in Stockholm, and the master saw that it got a good press.

Sartre's attitude, in international politics, seems to have become that of a convinced pacifist. He may remember that he is Albert Schweitzer's second cousin, and above all that he taught philosophy at the Institut Français in Berlin during the stormy years, 1933 and 1934, when the waves of totalitarism and were dragging Germany toward a cruel fate.[105]

The position adopted by Albert Camus was more subtle. Born to a poor family of French colonials in Algeria, this brilliant essayist expresses in his books the feeling he has always had of being "a stranger" in a Moslem world. In opposition to Sartre, he is a believer who preaches love through his own suffering. Camus fought injustice wherever he found it, under all its forms, without concerning himself with politics or popularity. He supported the Greek communists pursued by fascist-royalist governments, was against the Soviet concentration camps, supported the Hungarian revolution and was against certain repressive measures of the Franco régime.

For him, more than for anyone else, the drama lay in Algeria. He felt himself attached to what was his native soil. To those who reproached him for his attachment to the Algeria of his birth as opposed to the Algeria of the nationalists, he replied: "I prefer my mother to justice." *"Algerie algérienne"* is an absurd solution, inevitable probably, but which broke something within him. The more the war developed, the more Camus felt himself involved, both anxious and guilty at the same time. He would not admit the historic determinism of Marx and refused to make the difficult present subordinate to a conditioned and pre-established

⚜

future. He broke with Sartre and was condemned by the communists. He aligned himself with the proposals for a compromise
peace between the Algerian communities, but when this failed,
he withdrew into isolation and left unanswered the questions of
the young French on Algeria, together with those on Europe or
Vietnam.

His spiritual and moral thinking, sad but not pessimistic, continues to exercise over French youth a stimulating influence: their
destiny belongs to them alone and will be what they make of it.

In citing these masters of their thinking, their favorite writers,
one can place French youth politically.

General de Gaulle does not feel the interest for youth which
military leaders normally display, *i.e.*, to see good human material
in healthy youth. His attitude is rather one of indulgence.

When clever press agents presented their "pop" idols (Halliday, Gal, Enrico, and Françoise Hardy) to 100,000 young Parisians in the Place de la République, the event nearly became a
riot. Roger Frey, minister of the interior, expressed his anxiety
to the Council of Ministers and suggested "severe measures."

The General looked at his minister quizzically.

"Of course these young people are a little noisy, but I find it
comforting; it is a proof of the vitality of the nation. In 1939,
youth was good, well behaved, very 'correct.' They were asleep!
You probably remember what happened. So what are you com-
plaining about?" [69]

As for the aspirations of youth, de Gaulle seems to ignore them.
He carefully follows the evolution of the demographic chart, but
offers no ideal, no objective to youth. This is all the more serious
because, according to statistics and discounting another war, in
1980 France will be a young country surrounded by an aging
Germany, England and Belgium, whose shrinking populations will
have to bear the increasing cost of old-age pensioners.

Having been lucky enough to find himself at the start of a

national regeneration, de Gaulle was offered an opportunity of creating new points of departure. He did nothing of the kind. The governments who will succeed him can congratulate themselves on results which they did not deserve and on which de Gaulle will have omitted to leave his mark.

In 1971, one worker in four will be under twenty-five, but today, many economic factors are already in recession and do not offer the young an acceptable opportunity. They are leaving agriculture in greater and greater numbers. Too many unqualified young workers are used in the sectors in regression: textiles or clothing, food, mines. The expanding industries do not make it easy for the young to acquire a good professional training in construction, engineering, chemistry, public or private services. Instead of remaining in their native regions, the young migrate west in a Grenoble to Paris and Le Havre direction.[106]

The substitution of national service (army, defense, technical co-operation with the *Tiers Monde* or overseas) instead of military service has only been achieved minimally and without great enthusiasm. The General has not given the young the wide economic and cultural expansion of their horizon they could have expected.

Disappointed with de Gaulle on a domestic level, the French youth in 1967, unlike French youth in 1958, no longer need to put an end to a stupid war and have only the vaguest memories of the Fourth Republic and its régime of parties. Of the state newly desired and created by de Gaulle, they appreciate only the shortcomings and wonder if the present social and political peace requires the maintenance of such a well-meaning dictatorship.

As the years pass, the unhappy memories fade. When the majority of the electorate has forgotten, the door will be opened to adventure.

Observers would like to see an economic and social reform,

❧

which will have to be applied as soon as a crisis appears. As to the revision of foreign policy, it is very unlikely, since 76 per cent of the French, Gaullist or not, approve of the General's diplomatic actions.[109]

In spite of the stability of the French electorate with its party of order (Conservative), and its Progressivist party, separated by a thin layer of floating electors who will decide the political future of France, the defeat of the Gaullists—who will undoubtedly split up after the General's departure—seems probable. The final victory of the left will create the necessary conditions for economic reform, but this can only succeed in the framework of a solid constitution, in *l'État* created by de Gaulle (or something similar) with a strong executive, and a legislative power, distinct but controlled.

An immediate reform of the Constitution will undoubtedly be the first concern of the political troubles which will restrain the economic and social progress and will bring the dictatorship to an end.

When we speak to de Gaulle of his political antecedents, he says: "De Gaulle had no predecessors!" [69]

He will have no successors, either.

CRITICS AND CRITICISM

At the end of this long and complicated journey, we can reckon on almost as many detractors as admirers for de Gaulle. Churchill said one day:

"Of all the crosses I have to bear, the Cross of Lorraine is the heaviest," and de Gaulle, seeing the French applauding Churchill in 1944, was able to say aside: "The fools! The idiots! Just look at them, cheering that brigand, that scoundrel!" [69]

What does it matter what accusations are leveled at de Gaulle, the man who was born politically on June 18, 1940, and leaving France virtually unknown, returned to his country in the midst of cheers? He has been accused:

1. Of having been a rebel and spoiling the relations between London and Vichy.

2. Of dragging England into the Dakar adventure.

3. Of stirring up troubles in Anglo-American relations (notably over Saint-Pierre and Miquelon).

4. Of favoring the development of a communist Resistance and bringing Thorez back into power.

5. Of quarreling with the Anglo-Americans over North Africa (the Darlan, Giraud affairs).

6. Of slowing down the advance of the Allied armies in order to liberate Paris.

7. Of refusing to go and see Roosevelt in Algiers.

8. Of nearly spoiling Allied unity at the end of the war (events in Strasbourg, Stuttgart, and La Brigue).

After his return to power in 1958, he has been accused:

1. Of having abandoned the plans for a European union to sacrifice everything to his friendship with the Soviet Union.

2. Of compromising the Atlantic Alliance.

3. Of keeping Britain out of the Common Market.

4. Of carrying out numerous political actions according to his own personal likes and dislikes (recognition of Red China, neutrality in Vietnam, interference in Canadian affairs, embarrassing the United States to the point of dividing "the free world").

On the question of French internal policy, the principal critics concentrate on two essentials: 1) He exercises power personally and despises parliament; 2) He takes himself for Joan of Arc,

Louis XIV (*l'État, c'est moi*), Napoleon. The psychoanalysts interpret this as a constant struggle to emulate, equal, and then destroy Pétain's image.

For the period from June 18, 1940, to his resignation on January 20, 1946, de Gaulle's admirers and he himself would answer his accusers by saying:

1. The summons of June 18, 1940, was of great importance for France and the French, for the government of that country was the only one that had not emigrated to London, and it was essential to ensure the presence of France on the side of the Allies.

2. Diplomatic relations between London and Vichy were broken off by London. Washington maintained its relations with Vichy for reasons which have never been made clear, perhaps espionage, or to prevent France and her fleet from joining Germany.

3. The expedition to Dakar was urged by the British, particularly in order to recover the French, Belgian, and Polish gold reserves.[69]

4. The expedition to Saint-Pierre and Miquelon was instigated by the British to block the Americans.

5. Roosevelt's ambiguous diplomacy led to the recognition of Darlan, "the provisional expedient," and later to that of Laval in 1944 (Roosevelt to André Philip in 1943).

6. The handshake in Anfa (Casablanca) insisted upon by Roosevelt was at the root of the cross purposes of de Gaulle and Giraud, whereas it was essential to establish a strong political power in Algeria. Giraud, who was incapable of creating or directing it, irresponsibly organized the liberation of Corsica by using only communist forces.

7. The recall of Thorez was intended only to facilitate the dissolution of the military units of the Resistance.

8. Not to liberate Paris was madness, for the capital would have been seized by the communists, who would have stirred up troubles in the rear of the Allied armies.

9. The refusal to visit Roosevelt in Algiers was decided on by the French government and constituted a repudiation of the Yalta agreements, concluded without France.

After 1958, the General's supporters consider that he:

1. Has been the fervent advocate of the political union of Europe, which he tried to establish with the help of Dr. Adenauer.

2. Has remained faithful to the Atlantic Alliance, though he has asked for the revision of NATO, whose conditions he considers detrimental to France.

3. Has never opposed the unconventional entry of Britain into the Common Market.

4. Has only tried to avoid the extension of the war in Vietnam by preaching neutrality.

Finally, in domestic terms, de Gaulle has: 1) given a Constitution to France; 2) recreated the state; 3) reorganized the French Army, so that it is now one of the most effective in Europe.

Psychologists suggest that France and the French people have always wished to be guided by a father figure, wise and authoritarian. They wonder whether de Gaulle is not precisely the leader the French deserve and that France has always desired.

It is hard to settle the debate, but all admit that: 1) June 18, 1940, is an important date in the history of France; 2) the Gaullist policy is formed with great logic and remarkable continuity.

The criticisms leveled at de Gaulle are made by supporters of British, American, or Soviet policy. But from the French point of view, the Gaullist policy is certainly a solution to French problems, conceived on a worldwide scale, as the great men of World War II, each in his own national context—Roosevelt, Stalin, and

❧

Churchill—had done. De Gaulle is the last of the great men of this period, which will long reverberate in future history.

BIOGRAPHIES AND HISTORIES

Outstanding personalities arouse in their lifetime the creative interest of men of letters. One must distinguish between the men of letters, the eyewitnesses, the chroniclers, the historiographers, and the historians.

Of the eyewitnesses on the military side, we have included Auburtin, Laffargue, Nachin, and Paul Reynaud; from the great days of the Free French, d'Astier, Churchill, Larminat, Muselier, Passy, Pineau, Schumann, Sice, Soustelle; from the Fifth Republic, Buron, Guéna, and Soustelle.

Working from this first-hand material and other indirect sources—either little known or unpublished—chroniclers have built up very lively accounts: Amouroux, Elgey, Paillat, and Tournoux are the best. Criticism and time will say which are to be remembered. The climate in which they are writing is in any case evidence in itself.

What is to be said of the historiographers, Barrès, Cattaui, Debu-Bridel, and the fine triumphal arches which they have built for the General, whose actions they approve? The historians have weakened their work. Equipped with their index cards, their analogical scales, their critical equipage, they dissect and offer their explanations to the judgment of their fellow citizens. Barfod, Schoenbrun, Vinde, Werth, among the foreigners, and Grosser, Jouve, P. M. de la Gorce, Lacouture, Tournoux among the French writers have already published very estimable books that the publication of state papers in the year 2020 will only slightly correct.

But room must also be found for political moralists such as

Eugene Mannoni or Georges Izard and authors who, each in his own style, have used a distorting mirror to reflect a surprising image of de Gaulle.

The most distinguished among them we would consider to be the baron Alfred Fabre-Luce. This grandson of Henri Germain, the founder of the Crédit Lyonnais, has made a speciality of speaking in the name of the opposition. Born in 1899, he belongs to the same generation as Charles de Gaulle, but his career of nonconformist oracle has followed very different paths. At twenty-four, he attacked the Treaty of Versailles in *La Victoire*. In the radical line, he followed Caillaux, then Briand, and fought for a while under a pan-European banner. At the time of the *Front Populaire*, in 1936, he founded an ephemeral party of the young right. Beaten in the 1932 and 1936 elections, he continued to publish political studies that were as witty as they were clairvoyant. Anti-Soviet ever since he visited Russia in 1928, he advocated a Franco–German *rapprochement* and approved the official theories of Vichy in the first volume of his *Journal de la France*. In volume II he became more independent, omitting to ask the censor's permission; on the publication of volume III, he was arrested by the Germans. He was set free after three and a half months in prison, but was arrested again immediately after the Liberation as a collaborator. Writing in secret, he spoke "in the name of the silent," criticized the injustice of the purges, and showed that the Gaullist movement contained contradictions and inadequacies.

His ironic criticism of the eccentricities of the General, his mockery of the megalomaniac dreams of "Gaulle II" should have helped remove from the Gaullist system part of its extremes and fantasies. But nothing of the sort has happened. Charles de Gaulle is incapable of appreciating ridicule and brushes aside all critics, even if they are witty. Regretfully, it must be concluded that exercises in the style of Alfred Fabre-Luce are totally ineffectual.

The most *desinvolte* of the critics of the Gaullien manner is un-

❧

doubtedly Jacques Laurent. He is much younger, having been
born in 1919. Brilliant and free of all political commitment, he has
a great many readers in France, nearly two million, but they are
more interested in the adventures of his heroines Caroline Chérie,
Clotilde, and Hortense, extremely attractive young women who
do not hesitate to use their charms on their political and military
companions.

Jacques Laurent's pamphlets are aimed at the *monstres sacrés*
who make themselves adored. Sartre was shot down in flames in
one diatribe, and de Gaulle also has been the subject of a savage
attack. Without fearing any action from the zealous but narrow-
minded police, he writes virulent pages in beautiful language, tear-
ing to pieces a doddering old academician, and through him,
aiming at de Gaulle. Jacques Laurent complains that the General
has divided France, exploited the defeat of his country for his
own benefit, and followed a grandiose political program beyond
the means of the country. Fundamentally, the main reproach
Jacques Laurent levels at de Gaulle is his aggressiveness, an aggressiveness directed particularly against the French. Our readers
will form their own opinion on the subject, but it is interesting
to note the violence of the young writer himself, particularly because it expresses the feelings of a section of the conservative
opposition. Fear is at the base of this violence, fear that is shared
by certain Frenchmen that they will see themselves dragged,
willy-nilly, in a direction which is not necessarily good. The General seized power by a *coup d'état,* and he means to impose "a
certain image of France" on his country and on the world. It
has not yet been proved whetther this image is true or representative.

When a man succeeds in incarnating the aggressive powers of
a not inconsiderable number of his countrymen, it may demonstrate that we are dealing with an outstanding personality, but
also a statesman who has not managed to express or collect the

peaceful aspirations of all his compatriots. A lack of political sense, perhaps, but above all a disquieting lack of perception and sensitivity. By despising his fellow men, de Gaulle has disturbed a good many Frenchmen.

With François Mauriac, the most distinguished of his critical biographers, we meet de Gaulle under a different aspect. Five years senior to de Gaulle, this author is a bourgeois from Bordeaux, unhappy and sinful, a moralizer and a tortured spirit. Dissatisfied with himself and the world, Mauriac has salved his conscience as an out-of-date conservative by subscribing to all the movements of the left: the *Front Populaire* in 1936, the International Brigade in the Spanish Civil War, the *Front National* in 1942, the *Front Republicain* of Mendès-France in 1953. He constituted himself the judge of his fellow authors during the painful purging of 1944 and totally condemned Pétain, except for his desire to expiate the errors of the past.

After 1958, in the name of a Christian truth which he sees himself as upholding, he rallied again to de Gaulle, whom he had betrayed like all his other friends. Although Mauriac's personality is utterly detestable, with his hypocritical habit of using Christian terms for scabrous subjects, through his wide-reading public he is representative of the facileness with which a great many French see in de Gaulle the assurance of a craven ease. Louis Guitard [110] has listed the more extravagant terms used by Mauriac to describe de Gaulle: "genius of simplification," "the most positive of positive intelligences," "the elect of history," "Baron of the north," "look-out man," "David facing two Goliaths," "Knight of the West." This is adoration. The captain is at the helm, the passengers in "France" can dance in peace. The great leader, bearing all our sins, works alone for our salvation.

❧

THE CRISIS OF 1968

The great leader emerged again at the time of the dissolution of the National Assembly on May 30, 1968. His willpower is very clear, his impulses are controlled and placed at the service of a final goal which is always passionately pursued. He said on the radio:

> "Being the holder of national and Republican power, during the last twenty-four hours I have examined all the possibilities which would enable me to maintain it. I have made my decision. I shall not resign. I have a mandate from the people. I will fulfill it. I am today dissolving the National Assembly."

How did the General reach this vital decision in this revolutionary situation? On May 10, 1968, simultaneously with the incidents created by the students in Berlin, rioting broke out in Paris; 30,000 out of 150,000 students barricaded themselves in the Latin Quarter and a pitched battle was fought, during which the police took the sixty-odd barricades by storm: 367 injured were reported. First the trades unions, then the Opposition, used this outburst to unleash a vast strike, which by May 21 involved 7 million workers and brought the entire economy to a halt.

It is clear that agitators increased the tension between the rioting students and the forces of order. Molotov cocktails were distributed to the young people, and "technicians" brought in power shovels and their compressors to rip up the paving stones and stretch wires among the improvised barricades at ankle height to stop the police charges. Rumors carefully spread announced that soldiers had killed babies, raped young girls and abducted young men.

These provocative maneuvers were denounced by the Communist leaders and the Pompidou government, in spite of which the students rioted again on May 24, when there were 178 casualties.

On May 27, 35,000 students and young workers surrounded Mendès-France at the Charlety stadium, chanting "Neither Mitterrand nor de Gaulle" and booing the Communist leaders. It was obvious that the Trotskyites, the anarchists, and followers of Mao were pulling the strings.

The General at first allowed the National Assembly to debate a vote of censure on May 22, which was defeated, giving his government a majority of 244 votes against 233. The Opposition continued to demonstrate: on May 28, M. Mitterrand declared himself ready to take office and reserve a small place for M. Mendès-France. He even spoke of forming a Provisional government, implying that a *coup d'état* would take place.

General de Gaulle seemed at first to hesitate.

On May 24 he announced that on June 16 a referendum would be held aimed at giving the President of the Republic a mandate for "university, social and economic revisions."

Then he allowed his Prime Minister, Georges Pompidou, to negotiate with the trades unions various agreements over social benefits for the workers. But the latter, partly maneuvered by the extremists, rejected the "Grenelle agreements."

On May 29 at 11:44, the General and Madame de Gaulle left the Elysée, ostensibly for Colombey. "The only solution was for him to go," wrote Viansson-Ponté in a leftist paper, *Le monde.* He explained the General's desire "to mark that he has gone home, as a private citizen, to nurse his grief."

De Gaulle returned to Paris next day to announce his decision to dissolve the National Assembly. What had happened? "During the past twenty-four hours I have considered all the possibilities without exception," he said.

What were these possibilities?

๛

1. Strong-arm methods: to break the strike, using the army and the police. This was unthinkable; it would lead to civil war.
2. Resignation of the government. M. Pompidou seems to have drawn the General's attention to the only two possible alternatives according to him: resignation or a general election.
3. Dismissal of the Prime Minister and a summons to a leader from the Left to form a government. The most qualified seems to have been M. Mendès-France, but he refused categorically. His chances of success were very limited, because he was rejected by the left-wing politicians.

In fact, the only alternatives confronting the General were to stay or to resign. We know that de Gaulle is a man who resists opposition: he chose to stay. If he were to stay, he must dissolve the Assembly, but this would risk inciting the Left who could, if they so desired, prevent the normal process of the elections, and through a *coup d'état,* seize power.

De Gaulle did indeed go to Colombey, but his helicopter landed first in Germany, at Baden Oos, where he met General Massu, Commander of the French Forces in Germany, and General Beauvallet, Governor of Metz. He asked them if he could rely on the loyalty of their 60,000 troops to enforce public order and guarantee the freedom of the elections if the extremists took to the streets.

In his speech of May 30, de Gaulle concluded: "The legislative elections will take place as planned unless an attempt is made to gag the entire French people by preventing them from expressing themselves while they are also prevented from living. . . . The methods used will be intimidation, intoxication, the tyranny exercised by groups organized at long distance and by a party with totalitarian aims, even if it already has rivals in this respect."

The assurance and the firmness of the message struck all observers. The demonstrations which were organized after the

General's speech showed that the head of State had struck the right note, and that the forces of order could still command a majority. The elections of June 30 gave the General's supporters 47 per cent of votes against 21 per cent to the Communist party and 22 per cent to the various left-wing organizations.

After this victory, de Gaulle accepted the resignation of Pompidou who, he hopes, will be his successor, and called M. Couve de Murville to the position of Prime Minister.

The supporters of the General will say that once again, he had saved France.

NOTES : INTRODUCTION

1. The Club of Tall Men. (*Klub langer Menschen*, K.L.M.) was founded in Federal Germany after the war. It offered honorary presidency to King Ibn Saud (2.12 m.—6' 7''), to President de Gaulle, and Chancellor Kiesinger. It includes among its 2,200 members Paul Adenauer (1.96 m. —6' 1''), son of the chancellor. This club has studied the problems that daily life sets tall men. In particular: increased expenditure owing to special circumstances, size of clothes and underclothes, larger sizes of furniture (beds, cupboards, baths), the cost of food, the fact that the tax collector makes no special allowances for tall men, difficulties in dealings with fellow men (chances of marriage, for instance, particularly for tall women) and sometimes even a tendency to depression and suicide.

2. Spears: *Assignment to Catastrophe*, London, 1963. Vol. II.

NOTES : PART I

All the quotations from C. de Gaulle are extracts from his *Mémoires*, except where indicated.

1. On his childhood, there are witnesses in P. Barrès, *Charles de Gaulle*, page 16, and particularly J. R. Tournoux, *Pétain et de Gaulle*, and also G. Bonheur, *C. de Gaulle*. See also the study by Roger Wild, "De Vaugirard au quartier latin," in the *Revue des Deux Mondes*, Paris, 1963. Interviews with Pierre Bourget (*Ici Paris*, December 24, 1958), M. Joseph Teilhard de Chardin, and R. P. François Lepoutre, who were Charles de Gaulle's fellow students at Antoing. We have ourselves talked to three other college friends.

2. Text of the R. P. A. Butin, in author's personal papers: In a lecture lasting half an hour, he describes Marshal Saxe who "has no nobility or elevation of mind except during the hours when he is dealing with matters of war, describing the soldier's soul, planning a campaign, or engaging a battle . . . for the man isn't defendable."

He justifies the reproaches addressed to the Marshal for his repeated cavalry charges: "These reproaches are based on the false principle that 'the whole art of conquest is the art of avoiding losses.' This ridiculous principle the great military leaders have never known. Very careful, deliberately, of the blood of their infantry, they never needlessly sacrifice a single platoon, or a man; they do not hesitate, when needs must, to hurl into the battle brigades, divisions, and even whole corps of cavalry."

He points to the Irish battalions of Lally-Tollendal, which were quickly reorganized and thrown again into the attack on the right flank of the English army.

Marshal Saxe was ill and was drawn from one end of the battle to the other in a wicker carriage, but at the decisive moment he demanded a horse, was hoisted on its back, and rallied his cavalry for a final charge.

He heard that it had been suggested to Louis XV, who was present on the battlefield, that he should cross the Scheldt. "What fool is it," said the Marshal aloud, "who offers such advice? I was all for it a moment ago; now it is too late."

With the help of the duc de Richelieu and the king's bodyguard, the

⚜

English were put to flight. And Father Butin concludes his description: "If courage is worthy of esteem, even amongst the enemy, how much more should it be recognized amongst brothers-in-arms. We have always loved the chivalrous Irish nation, great through its past history, its glories and its griefs: we salute with respect the heroism of her children, but this inscription of 1902 cannot be accepted without explanation. Here, as elsewhere, *Amicus, Plato, magis amica veritas.*"

Working in the laboratory of phonetics of the University of Strasbourg on four speeches by General de Gaulle, that of Brazzaville (1940), the Battle of France (1944), the Forum of Algiers (1958), and the press conference of March 25, 1959, M. Jacques Laurin has put forward a theory on "Rhythm in the speeches of General de Gaulle" (University of Strasbourg, June 1964). Analyzed by a cathode oscillograph, translated into graphs, and compared, these recordings enable the volume to be measured, the length of syllables, the accentuation, the strong and weak beats, and the over-all rhythm. M. Laurin has extracted five permanent factors which show how much continuity there is in the oratorial rhythm of the General. Among these factors can be noted ternary groups of words, expressions, or phrases; alliterations; and anapaests. A striking point: the rhythm is very close to that of Father Butin.

3. Butin, A.: *Une frontière en péril,* Lille, 1904; Appendix, Lille, 1905; *Gribeauval et ses précurseurs,* Lille, 1906. (Study on the artillery and its role.) We know that Gribeauval was the father of mobile artillery, a preliminary sketch for the armored division.

4. Account by Madame Denquin as told to Georges Menant, *Paris-Match,* September, 1964.

5. On his period at the Ecole de Guerre, see General Chauvin, in *Miroir de l'histoire,* Paris, July, 1960, and author's personal papers.

6. As J. R. Tournoux has so ably demonstrated (*Pétain et de Gaulle*), at the same time the Austrian general von Eimannsberger published in Munich *Kampfwagenkrieg,* 1935. This book was translated and published in France in 1936 by Berger-Levrault, de Gaulle's publisher. Eimannsberger's ideas inspired General Guderian who wrote on the same theme in May, 1936 in the *Militär Wissenschaftliche Rundschau:* Colonel de Gaulle never denied having refurnished known ideas. The legend of the "prophet of tanks" was born in London in 1940.

The conception of a self-contained armored division was in the air.

In 1927, Colonel Doumenc had submitted a project to headquarters on these lines. The year de Gaulle wrote his book (1933), an analytic study appeared in Paris, nineteen pages, entitled "Tactique générale allemande." It was a résumé of a long publication from the *Militär-Wochenblatt*. This text must have appeared on Charles de Gaulle's desk, together with those of the English General Fuller and the military historian Liddell Hart. By the same token, if, as Jean Lacouture says, from 1932 to 1937 no German military memorandum or any note from the German ambassador in Paris, mentions de Gaulle's books, it should be noted that the book *Vers l'armée de métier* was published in 1935 in Germany, in the United States, and in Russia, in editions very much larger than those of the French publication (2000 copies of which 700 were sold).

De Gaulle's and Guderian's ideas deserve to be compared:

Armored division	*Panzerdivision*
De Gaulle plan 1933	Guderian plan 1935
1. A reconnaissance group. (Mobile machine guns and infantry transport)	1. A reconnaissance group. (Mobile machine guns and infantry transport)
2. A brigade of 500 tanks.	2. A brigade of 540 tanks.
3. A brigade of infantry. 6 motorized battalions with guns and antitank weapons.	3. A brigade of fusilliers. 5 motorized battalions with guns and antitank weapons.
4. A brigade of mobile artillery, including a regiment of 75's, a regiment of 105's, a battalion of engineers, a camouflage battalion.	4. A regiment of 105's, a pioneer detachment, and a camouflage group.

7. In *Vers l'armée de métier*, de Gaulle mentioned only tanks. He did not foresee the tank-airplane tandem of World War II. In the revised edition of the book (Algiers, 1944), the author added the following phrase (p. 109): "But above all, by its capacity to strike at a visible target, airplane becomes par excellence the weapon whose shattering effects can best be combined with the virtues and mobility of heavy mechanized units."

If de Gaulle's plan had been applied in 1940, the French armored divisions would probably have been pinned down by the German air

❧

power, which had control of the air. The latest editions of *Vers l'armée de métier* (Presses de la Cité, 1963) are without the 1944 addition.

8. Launay, J. de.: *Grandes Controverses du temps présent*, Vol. I, pages 150–155.

9. Auburtin, J.: *Le Colonel de Gaulle, Paris, 1965*, page 15. De Gaulle spoke in 1934 at the Cercle Fustel de Coulanges, then at the Club du Faubourg.

10. This book is a collection of four studies made by de Gaulle at Marshall Pétain's request between 1925 and 1927, and three original chapters. This publication gave rise to a sharp exchange between de Gaulle and Pétain. See the accounts of general Héring and Daniel-Rops related by J. R. Tournoux, *Pétain et de Gaulle*, and the very careful study made by this writer.

11. "M. Paul Reynaud gave the impression of being a man who had his future before him. I saw him, convinced him, and from then on, worked with him." De Gaulle, *Mémoires*, Vol I, page 20. It is likely that de Gaulle collaborated on the editing of a small book by Paul Reynaud, *Le Problème militaire français*, Flammarion, Paris, 1937. P. Reynaud published his letters from de Gaulle between April 2, 1936 and May 3, 1940, in *Envers et contre tous*, Paris, 1963.

12. General de Gaulle collected a history of the battles of the Fourth Armored Division. The text is in Tournoux, *Pétain et de Gaulle*, pages 412–425.

13. Approximately 59° Fahrenheit.

14. Approximately 65° Fahrenheit.

15. Sterniot, J.: "Les de Gaulle," in *L'Express*, Paris, July 19, 1966, and private papers.

16. Author's personal papers.

17. Passeron, A.: *de Gaulle parle, 1962–1966*, Paris, 1966, page 376.

18. These tendencies are mostly hereditary. Would this be the result of consanguinity? It is certain that the warm and intimate atmosphere created around the General by Madame de Gaulle has restrained disquieting tendencies.

19. Lacouture, Jean: *de Gaulle*, pages 62–64.

20. Guitard, Louis: *Lettre sans malice à François Mauriac*, Paris, 1967, page 271.

21. On the behavior of de Gaulle during the Battle of France in 1940, see Gallimard, L.: *Vive Pétain, vive de Gaulle*, Paris, 1948, and the novel by Molaine, P.: *Le sang*, Paris, 1967.

22. Barrès, P.: *Charles de Gaulle*, Paris, 1945, page 68.

23. On the machine-gunning of Notre-Dame, Aron, R.: *Charles de Gaulle*, pages 52–54, who took down the evidence of the gendarme responsible.

24. Menant, G.: "Account by Madame Denquin."

25. Gorce, P. M. de la: *De Gaulle entre deux mondes*, Paris, 1964, pages 39–40.

26. Account by R. Prigent related to J. R. Tournoux, *Pétain et de Gaulle*, page 494.

27. Buron, R.: *Carnets politiques de la guerre d'Algérie*, Paris, 1965.

28. Amouroux, H.: *Le 18 juin*, Paris, 1964.

29. Launay, J. de: *Histoire de la diplomatie secrète 1914–1945*, pages 271–274.

30. On the check kept on de Gaulle at Bordeaux, see the evidence of the police officer responsible, in Aron, R.: *Charles de Gaulle*, page 195.

31. Schumann, M.: *Honneur et Patrie*, Paris, 1946; and *Les Voix du couvre-feu*, Paris, 1964.

There is no recording of the appeal of June 18, 1940. See Schoenbrun, D.: *Les trois vies de C. de Gaulle*, Paris, 1965. The rough notes of the General still exist. The innumerable alterations show the hesitations of the writer regarding the form, but not the contents.

32. From June 28, de Gaulle was recognized as the de facto leader of Free France. This date coincides with the failure of the Gort-Duff Cooper mission to Mandel in Casablanca.

33. The official historian of the Resistance, Henri Michel, says: "There are not many men of the Left: a few universitarians, trades-unionists, or journalists; on the other hand, the militants of the Extreme Right are increasing, those of the *Action française* or the Cagoule. (*Histoire de la*

❧

France-Libre, Paris, 1963, page 29). This is the socialist theory pushed to the extreme, as it is customarily expressed by this committed historian.

34. We have seen that there was no plotting on the Marshal's part to seize power, contrary to certain assertions. Launay, J. de: *Le Dossier de Vichy,* Julliard, Paris, 1967.

35. Bromberger, M.: *Le Destin secret de G. Pompidou,* Paris, 1965, page 254.

36. Text in Passeron, A.: *de Gaulle parle,* Vol. I, pages 99, 101, 134; Vol. II, pages 21, 22, 29.

37. The Ministers' opinions are in Passeron, *op. cit.,* Vol. II, 33 to 38.

38. Churchill. *Memoirs,* Vol. III, page 226. (Edition: Cercle du Bibliophile.)

39. Launay, J. de: *Grandes Controverses 1945–1965,* Vol. II, page 256.

40. Passeron, A.: *op. cit.* Vol. I, page 298.

41. Le Senne, R.: *Traité de caractérologie,* Paris, 1963, page 399.

42. Photocopy in Tournoux, J. R.: *Pétain et de Gaulle,* page 506.

43. Isorni collection.

44. Photocopies in Sebastien, A., and Philippe, J.: *Pétain et de Gaulle,* Paris, 1965, pages 94–95.

45. See example. Jouve, E.: *Le général de Gaulle et la construction de l'Europe,* Vol. II, pages 69–74.

46. Military notes by de Gaulle in Tournoux: *Pétain et de Gaulle,* pages 380–391.

47. See de Gaulle, *La France et son armée.*

48. C. de Gaulle, in *Revue militaire d'information,* Paris, March 1928, June 1930, June 1931. The three lectures given by de Gaulle at the Ecole de Guerre were repeated at the Sorbonne at the end of 1927, before publication in his book *Le Fil de l'épée,* Berger-Levrault, Paris, 1932.

49. C. de Gaulle, *La France et son armée.*

50. In his *Mémoires,* de Gaulle mentions that 39,000 prison sentences were pronounced as against 55,000 in Belgium and more than 50,000 in Holland.

⚜

51. Mauriac, Claude: *Malraux ou le mal du béros*, Grasset, Paris. The complete works of Malraux have been published in seven volumes by Skira at Geneva. *La Condition humaine* (Gallimard) won the Prix Goncourt in 1933. It is not uninteresting to note that Malraux wrote an essay on Choderlos de Laclos and another on Lawrence, "Le Démon de l'absolu."

NOTES : PART II

1. Author's personal papers.

2. General de Gaulle's genealogy has been studied by distinguished scholars. Contrary to certain historians who thought they could trace it back to Richard de Gaulle, groom to Philippe-Auguste and to Jehan de Gaulle, who fought at Agincourt, the French experts cannot get beyond Jean-Baptiste de Gaulle, borne at the beginning of the eighteenth century. He had two children, of whom one, J. B. Philippe, born and died in Paris (1756–1832), was a lawyer at the Court of Paris. Imprisoned by the Revolution, he was released on the 10th Thermidor, then married Anne-Sophie Gaussen on the 14th Thermidor, year III. Later, he was attached to the postal services of the Grand Army. Their son was Julien-Philippe de Gaulle, born and died in Paris (1801–1883), the historian of Paris and Saint-Louis. He married a woman of letters, the biographer of Chateaubriand and editress of the revue *Correspondance des familles*, Joséphine Maillot (1805–1885), daughter of an industrialist of Dunkirk. The de Gaulle-Maillots had three sons: Charles, Henri, and Jules. Henri, born and died in Paris (1848–1933), married his cousin Jeanne Maillot and Charles de Gaulle was their second son. See *La France généalogique*, Paris, April 1966.

A Flemish genealogist, Ludo Poplemont, has carried out researches in Burgundy. He has established that the de Gaulles, a family of bourgeois and tradespeople, lived at Châlons-sur-Marne from the sixteenth century. Claude de Gaulle (1630–1691) a tradesman, had married Madeleine Fastret, and was the father of Antoine de Gaulle (1669–1730), a merchant. He married Anne Regnault, and had four children. The second was Jean-Baptiste (1720–1798), an attorney, father of J. B. Philippe. See L. Poplemont, *Vlaamse Stam*, October, 1966.

3. Quoted by Lacouture, Jean: *de Gaulle*, page 3. Charles de Gaulle's maternal ancestry is equally bourgeois. The mother of Madame Henri de Gaulle-Maillot is Julia Maillot-Delannoy, a daughter of a Delannoy-MacCartan. The Delannoys, a bourgeois family of the North, are descended from numerous bastards of the Seigneurs de Lannoy, whose most illustrious members are: Jehan de Lannoy (1410–1493), stadtholder of Holland, then Louis XI's ambassador to Edward IV of England, and

Charles de Lannoy (1487–1527), viceroy of Naples and conqueror of François I of France at Pavia, whose descendants are still living in Belgium.

4. On January 20, 1952, Mrs. Roosevelt was made a freeman of the city of Lannoy. During the years 1900 to 1910, an obscure officer, Maurice Gamelin, sometimes came to Lannoy to visit his cousins the Mulles. At Lille, in 1900, Commandant Weygand married the daughter of Colonel de Forsanz.

5. Among Henri de Gaulle's pupils can be noted Philippe de Haute-cloque, the future Marshal Leclerc, and Jean de Lattre, the future Marshal de Lattre de Tassigny.

6. Noted by Lacouture, Jean: *op. cit.* page 8. De Gaulle in *Le Fil de l'épée*, pages 12–13, has pointed out this preoccupation. What Alexander calls his hopes, Caesar his fortune, Napoleon his star, is it not merely the certainty that a particular talent puts them into such close contact with realities that they can always be masters of their fate?

7. Eyewitness account by the author's father who was present at Dinant and finally captured by the Germans on August 22 in the citadel of Namur.

8. Laffargue, A.: *Fantassin de Gascogne.*

9. Molaine, P.: *Le sang.*

10. This summons was broadcast from Studio B2 in the presence of a French announcer, Maurice Thierry, and Elizabeth Barker of the diplomatic service of the BBC (and not Gibson Barker, as J. Lacouture has it). In the adjoining room were the Director-General of the BBC, Sir Stephen Tallents, who had been ordered to receive him, and Lieutenant Geoffroy de Courcel who accompanied the General.

The appeal of June 18 is a call to dissidence. "De Gaulle was not a general like the others because the previous day he had formed part of the government. It was, in fact, a minister rejecting the idea of the Armistice without yet being able to say what means he would be able to use to annul the effects." (Marshal Juin: *Trois siècles d'obéissance militaire, 1650–1963.* Paris, 1963.) Always, according to Juin, de Gaulle remained a soldier and endeavored to obey army regulations: "To make the laws of the Republic be obeyed, and safeguard the independence and honor of the country." The fleet for the most part refused all contact

✤

with de Gaulle, by virtue of the same principles. The ambiguity of de Gaulle's situation arose from the existence of a legal and lawful government in Vichy, and his action, which was at first exclusively directed toward the army.

11. De Gaulle: *Mémoires, op. cit.*, Vol. I, page 96.

12. Passy, A. D.: *Souvenirs*, Vol. I, pages 13–40.

13. Admiral Muselier's *Mémoires*, pages 13–14. On St. Pierre and Miquelon, see White, D. S.: *Seeds of Discord*, Soustelle, J.: *Envers et contre tout*, Sherwood, R. E.: *Roosevelt and Hopkins*, Villefosse, L. de: *Souvenirs d'un marin de la France libre*, Paris, 1951.

14. Soustelle, J.: *op. cit.*, pages 30–31. On the atmosphere of Carlton Gardens, see also in the opposite sense Mengin, R.: *De Gaulle à Londres*, Paris, 1965.

15. Lacouture, Jean: *op. cit.*, page 96. Tournoux: *Pétain et de Gaulle*, page 297.

16. De Gaulle: *Mémoires*, Vol. II, page 52.

17. D'Astier, E.: *Sept fois, sept jours*, Paris, 1961.

18. Roosevelt, E.: *As He Saw It*, New York, 1946. It should be added that de Gaulle had several times proposed to General Giraud a meeting to unite the French Forces of the Exterior, notably on December 25, 1942, January 1, 7, and 17, 1943, and that these proposals do not seem to have been delivered. See de Gaulle—*Mémoires*, Vol. II, pages 431–432.

To speed up events, de Gaulle had named as delegate to Algiers General of the Air Force François d'Astier de la Vigerie. Arriving on December 19, 1942, he saw Darlan and Giraud briefly, but spent more time with the leaders of the Gaullist Resistance. They had formed a triumvirate in charge of political action: René Capitant, Henri d'Astier de la Vigerie, Louis Joxe. General d'Astier returned to London on December 23, 1942. Next day, Darlan was assassinated. The mystery of this assassination remains. An enquiry was opened against Henri d'Astier and the Abbé Cordier, for a time accused of complicity in the murder. A search made of Henri d'Astier's house uncovered a bundle of dollars that had come from London. The assassin had had a similar bankroll, probably to facilitate his flight. Henri d'Astier and Cordier were both non-suited. See Paillat, C.: *L'échiquier d'Alger*, Paris, 1967, page 172. Our own conversations with General d'Astier and Henri d'Astier in

October 1947 shed no more light. Giraud's position was maintained by R. Murphy and the State Department. Giraud had been chosen by Murphy to block General de Gaulle. Before Giraud's escape from Germany, Murphy had thought of the former commander of the Cavalry School at Saumur, General de la Laurencie. He had served on the military tribunal of Clermont-Ferrand which on August 4, 1940, had sentenced de Gaulle to death. The political councillor of de la Laurencie was Colonel Salan. To promote his candidacy, the General from June 1941 had had pamphlets distributed by Mademoiselle L. of the *corps de ballet* of the Opera. This says a good deal about the seriousness of the de la Laurencie solution and the political thinking of the future General Salan.

19. In Washington, as in London, de Gaulle was at the bottom of the list. Here are a few samples of the official correspondence:

May 8, 1945: Roosevelt to Churchill:

". . . The fiancé's behavior gets worse and worse. His politics and his attitude are becoming intolerable, . . . De Gaulle thinks he is the Messiah . . . even when we are in France, we must consider the situation under the aspect of a military occupation directed by English and American generals. . . . I don't know what to do with de Gaulle. Perhaps you could make him Governor of Madagascar."

May 13, 1945: Conversation Cordell Hull and Churchill: (résumé):

". . . I said that if the question of de Gaulle continued as before, it would undoubtedly cause serious friction between our two governments. . . ."

May 30, 1943: Wiley, American General in Algiers, to Cordell Hull:

". . . The English financial subsidies which according to what he (Churchill) tells me amount to nearly 20 million sterling a year, will come to an end in June. . . ."

June 1, 1943: Wiley to Cordell Hull:

". . . Eden has had enough of de Gaulle and can't stand him. (Churchill) has warned us that de Gaulle is capable of a *coup d'état* and wants to know if Giraud has taken police measures in consequence. . . ."

June 10, 1943: Roosevelt to Eisenhower, Algiers:

". . . for transmission to de Gaulle: having named Governor-General Boisson as French administrator, revocation would be contrary to our aims. F.D.R."

June 10, 1943: Roosevelt to Churchill:

⚜

". . . Neither you nor I can know where de Gaulle will stop. I consider that it is impossible to imagine him in charge of French West Africa. I must consider the possibility of sending troops and ships to Dakar, where there is some thought that de Gaulle may lay his hands on the A.O.F."

June 16, 1943: R. Murphy to Roosevelt and Cordell Hull:

". . . Growing number of the members of the *Comité français* assures the supremacy of de Gaulle. Giraud says that Monnet has betrayed him. . . . Necessary to review the political rearmament of the French troops."

June 17, 1943: Roosevelt to Churchill:

". . . I am fed up with de Gaulle, and the secret and personal maneuvers of the *Comité français* show that it is impossible to work with de Gaulle. . . . He is upsetting our war effort. . . . We must break with him. . . . When we get to France, the Allies will have a project for civil government. . . . We cannot allow General de Gaulle to command the French African Army in person. . . ."

June 18, 1943: Churchill to Roosevelt:

". . . I sent a telegram to the White House, when we were together, but as I told you at the time, the Cabinet (British) doesn't agree with the suggestion (the elimination of de Gaulle) because among other reasons, de Gaulle has just left for Algiers to meet Giraud. This is a new development and we are all inclined to give him his chance. Apart from that, we have all watched their behavior with growing discontent. But it wouldn't be just to say we have decided that "the time has come to break off with him." It may be that this will happen, but it will only be as a result of his refusal to accept the military conditions necessary to guarantee that the French army remains in the hands of someone we can trust. . . ."

June 21, 1943: Roosevelt to Churchill:

". . . it seems that the *Comité* (*français d'Alger*) is now completely Gaullist. He is demanding full authority over the French war effort. I am sure that, for military reasons, you will agree that this control cannot be accepted. . . ."

June 23, 1943: Churchill to Roosevelt:

". . . if de Gaulle were to break with the *Comité* and resign, our obligations would cease to be personal to him and give way to fresh relations with the majority of the *Comité*, which would be a much more powerful means of control."

December 21, 1943: Roosevelt to Churchill:

". . . to be given to de Gaulle by Eisenhower. . . . In view of the help given to the Allies by Boisson, Peyrouton, and Flandin, you are ordered not to take any action against these persons for the time being."

All this correspondence has been published by the State Department: *Foreign Relations of the US for 1943*, II, *Europe*. It will be noted that this publication appeared on the June 11, 1964, the very day President Johnson wrote to de Gaulle to stress the necessity of "maintaining cordial and constant communications" between them. See Schoenbrun, D.: *Les trois vies de C. de Gaulle*, Paris, 1965.

It will also be noted:

1. That Churchill in fact supported de Gaulle vis-à-vis Roosevelt.

2. That Roosevelt did not hesitate to meddle in French affairs and give orders to de Gaulle.

20. de Gaulle: *Mémoires*, Vol. II, pages 473–475.

21. *Ibid.*, pages 360–361.

22. Lattre, J. de: *Histoire de la 1ère armée française*, Paris, 1950, page 351.

23. On Roosevelt's opposition see Viorst, M.: *Hostile Allies, F. D. R. and Charles de Gaulle*, New York, 1965, page 297. It should be noted that at the same time Eisenhower was expecting a winter campaign and was wary of economic difficulties that might hinder operations. He had asked his chief, General Marshall, to support a single central authority in France, and added that "the *Conseil des Ministres* should be supported by every means and recognized as the provisional government of France." (October 20, 1944.)

24. For an appreciation of the Moscow discussions, see Laloy, J.: *Entre guerres et paix*, Paris, 1966, pages 86–88.

25. *Roosevelt—His Personal Papers* (ed. E. Roosevelt), New York, 1950, page 572. At Yalta, Roosevelt expressed his dislike of de Gaulle in no uncertain terms. The French point of view was supported by Churchill and Eden. On the American side, Hopkins, Stettinius, Harriman, Byrnes did their best to win Roosevelt from his antipathy to de Gaulle. The President then told them about Joan of Arc, and other stories about de Gaulle which he had invented himself.

26. de Gaulle: *Mémoires*, 1945, Vol. III.

27. Butcher, H.: *Three Years with Eisenhower*, New York, 1946.

28. Roosevelt, E.: *op. cit.* The writings of the President's son are lively and imaginative. It is open to question whether he has not accentuated his father's opinions to make them more colorful, but the publication of the diplomatic papers corroborates his views, and frequently his actual words.

29. On the departure of General de Gaulle the author is better informed than Elgey, G.: *La République des illusions.* Paris, 1965, pages 49–95.

30. Bromberger, M.: *Le Destin secret de G. Pompidou.* Paris, 1965, page 117. The statutes of the R.P.F. were drawn up by MM. Malraux, Mazeaud, Rémy, Soustelle, and Vallery-Radot on May 29, 1947. The movement was, in fact, directed by seven personalities: Jacques Soustelle, secretary general; André Malraux, *délogué général;* Christian Fouchet, *délégué général* for the Paris region; Jacques Baumel; Louis Vallon; Gaston Palewski; Charles Bozel, treasurer. The General's closest collaborator from 1948 to 1954 was Georges Pompidou, assisted by two colleagues, Olivier Guichard and Roger Frey.

The list of the R.P.F. candidates at the 1951 elections was drawn up at Colombey by the General himself, together with MM. Pompidou, Soustelle, Fouchet, and Baumel.

On the history of the R.P.F., see Purtschet, C.: *Le Rassemblement du peuple français (1947–1953)*, Paris, 1965; and Debu-Bridel, J.: *Les Partis contre de Gaulle,* Paris, 1948. On the financing of the R.P.F. see de Launay, J.: *Grandes Controverses,* Vol. II, page 112. The expenditure came to 821 million francs between 1947 and 1953; 320 million francs came from members and sympathizers and the balance was provided by the Rothschild Bank.

31. L. Chassin has written a *Histoire militaire de la 2ème guerre mondiale* and *La conquête de la Chine par Mao Tse Toung.*

32. Cf. letter from Michel Debré to Robert Lacoste, dated May 8, 1958 quoted by Paillat, *Dossier secret de l'Algérie,* Vol. II, page 528, and on the same date, meeting between Parodi and Mohammed V. *Ibid.,* page 525.

33. The previous day, May 8, Monsieur Coty, President of the Republic, sent the head of his military establishment, General Ganeval, to make contact with MM. Guichard, Foccart, and de Bonneval. After having been

to Colombey, they relayed to him the conditions laid down by de Gaulle for his return to office.

34. For further details, see de Launay, J.: *Grandes Controverses*, Vol. II, pages 110–118. De Gaulle read Machiavelli and the Cardinal de Retz. We do not know if on May 13, 1958, he read this piece of advice given by Machiavelli:

> To profit by the discord within a town in order to capture it, is often a bad method. . . . One of the surest ways [to power] is to seek to gain the confidence of a town which is in the grip of dissensions, and to offer to arbitrate between the parties just as they are prepared to take arms. When they are armed, the weaker party should be encouraged by some slight assistance, enough to enable them to fight and destroy themselves, but not enough to anger them and give them cause to believe you wish to oppress them and bend them to your own power. If you conduct yourself with wisdom in these circumstances, you cannot fail to reach your goal.

35. On the emancipation of Central Africa see Lacouture, J.: *Cinq hommes et la France*. Paris, 1961; Guéna, Y.: *Historique de la Communauté*. Paris, 1962; Chaffard, G.: *Les Carnets secrets de la decolonisation*. Paris, 1965.

36. On the attitude of the Gaullists favorable to decolonization before 1958 (Capitant, Malraux, Michelet) see Gorce, P. M. de la: *De Gaulle entre deux mondes*, pages 526–527. On the General's opinion toward decolonization before 1958 see *ibidem*, pages 518–519; Launay, J. de: *Grandes Controverses*, Vol. II, pages 234–235; Lacouture, J.: *De Gaulle*, pages 169–170. On the evolution of his opinion after May 13, see P. M. de la Gorce, *op. cit.*, J. de Launay, *op. cit.*, Buron, R.: *Carnets politiques de la guerre d'Algérie*.

37. On the tentatives of peace, see Launay, J. de: *Grandes Controverses*.

NOTES : PART III

1. On August 20, Auphan had been to see M. Caous, *procureur général* at the Court of Appeal who, in his presence, opened the confidential note from Marshal Pétain. The Marshal had decided to create a "governing body of seven members" authorized to exercise provisional governmental power, if necessary, and to summon the National Assembly. Of the seven persons chosen, Auphan, Caous, Gidel, Noël, Porché, Bourhillier, and Weygand, the last two were prisoners in Germany. Caous arranged for the five members still in France to meet on August 21 at 15:30. Auphan and Caous were the only two to arrive, and realized the impossibility of implementing their task. In any case, the Marshal's plan seemed difficult to carry out. Auphan, at least, tried to respect the spirit, in default of carrying out the letter. See also Juin: *Mémoires*, Paris, 1960. Vol. II, page 43.

2. According to Stalin, it seems that it was de Gaulle who requested the invitation. Letter from Stalin to Churchill, November 20, 1944.

3. The text of these talks was published in *Mejdounarodnaia Jizn*, Moscow, No. IV, April 1959.

4. Duroselle, J. B.: *European Resistance Movements*, Pergamon Press, Oxford, 1964.

5. *Franco-Soviet Relations*. Ministry of Foreign Affairs of the U.S.S.R., 1959. (*In Russian*.)

6. Launay, J. de: *Histoire de la diplomatie secrète, 1914–1945*. 1966.

7. Byrnes, J. F.: *Speaking Frankly*, New York, 1947. Byrnes was Roosevelt's Secretary.

8. Gannon, R. I.: *The Cardinal Spellman Story*, New York, 1962, pages 222–224.

9. The decision to rebuff Roosevelt had been taken at a *Conseil des Ministres*: the French government did not wish in any way to ratify the Yalta agreements.

10. Hull, Cordell: *Memoirs*, New York, 1957, pages 1239–1245.

11. Paillat, C.: *L'échiquier d'Alger*, Paris, 1967, Vol. II, page 394.

12. Leahy, W. D.: *I Was There*, New York, 1950, page 273.

13. Sherwood, Robert E.: *Roosevelt and Hopkins*, New York, 1948.

14. Viorst, M.: *Hostile Allies, F.D.R. and Charles de Gaulle*, New York, 1965.

15. *Ibid*. See also White, D. S.: *Seeds of Discord*. Syracuse, 1964.

16. *Ibid*.

17. "We did not wish La Brigue and Tende to alienate us from our French friends. English and American democracy is as far removed from French as from Italian democracy, which are both colored by Christian socialism. It was on the basis of Franco-Italian friendship that we considered the problem." Statement by Alcide de Gasperi, president of the Italian Council, to the author. August 21, 1946.

18. Author's personal papers.

19. Launay, J. de: *Controverses*, Vol. II, pages 92–109.

20. Text in Jouve, E.: *Le général de Gaulle et la construction de l'Europe*, Vol. II, pages 414–421. It should be noted that the two leaders of the French Army, Marshal Juin and General Weygand, both spoke against the EDC as well as de Gaulle.

21. *Ibid.*, Vol. II, pages 410–414.

22. These two sketches of Debré and Soustelle were written by the author after conversations he had at the time with the two men in question.

23. J. Soustelle had been nominated Governor-General of Algeria on June 18, 1954.

24. Text in Jouve, E.: *op. cit.*, Vol. II, pages 421–426. It should be noted that the General's European views have always been confederal. One of the first moves toward a united Europe constituted in France after the Liberation was the "International Confederation of Europe." President: J. A. d'Astier de la Vigerie. General secretary: J. de Launay. This organization, which included representatives of countries from Eastern Europe, was headed by Gaullist personalities.

R. de Coudenhove-Kalergi, apostle of the Pan-European Union, on several occasions expressed his agreement with the General's European policy: "No one has done more for the Union of Europe than de Gaulle and Adenauer." (*Le Monde*, October 28, 1965.) The French section of

❧

the organization was composed in the main of personalities favorable to de Gaulle's European views. On the other hand, the European Movement was openly anti-Gaullist. (Congress of Cannes, 1965.)

25. Couve was judged undesirable by Morgenthau and sent on a mission to Italy. Giraud has penned the following appreciation of Couve: "He has one of the finest brains, an outstanding Inspector of Finances who has shown himself an eminent diplomat. He has not compromised himself by keeping up any connections with me. He is a wise man!" Giraud, H. H.: *Un seul but, la victoire*. Paris, 1949, page 130.

26. Beloff, N.: *Le Général dit non*, Paris, 1964.

27. Text of a Peyrefitte project, in Jouve, E.: *op. cit.*, Vol. II, pages 427–441.

28. We follow E. Jouve throughout. His work is remarkable on all points.

29. Text of the Fouchet proposals in Jouve, E.: *op. cit.*, Vol. II, pages 441–449.

30. The phrase *"Europe des patries"* was by M. Guy Mollet. M. Spaak largely echoed him. It should be noted that the General's adversaries have continually travestied and deformed his thoughts. Among many examples, the publication on August 29, 1960 by *La dernière Heure* of Brussels of a "document" revealing the "Europe tactics" of France, which pretend to give way, the better to torpedo the European Union. This text was taken from a confidential note from M. Peyrefitte, which was then cut and modified by 22 additions, 20 cuts, and 74 complements. This says a good deal for the good faith of the General's adversaries. Cf. Jouve, E.: *op. cit.* Vol. II, pages 487–502.

31. Text of the treaty in Jouve, E.: *op. cit.*, Vol. II, pages 460–471. De Gaulle would have been satisfied with a protocol. It was Adenauer who wished to give the agreements the form of a treaty so as to be able to submit it to ratification by the Bundestag.

32. Rouanet, P.: *Mendès-France au pouvoir*, Paris, 1965, page 349.

33. Guéna, Y.: *Historique de la Communauté*, Paris, 1962; and Gorce, P. M. de la: *De Gaulle entre deux mondes*, pages 575–612.

34. It can be questioned if the grave incidents at Sétif, May-June 1945, with their several thousand dead, were not behind the lightning development of the Nationalist Algerian movement. If so, the responsibility of

⚜

General de Gaulle and his Provisional Government of 1945 is very great. General Hubert's report to the National Assembly dated July 10, 1945 does not pin down the responsibility, nor give the number of victims. I questioned General Hubert at the time, and his answer was equally evasive. It should be noted that the Communists took an active part in the repressions, on a civilian as well as a military plane. See Aron, R.: *Les Origines de la guerre d'Algérie*, Paris, 1962.

In my own notes made at the time, I said: "The Governor General of Algeria, M. Chataigneau, called in the police and the army to re-establish order. Paris informed of events several times a day: General de Gaulle telegraphs to Chataigneau: "Proclaim publicly France determined on victory. Allow no attempt on French sovereignty over Algeria. Take all necessary measures to repress anti-French agitations by a minority of agitators." Author's personal papers.

35. Grosser, A.: *La politique extérieure de la V République*, Paris, 1965, page 44.

36. Buron, R.: *Carnets politiques de la guerre d'Algérie*, Paris, 1965.

37. Chronology of attacks in Passeron, A.: *De Gaulle parle, 1962–1966*, Paris, 1966, pages 435–436.

38. Viansson-Ponté, P.: *Les politiques*, Paris, 1967, page 159. Carmoy, G. de: *Les politiques étrangères de la France 1944–1966*, Paris, 1967.

39. There is a political history of the Algerian war in Launay, J. de: *Controverses*, Vol. II, pages 207–277.

40. On the de Gaulle-Dulles talks see Schoenbrun, D.: *Les trois vies de C. de Gaulle*, Paris, 1965, pages 401–407. The Dulles papers are at Princeton University; their forthcoming publication will include an analysis of this conversation.

The question of the Levant had recurred in the spring of 1958. It was settled on July 15 and 17 by English intervention in Jordan and American intervention in Libya. Dulles informed de Gaulle of this plan to intervene, at the same time asking him not to participate.

41. The contents of this memorandum are known through leakages. See notably Schoenbrun, D.: *op. cit.*, pages 408–410 and *"Déclaration de Maurice Schumann,"* in *Journal Officiel* of December 29, 1959, page 3675.

❧

42. At home his brothers called him "the Emperor." In 1948, when Britain wished to create agreements for bilateral military defense with France and the three Benelux countries, it was M. Spaak who made this modification in the traditional military policy of alliances between the countries of Benelux and Britain, the protecting power: and put forward the counterproposal of an Atlantic alliance as a substitute for the Brussels pact. This reversal in the alliances of the Benelux countries had incalculable historic results. M. Spaak has summed up his point of view on the role of small nations: "We know that the Great Powers, whose responsibilities and duties we do not forget, and which give them a special role, should be our trusted leaders, willingly accepted. But we want to be allowed to express our opinions freely, to participate in the measures world security demands, and share the general responsibility proportionate to our forces, all this while respecting the essential rights of all countries." (Letter to the author, March 13, 1946.)

This attitude, in the Geneva tradition, was the opposite to that of the Great Powers: Roosevelt, Churchill, and Stalin had agreed at Yalta not to allow any decision by the Great Powers to be blocked by a small country. See Byrnes, J. F.: *op. cit.*, Roosevelt, E.: *As He Saw It*, New York, 1946; and Churchill, *Memoirs*.

43. Mignon, E.: *Les mots du général*, Paris, 1962.

44. Eisenhower to Schoenbrun, D.: *op. cit.*, pages 457–466, August 25, 1964.

45. De Gaulle: *Mémoires*, Vol. III, page 210.

46. The Paris conference was torpedoed by Khrushchev following the U2 affair. Eisenhower had to admit responsibility. Later, Khrushchev visited the United States.

47. The texts, either in full or abridged, are in the *aide-mémoire* published by Dean Rusk, Department of State, Washington, August 1966. When they left the White House, Truman and Eisenhower took many of their papers away. The Kennedy documents have been divided between the Kennedy Library and the National Library, but the family has made certain selections. Historians of the year 2,020 will have difficulty in establishing the truth.

48. Schlesinger, A. M.: *A Thousand Days—John F. Kennedy*, New York, 1965.

49. Schoenbrun, D.: *op. cit.*, pages 429 et seq.

50. Sorensen, T. C.: *Kennedy*, New York, 1965.

51. According to Schlesinger, A. M.: *op. cit.*

52. On this point, see General Gallois: *Paradoxes de la Paix*, Paris, 1967; Hamon, Léo: *La stratégie contre la guerre*, Paris, 1967 (Preface by General Ailleret); General Ailleret: *Etudes* in *Revue de la défense nationale*, Paris, 1966. These works put forward the French strategic thesis favoring nuclear dissemination. Citing a different viewpoint: Aron, Raymond: *Le grand Débat*, Paris, 1963. General Beaufré: *Introduction à la stratégie*, Paris, 1963, and *Dissuasion et stratégie*, Paris, 1965. General Paul Stehlin: interview, in *Enterprise*, Paris, November 28, 1964, all express the idea that France cannot, for political and financial reasons, fully dissociate her nuclear armament from that of the United States. They are opposed to nuclear dissemination, but defend the right of France to participate in common decisions and to possess national nuclear weapons. The American point of view opposing nuclear dissemination is put forward, notably by Herman Kahn, Albert Wohlstetter, W. Kaufmann. See *La guerre nucléaire*. Stock, Paris, 1965. H. Kissinger has stated that the United States would never prevent the dissemination, and puts forward a theory which on its negative side supports the French view.

53. Communiqué from the *Conseil des Ministres* of August 29, 1963 read by M. Peyrefitte. Text in Chaffard, G.: *Indochine, dix ans d'indépendence*, Paris, 1964, page 285.

54. On the Rumanian mediation, see Launay, J. de: in *Dossiers de la guerre froide*, Marabout-Université, Brussels, 1968.

55. On the English position toward Europe, see Launay, J. de: *Grandes Controverses*, Vol. II, pages 92–109. We quote Macmillan's *Memoirs*, II. London, 1967, Vol. II. *General de Gaulle et la construction de l'Europe*.

56. We quote de Gaulle according to Jouve, E.: *op. cit.*, Vol. I, pages 174–188. We follow this author on the whole of this question.

57. Beloff, N.: *Le général dit non, op. cit.*, page 200.

58. See the analysis of Jouve, E.: *op. cit.*

59. Criticism of General de Gaulle increased in England, to such a degree

⚜

that two British historians, A. L. Rowse and Sir Arthur Bryant, published a protest in *The Times*, August 16 and 17, 1967. To quote Sir Arthur:

> May I support the plea of my friend and fellow historian, A. L. Rowse, that we should try to understand de Gaulle's point of view instead of merely denigrating him because his policies run counter to ours. He is, as Dr. Rowse says, a historically minded statesman with a historian's memory.
>
> His twin objectives have been to restore, after a period of national eclipse and defeatism, the faith and vitality of the French people—something which a statesman has still to do for Britain— and to create a union of Western, or Roman Europe, based on the value of French civilization which, whatever an Anglo-Saxon may think, a Frenchman may be forgiven for regarding as the finest and most civilizing of all. To create that union out of six historic nations speaking at least four different languages must seem to him quite difficult enough without the entry of another whose language, traditions, and maritime and commercial interests instinctively link her with the United States and the English-speaking ocean-nations of the old and new Commonwealth.
>
> The truth is that the Europe we envisage—an outward-looking commercial one with close ties with America—is a fundamentally different ideal to de Gaulle's. That we, or many of us, think it a better one is no reason why we should belittle him. What matters to him about the European Economic Community is that it should succeed, not that we should be in it.

60. de Gaulle, C.: *Vers l'armée de métier*, page 87.

61. de Gaulle, C.: *Mémoires*, Vol. III, page 260.

62. Jouve, E.: *op. cit.*, Vol. I, pages 172–174, 525–529.

62 bis. de Gaulle might have been better advised to note the closeness of his ideas to those of the Rapacki plan.

63. See Kroll, Hans: *Mémoires*, Cologne, 1967; and Launay, J. de: *Grandes Controverses du temps présent*, Vol. II, page 109.

64. In 1966, French imports from Israel were 85 millions of French francs, exports to Israel were 232 millions. Imports from the United Arab

Republic were 73 millions, exports 190 millions. French exports to Libya, Kuwait, and Saudi Arabia rose from 57 millions in 1961 to 250 millions in 1966. France is the leading supplier to Tunis (more than 450 millions), Algeria (more than 2 billions) and Morocco (nearly one billion). She is only the fourth supplier of Israel.

65. Tournoux, J. R.: *Pétain et de Gaulle*, page 343.

66. Mauriac, F.: *De Gaulle*, Paris, 1964, page 72.

67. De Gaulle: *Mémoires*, Vol. III, pages 16 et seq.

68. Tesson, P.: *De Gaulle Ier*, page 80; see also for the Communist point of view Tillon, C.: *Les F.T.P.*, Paris, 1962, and particularly Kriegel-Valrimont, M.: *Les archives du COMAC*, Paris, 1964.

69. Author's personal papers.

70. Elgey, G.: *La Republique des illusions*. Paris, 1965, page 23.

71. Bourdet, C.: "*La politique intérieure de la résistance*," in *Les Temps modernes*, Paris, May 1955.

72. On Mendès-France, see his authorized biography by Jacques Nantet, Paris, 1967.

73. Quoted by Elgey, G.: *op. cit.*, pages 33–45.

74. The financial experts of the government were, on the one hand, members of the financial commission of the *Comité général d'etudes du conseil national de la résistance*: MM. Courtin, P. H. Teitgen, and R. Lacoste, and on the other hand, MM. Bloch-Lainé; Bartoux, director of the Crédit; Calvet, director of the Treasury; Belin, controller-general of the Bank of France; Bizot, director of the Comptoir d'Escompte. All these men were in favor of a liberal solution. It should be noted that the three secretaries-general of the key ministries, Monick, (Finance), Lacoste (Production), Courtin (Economy), the latter a close collaborator of Mendès-France, were opposed to the austerity plan.

75. De Gaulle: *Mémoires*, Vol. III, pages 141–149.

76. *Ibid*.

77. On the attitude of the Communists toward nationalization, see G. Elgey, *op. cit.*, and P. Tesson, *op. cit.*

78. Biographical details on J. Monnet in Launay, J. de: *Histoire de la diplomatie secrète*, page 273. Monnet was later given honorary degrees by three universities.

⚜

79. Text in de Gaulle, *Mémoires*, Vol. III, Annexes.

80. Fontaine, F.: *Jean Monnet*, Lausanne, 1963.

81. J. Monnet in *Le Monde*, January 4, 1966.

82. P. Drouin, *ibid*.

83. On the history of the plan, see Bauchet, P.: *La Planification fran-caise*, Paris, 1961; Bauchand, P.: *La mystique du plan*, Paris, 1963; Lecerf, J.: *La Percée de l'économie française*, Paris, 1963.

84. Letter from Nicolo Machiavelli to F. Vettori, April, 1527.

85. Those attending these reunions included MM. Debré, Janot, Mollet, Pflimlin, Jacquinot, Houphouet-Boigny, ministers of State; the *président du Conseil d'Etat* René Cassin; and Georges Pompidou, *directeur du cabinet du général*.

86. On the Constitution of the Fifth Republic, see Launay, J. de: *Le dossier de Vichy*, Julliard, Paris, 1967.

A few essential comparisons can be made:

	Pétain Plan 1944	Monick-Debré Plan 1944	IVth Republic 1946	Vth Republic 1958
Head of State	for 10 years	for 12 years	for 7 years	for 7 years
Président du conseil	nonexistent	head of govern-ment	head of govern-ment	head of government
Government	responsible to head of state	responsible to parliament	responsible to parliament	responsible to parliament
Executive power	head of state	*Président du Conseil*	government assembly	government
Legislative power	2 assemblies & head of state	parliament & government	parliament	parliament & government

The Constitution of the Fifth Republic arose above all from ideas expressed by de Gaulle at Bayeux on June 16, 1946. Text in de Gaulle: *La France sera la France.*

The important dates of the elaboration of the constitution of the Fifth Republic in 1958 were as follows:

August 1–14	Work of the *Comité consultatif constitutionel* (CCC).
August 8	Message from General de Gaulle to the CCC on the liaisons France-Overseas possessions.
August 14	End of the work of the CCC approved by 30 votes with seven abstentions.
August 19	Adoption by the Government of the advanced plan of the Constitution.
August 27–28	Discussions of the advance project by the Council of State. The project becomes definitive.
September 3	Adoption by the government of the definitive project.
September 4	De Gaulle presents the outlines of the project to the public, Place de la République in Paris.
September 28	Constitutional referendum: 84.9 per cent votes registered, 79.25 per cent in the affirmative.

87. Tournoux, J. R.: *Pétain et de Gaulle*, page 363.

88. See Launay, J. de: *Le Dossier de Vichy, op. cit.*, page 46. The eighty members of parliament who voted on July 10, 1940 against the delegation of constitutional power to Marshal Pétain were not all opposed to the Marshal, but favored a different formula. See Debu-Bridel, J.: *Les partis contre de Gaulle*, Paris, 1948; Moch, J.: *Souvenirs sur les quartre-vingts,"* in *Le Monde*, July 24, 1965 and Pébellier, E.: *ibid.*, July 29, 1965.

89. We have followed Gorce, P. M. de la: *De Gaulle entre deux mondes*, pages 737–742.

90. Bromberger, M.: *Le Destin secret de G. Pompidou*, page 232.

91. Launay, J. de: *Le dossier de Vichy, op. cit.*, pages 59–77 to 92.

92. Viansson-Ponté, P.: *Les politiques, op. cit.*, pages 77 to 81.

93. Personal papers of the author. On the filiation of the Gaullist economic thinking (de Gaulle, Vallon) see Launay, J. de: *Le dossier de Vichy.* The General's thinking and that of Marshal Pétain had had the same origins.

⚜

94. Grégoire, Marcel: *"l'incident franco-canadien et la Belgique,"* in *Le Soir*, Brussels, August 10, 1967.

95. Viansson-Ponté, P.: *Les Gaullistes*, page 7.

96. Sociétaire of the Théâtre Français.

97. Bloch-Morhange, J.: *Réponse à de Gaulle*, Paris, 1967.

98. Viansson-Ponté, P.: *Les Gaullistes*, page 153.

99. It is significant that MM. Cazenave and Fischer, the directors of the U.J.P., on July 15, 1967 founded a political club: "Gaullisme et prospective" (10 rue Thureau-Dangin, Paris, XV) with a view to basic study of the philosophy expressed by the Head of State, and its future development.

100. Faucher, J. A.: *Les clubs politiques en France*, Paris, 1965.

101. Mendès-France, P.: *La République moderne*, Paris, 1962.

102. Defferre was chosen by the weekly paper, *L'Express*, in 1964 as the "Monsieur X" in a future electoral campaign for president of the Republic. He conducted a clever and dignified campaign, but was set aside by the Communists and the Socialist followers of Mollet after tortuous intrigues. For his program, see Defferre, G.: *Un nouvel horizon*, Paris, 1965.

103. At the same time, the Socialist vote fluctuated between 2 millions in 1936 and 4.5 millions in 1945, 2.7 millions in 1951, 3.2 millions in 1956, 3.1 millions in 1958, 2.3 millions in 1962.

104. Marchant, P.: in *Réalités*, Paris, January, 1967.

105. Burnier, M. A.: *Les existentialistes et la politique*, Paris, 1966, and Bon, F. and Burnier, M. A.: *Les nouveaux intellectuels*, Paris, 1967.

106. Duquesne, J.: *Les 16/24 ans*, Paris, 1963. Report of the Bureau Européen de la Jeunesse et de l'Enfance (Director General, J. de Launay) by the I.F.O.P. The report published by the *Ministère de la Jeunesse*, Paris, 1967, confirms these tendencies.

107. Teindas, G., and Thireau, Y.: *La jeunesse dans la famille et la société moderne*, Paris, 1961. Garric, R.: *Les jeunes et la lecture*, Paris, 1960.

108. Sauvy, A.: *La montée des jeunes*, Paris, 1959.

⚜

109. Researches I.F.O.P. at the end of 1965. This figure closely corresponds to the increase in the votes gained by de Gaulle and Mitterrand on December 5, 1965 (81%). The two foreign policies proposed have many points in common. See M. Duverger, in *Le Monde*, December 28, 1965. The presidential elections definitely strengthened de Gaulle's foreign policy.

110. Launay, J. de: *Histoire de la diplomatie secrète 1914–1945*, pages 281–283.

111. Guitard, L.: *Lettre sans malice à François Mauriac*, Paris, 1967, pages 41, 45, 69, 70, 71, 76.

SELECTED BIBLIOGRAPHY

1. *Charles de Gaulle's writings:*
Books: *La Discorde chez l'ennemi.* Berger-Levrault, Paris, 1924; *Le fil de l'épée. Ibid.*, 1932; *Vers l'armée de métier. Ibid.*, 1934. All three books were republished in 1944.
La France et son armée. Plon, Paris, 1938. Republished in 1945.
Mémoires de guerre. Plon, Paris, Vol. I, *L'Appel*, 1954; Vol. II, *L'Unité*, 1956; Vol. III, *Le Salut*, 1959.
Between 1920 and 1936, 17 articles in various revues (list in Jouve, E.: *Le general de Gaulle et la construction de l'Europe*, Vol. II, pages 43–44).
Three of these articles were combined in: *Trois études, suivies du memorandum du 26 janvier 1940*, Berger-Levrault, Paris, 1945.
Prefaces to seven books (list in E. Jouve, op. cit., page 44).
His speeches, declarations and press conferences have been combined in *Discours 1940–1945*. Luf, Paris, 1945. 3 volumes. *Discours et messages 1940–1946*. Berger-Levrault, Paris, 1948; *La France sera la France.* Bouchy, Paris, 1951 (Speeches from 1937 to 1951, collected by a committee of the R.P.F. headed by G. Pompidou).
Passeron, A.: *de Gaulle parle, 1958–1962*. Plon, Paris, 1962.
Passeron, A.: *de Gaulle parle, 1962–1966*. Fayard, Paris, 1966.

2. *Evidence and sources:*
d'Astier, E.: *Sept fois, sept jours*. (Ed. de Minuit.) Paris, 1947; *Les Dieux et les hommes*. Julliard, Paris, 1952; *Les grands*. Gallimard, Paris, 1961. Auburtin, Jean: *Le Colonel de Gaulle*. Plon, Paris, 1965; *C. de Gaulle*. Seghers, Paris, 1966. Buron, R.: *Carnets politiques de la guerre d'Algérie*. Plon, Paris, 1965. Laffargue, André: *Fantassin de Gascogne*. Flammarion, Paris, 1962. Nachin, Louis: *C. de Gaulle*. (Ed. Colbert.) Paris, 1944; Passy, A. D.: *Souvenirs*. Solar et Plon, Paris, 1947–48; Schumann, M.: *L'homme des tempêtes*. Paris, 1946; Soustelle, J.: *Envers et contre tout*. Laffont, Paris, 1947–50 (2 vols.).
Various references to C. de Gaulle appear in numerous memoirs including those of: Adenauer, Blum, Churchill, Eden, Eisenhower, Macmillan, Reynaud, Truman; Marshals Juin and de Lattre de Tassigny; Generals Catroux, Giraud, de Larminat, Sicé, Spears; and Admiral Muselier.

Very fully documented studies have been published by: Bonheur, G.:
C. de Gaulle. Gallimard, Paris, 1958; Cattaui, G.: C. de Gaulle. Fayard,
Paris, 1960; Launay, J. de: Les grandes controverses du temps présent.
Marabout-Université, Paris, 1967; Tournoux, J. R.: Pétain et de Gaulle.
Plon, Paris, 1964 and Secrets d'État. Plon, Paris, 1960; Raissac, G.: Un
combat sans merci. Albin Michel, Paris, 1966.

3. Studies and works:

Numerous studies on the acts and policies of Charles de Gaulle have
been published. Among the best can be noted: Jouve, E.: Le général de
Gaulle et la construction de l'Europe. Pichon, Paris, 1967 (2 vols.);
Gorce, P. M. de la: De Gaulle entre deux mondes. Fayard, Paris, 1964;
Mannoni, E.: Moi, général de Gaulle. Seuil, Paris, 1964; Purtschet, C.:
Le Rassemblement du Peuple Français. Cujas, Paris, 1965; Robertson,
A. C.: La doctrine du général de Gaulle. Fayard, Paris, 1959; Schoen-
brun, D.: Les trois vies de C. de Gaulle. Juilliard, Paris, 1965; Viansson-
Ponté, P.: Les gaullistes. Seuil, Paris, 1963 and Les politiques. Calmann-
Levy, Paris, 1967; Viorst, M.: Hostile Allies, F.D.R. and Charles de
Gaulle. New York, 1965.

4. Biographies:

The gaullology is enormous. The majority of authors have used the
above cited sources, or numberless repetitions. We quote:

Andersen, C. A. Charles de Gaulle. Copenhagen, 1945.

Andersen, R. Charles de Gaulle. Copenhagen, 1962.

Aron, R. Charles de Gaulle. Paris, 1964.

Ashcroft, E. De Gaulle. London, 1962.

Barfod, G. De Gaulle og hans Republik. Copenhagen, 1965.

Barrès, P. Charles de Gaulle. Paris, 1945.

Bloch, P. Charles de Gaulle, premier ouvrier de France. Paris, 1945.

Brogan, D. W. De Gaulle: French Personalities. London, 1946.

Fabre-Luce, A. Le plus illustre des Français. Paris, 1960.

Funk, A. L. Charles de Gaulle. The crucial years, 1963–66. Norman,
Okla., 1960.

Garas, F. Charles de Gaulle seul contre les pouvoirs. Paris, 1957.

Gorce, P. M. de la. De Gaulle entre deux mondes. Paris, 1964.

Grinnel-Milne, D. The Triumph of Integrity. London, 1961. New York,
1962.

⚜

Hatch, A. *The De Gaulle Nobody Knows*. New York, 1961.

Lacouture, J. *De Gaulle*. Paris, 1965. New York, 1966.

Mauriac, F. *De Gaulle*. Paris, 1964. New York, 1966.

Montgomery, B. *General de Gaulle. The Path to Leadership*. London, 1961.

Remy. *De Gaulle, cet inconnu*. Monte Carlo, 1947.

Sandahl, P. *De Gaulle sans képi*. Paris, 1948.

Tesson, P. *De Gaulle J^{er}*. Paris, 1965.

Thomson, D. *Pierre Laval and Charles de Gaulle*. London, 1951.

Vinde, V. *de Gaulle och Frankrike*. Malmoe, 1962.

Werth, A. *De Gaulle*. London, 1965.

Williams, P. M. *De Gaulle's Republic*. London, 1960.

The most critical are those of Barfod, de la Gorce, and Lacouture.

5. *Bibliographies*:
The Memoirs cited in Section 2 are quoted in *The Two World Wars*. Pergamon Press, Oxford, 1964.
The works of E. Jouve (Section 3), P. M. de la Gorce (Sections 3 and 4), and J. de Launay (Section 2) quoted above also contain important bibliographies.

6. *Chronologies*:
The works of E. Jouve, A. Passeron, and P. Viansson-Ponté (notably *Les politiques*) include detailed chronologies. A. Passeron quotes the main statistics and figures of the elections and referendums. Hans Stercken (*De Gaulle hat gesagt*, Stuttgart, 1967) has listed chronologically and indexed under their themes and countries the various declarations made by the General between 1958 and 1967. A short *aide-mémoire* by E. Weisenfeld (*De Gaulle sieht Europa*, Frankfurt, 1966) is not without interest.

7. *Pictorial material*:
Several collections of photographs have been made and some published (For instance, Plon, Paris, 1966; Bücher, Lucerne, 1966). G. Oriol, 8 rue d'Oslo, Paris, (18e) has a very full collection. E. Jouve (*op. cit.*, Vol. II, 581–941) published a collection of 328 drawings and political caricatures made by 91 artists from 12 countries.

8. *Pamphlets:*
A certain number of critical texts and polemics have been published. Among the best should be noted: Fabre-Luce, A.: *Haute Cour*. Paris, 1962; Gavin, C.: *Liberated France*. New York, 1955; Izard, G.: *Lettres affligées au général de Gaulle*. Paris, 1964; Kérillis, H. de: *De Gaulle, dictateur*. Montreal, 1945; Laurent, J.: *Mauriac sous de Gaulle*. Paris, 1964; Wurmser, A.: *De Gaulle et les siens*. Paris, 1947.

INDEX OF FRENCH PERSONALITIES

Astier de la Vigerie, Emmanuel d' b. January 6, 1900. Naval officer (1921–1931), journalist, founder of the Resistance group "Southern Liberation." Commissioner at the Home Office of the C.F.L.N. (1943), home secretary (1945), deputy (1946–1958), vice-president of the World Council for Peace. Writer. Prix Lenin.

Baumel, Jacques b. March 6, 1918. Press agent. Deputy (1944–1950). General Secretary of the U.N.R. (1959–1967). Senator (1959). Deputy (1967).

Burin des Roziers, Étienne b. August 11, 1913. Diplomat. Embassy attaché (1939). Staff officer to General de Gaulle (1943), *chargé de mission* in the government of General de Gaulle (1945–1946), *chargé d'affaires* in Belgrade (1954), consul general in Milan (1956), ambassador to Warsaw (1958), general secretary to the Presidency of the Republic (1962–1967). Ambassador to Rome (1967).

Buron, Robert b. February 27, 1910. Journalist. Director of the Chamber of Commerce in Paris (1934–1937), director of the Trade Association of Confectioners (1937–1940), general secretary of the Committee for the Organization of the Cinema (1940–1944), president of Gaumont-Actualités (1944–1947), deputy (1945–1958), minister in the governments of Pleven, Faure, Mendès-France, de Gaulle, and Debré (1951–1962).

Catroux, Georges b. January 29, 1877. Lieut.-General. Military career in the colonies. Governor-General of Indochina (1940). Joined General de Gaulle (1940). Delegate to the Middle East. Ambassador to Moscow (1944–1948). Grand Chancellor of the Legion of Honor.

Chaban-Delmas, Jacques (pseudonym of Jacques Delmas) b. March 7, 1915. Inspector of finance (1943), national military delegate (1944), Brigadier (1944), deputy (since 1944), mayor of Bordeaux (since 1947), minister in the governments of Mendès-France, Mollet, and Gaillard (1954–1958). President of the National Assembly (since 1958).

Coty, René (1882–1962). Lawyer, deputy (1923–1935), senator (1935–1944), deputy (1945–1948), senator (1948–1953). Minister in the governments of Schuman and Marie (1947–1948). President of the Republic (1953–1959).

Courcel, Geoffroy Chodron de b. September 11, 1912. Diplomat. Attaché, then secretary to the Embassy (1937–1940). Principal private secretary to General de Gaulle (1940). Assistant-director private secretary to General de Gaulle (1940). Assistant-director in the same government (1943–1944), counsellor (1945), general secretary for National Defense (1955–1958). French representative at NATO (1958). General secretary to the Presidency of the Republic (1959–1962). Ambassador in London.

Couve de Murville, Maurice b. January 24, 1907. Inspector of finance (1930), director of foreign finance (1940), member of the C.F.L.N. (1943), ambassador to Rome (1945), to Cairo (1950), to Washington (1955), to Bonn (1956). Minister for Foreign Affairs (1958–1968). Prime minister since 1968.

Debré, Michel b. January 15, 1912. Career in the Council of State (1935–1942). *Chargé de mission* in the C.F.L.N., then in the provisional government (1943–1947). Senator (since 1948). Minister for justice (1958). Prime minister (1959–1962), minister of finance (1966–1968). Minister for foreign affairs since 1968.

Defferre, Gaston b. September 14, 1910. Lawyer. Member of the executive committee of the Underground Socialist Party (1940–1944), missions to Algiers and London. Mayor of Marseilles since 1944, deputy (1944–1959). Minister in the governments of Pleven, Queuille, and Mollet (1950 and 1957). Senator (1959). Deputy (1968).

Faure, Edgar b. August 18, 1908. Lawyer. Officer in the C.F.L.N. (1944). Assistant prosecutor at the Nuremburg Tribunal (1945), deputy (1946–1959), senator (since 1959), prime minister (1952 and 1953–1956). Minister in the governments of Pleven, Laniel, Mendès-France, Pflimlin, Pompidou, and Couve de Murville (1951, 1953, 1954, 1958, 1966, 1968).

⚜

Foccart, Jacques b. August 31, 1913. Exporter. General secretary of the R.P.F. (1954). Technical counsellor to the general secretariat of the Presidency of the Republic (1959). General secretary of the Community (1960).

Fouchet, Christian b. November 17, 1911. Diplomat. Secretary to the embassy in Moscow (1944). Delegate of the provisional government to Lublin, then Warsaw (1944–1945). Consul general in Calcutta (1945–1947), member of the directing committee of the R.P.F. (1947–1951), deputy (1951–1955), minister in the Mendès-France government (1954). Ambassador to Copenhagen (1958). Minister in the Pompidou governments since 1962.

Frey, Roger b. June 11, 1913. Industrialist. General secretary of the Republican Socialist Party (Gaullist) (1955). Minister in the de Gaulle, Debré, Pompidou, and Couve de Murville governments (since 1958).

Giscard d'Estaing, Valéry b. February 2, 1926. Inspector of finance (1954), deputy (since 1956). Minister of finance in the Debré and Pompidou governments (1959–1966).

Guichard, Olivier, baron b. July 27, 1920. Prefect. Chief of General de Gaulle's departmental staff (1947–1958). Assistant-director of the General's departmental staff (1958). Minister in the Pompidou government (1962).

Janot, Raymond b. March 9, 1917. Career in the Council of State (1946–1959). Technical counsellor in General de Gaulle's government (1958–1959). General secretary of the Community (1959–1960). General director of the R.T.F. (1960).

Joxe, Louis b. September 16, 1901. Professor. *Chargé de mission* in the government of Pierre Cot (1932–1934). Foreign service of the Havas Agency (1934–1939), General secretary of the C.F.L.N. (1942–1944), then in the provisional government (1944–1946). Ambassador to Moscow (1952–1955), then to Bonn (1955–1956). General secretary for foreign affairs (1956). Minister in the Debré and Pompidou governments (since 1959).

⚜

Juin, Alphonse (1888–1967). Marshal of France. Commander-in-Chief in North Africa (1941), then of the French Army in Tunis (1942–1943), in Italy (1943–1944), Chief of the General Staff for National Defense (1944–1947). President general in Morocco (1947–1951). Commander of the Allied Forces of Central Europe until 1956.

Koenig, Marie-Pierre b. October 18, 1898. General officer. Commandant (1940). Brigadier (1941). Defender of Bir Hakim (1942). Commander of the French Forces of the Interior (1944). Commander-in-chief in Germany (1945–1949). Deputy (1951–1958). Minister in the governments of Mendès-France and Faure (1954–1955).

de Lattre de Tassigny, Jean (1889–1952). Marshal of France. General (1939). Arrested for taking part in the Resistance (1942). Escaped. Commander of the First Army. Landed on the island of Elba, then on the coast of Provence. Campaigns in Germany and Austria. High commissioner in Indochina (1950).

Lecanuet, Jean b. March 4, 1920. Professor (1942). Director of the departmental staff of P. Pflimlin (1957–1959). Senator (since 1959).

Leclerc alias for (de Hautecloque, Philippe) (1902–1947). Marshal of France. Prisoner (1940). Escaped. Governor of the Cameroons (1940). Conquered Fez (1943). Commanded the Second Armored Division in the second Battle of France (1944). Commanded in Indochina (1945).

Malraux, André b. November 3, 1901. Writer. Missions to the Far East (1923–1927). Head of foreign aviation in the Spanish Republican Government (1936). Commander of the Alsace-Lorraine Brigade (1944). Minister in the governments of de Gaulle, Debré, and Pompidou (1945, 1946, and since 1958).

Mendès-France, Pierre b. January 11, 1907. Lawyer. Deputy (1932–1940). Under-secretary of state at the Treasury (1938), commission for finance of the C.F.L.N. (1943). Minister in the de Gaulle government (1944–1945), deputy (1946–1958). Governor of the International Monetary Fund (1947–1958). Prime minister (1954–1955). Deputy (1967–1968).

⚜

Mitterrand, François b. October 26, 1916. Lawyer. Deputy (1946–1958). Minister in the governments of Ramadier, Schuman, Faure, Mendès-France, Mollet (1947, 1948, 1954, 1955, 1956, 1957). Senator (1959). Deputy (1967).

Mollet, Guy b. December 31, 1905. Professor. Deputy since 1946. General secretary of the Socialist Party since 1946. Minister in the governments of Blum, Pleven, Queuille, and de Gaulle (1946, 1950, 1951, 1958). Prime minister (1956–1957).

Monnerville, Gaston b. January 2, 1897. Lawyer. Deputy (1932–1944). Senator since 1946. President of the Senate since 1958.

Palewski, Gaston b. March 20, 1901. Director of the departmental staff of Paul Reynaud (1928–1939). Director of the departmental staff of General de Gaulle (1942–1946). Member of the directing committee of the R.P.F. Deputy (1951–1955). Minister in the Faure government (1955). Ambassador to Rome (1957). Minister of state (1962).

Peyrefitte, Alain b. August 26, 1925. Diplomat. Secretary to the embassy (1949–1952). Deputy (1958). Minister in the Pompidou governments since 1962.

Pinay, Antoine b. December 30, 1891. Industrialist. Deputy (1936–1938). Senator (1938–1944). Deputy (1946–1958). Minister in the governments of Pleven, Queuille, Faure (1949–1952). Prime minister (1952). Minister in the governments of Faure, de Gaulle, and Debré (1955, 1956, 1958 to 1960).

Pisani, Edgard b. October 9, 1918. Prefect (1946–1953). Senator since 1954. Minister in the Pompidou governments (1962–1967).

Pleven, René b. April 15, 1901. Commissioner of the C.F.L.N. (1943). Minister five times (1944, 1949, 1958). Deputy since 1945. Prime minister (1950–1951).

Pompidou, Georges b. July 5, 1911. Professor. *Chargé de mission* on the departmental staff of General de Gaulle (1944–1946). *Maître des requêtes* to the Council of State (1946–1957). Director general of Rothschild Brothers (1957–1958). Director of the departmental staff of General de Gaulle (1958–1958). Prime minister (1962–1968). Deputy (1968).

Rochet, Waldeck b. April 5, 1905. Agriculturist. Communist deputy (1936–1940) and since 1945. General secretary of the Communist Party.

Salan, Raoul b. June 10, 1899. Professional soldier. Chief of the Second Bureau of the A.O.F. in Dakar (1941–1943). Brigadier (1944), Major-general (1947). Commander-in-chief of the troops of the Far East (1948). Lieut.-General commanding the Tenth Military Region (Algiers) (1956). Commander-in-chief in Algeria (1958). Place on the retired list (1960). Takes part in the "Algérie française" movement. Condemned.

Soustelle, Jacques b. February 3, 1912. Professor. Missions to Central America (1932–1939). Commissioner for information (1942). Minister in the de Gaulle government (1945). Deputy (1945–1946, 1951–1959). General secretary of the R.P.F. (1947–1952). Governor General of Algeria (1955–1956). Minister in the de Gaulle government (1958–1959). Takes part in the "Algérie française" movement. Lives in exile in Switzerland.

Vallon, Louis b. August 12, 1901. Engineer. Assistant-director of the departmental staff of General de Gaulle (1944–1946). Deputy (1951–1955, 1958–1967, 1968).

KEY TO ABBREVIATIONS

A.O.F.	French East Africa
C.E.C.A.	European Community of Coal and Steel
C.E.D.	European Defense Community
C.E.E.	European Economic Community
C.F.L.N.	French Committee of National Liberation
C.G.T.	General Confederation of Workers (Communist Trades Union)
C.N.R.	National Council of Resistance
C.O.M.A.C.	Military Committee for Action
D.S.T.	Direction of Safety of the Territory
M.R.P.	Popular Republican Movement (Christian-Democrat)
O.A.S.	Organization of the Secret Army
O.C.D.E. or O.E.E.C.	European Economic Development Council (E.E.D.C.)
O.T.A.N.	NATO
R.D.A.	East German Republic
R.P.F.	Assemblage of the French People
R.T.F.	French State Radio and Television
S.F.I.O.	French Socialist Party
U.N.R.	Union for the New Republic
U.S.R.A.F.	Union for the Safety and Renewal of French Algeria

GENERAL INDEX

⚜

⚜